Bird's Eye View

Dorothy Bird *and Joyce Greenberg*

with a foreword by Marcia B. Siegel

University of Pittsburgh Press

Bird's Eye View

Dancing

with

Martha

Graham

and on

Broadway

Published by the University of Pittsburgh Press, Pittsburgh, Pa. 15261
Manufactured in the United States of America
Printed on acid-free paper
10 9 8 7 6 5 4 3 2

This book is dedicated with love to my son, Casey, and his wife, Suzanne, and my grandchildren, Sarah, Brian, and Timothy.

Contents

Art, Aspiration, and the Body: The Emergence of Modern Dance

Marcia B. Siegel

Dancers record the first glimpse of their role models with unusual fervor. They know now, even if they didn't at the time, that they have seen Fate, and they remember the moment with exquisite clarity. The chemistry of these moments cannot be explained. But it is clear that very little in the dance environment of 1930 could have prepared young Dorothy Bird for her encounter with the small, pale dynamo that was Martha Graham.

By the end of the 1920s, American culture had emerged from its early dependence on European models, had passed through a sort of adolescence after the turn of the century, during which artists self-consciously examined their work, embraced and often rejected modernist trends, and tried to determine what it meant to have an individual style. Classical examples—the academic disciplines —never disappeared, but artists who thought themselves contemporary believed new techniques and new perspectives were needed to reflect the face of modernity. Painters and visual artists rallied around magnetic leaders such as Alfred Stieglitz, whose New York gallery at 291 Fifth Avenue promoted avant-gardists from Europe and North America; and Robert Henri, the influential teacher and center of the so-called Eight or Ashcan School, whose representatives tried to paint the rough, immediate realities of contemporary life. Louis Sullivan's *Autobiography of an Idea* (1924) traced the evolution of a philosophy that was to revolutionize American architecture. Poet and critic Vachel Lindsay made the first attempt at a theory of film, in *The Art of the Moving Picture* (1915), a farseeing look at the infant medium.

In 1920 the photographer Arnold Genthe published his *Book of the Dance*, a collection of images that challenged the overdecorated, codified personages of the typical ballet stage. In these pictures, taken before 1916, Genthe documented what he saw as a large-scale shift in the public's sensibility. In his foreword, he announced his goal of "permanently recording something of the fugitive charm of rhythmic motion, significant gesture and brilliant color which the dance has once more brought into our lives."[1] Genthe's subjects included not only the dissident stars Anna Pavlova, Ruth St. Denis, and Isadora Duncan, but a score of other exemplars, now unknown, of exotic, aesthetic, and naturalistic dance expression following in Duncan and St. Denis's footsteps, and reflecting the reforms of Michel Fokine on the Russian ballet of that early Diaghilev period.

The bodies Genthe captured on film are distinctly uncorseted, supple, curving, determined to break the sanctioned linear presentation of classroom ballet. The Duncanesque dancers look soft, filled with breath. They seem always to be rising upward with an open chest, taking pleasure in the expansiveness of their movement, even when they seem to be appealing to an invisible partner. Arms, heads, arching necks, and rounded upper torsos follow the thrust of the legs in unbroken lines from the propelling skip or prance. The exotics, costumed as primitives, peasants, or Asiatic deities, are more flamboyant. Their eyes flash, their bodies twist and angle more decoratively, their arms frame intense faces, their hands touch their skin sensuously, suggestively.

But whether spirited or demure, these dancers revel in a prodigious release of energy. The new forms of dancing allowed them to display their femininity more openly and completely than ever before. Men too were liberated from the strict courtliness and formal virtuosity of ballet protocol. Following the example of Nijinsky, Mordkin, Bolm, and later Lifar and Massine, they could be sensuous, playful, earthbound. Men and women acquired dignity as they took on the character of Greek choruses or Hindu deities, but whether they portrayed imps or angels they exuded a fierce dynamism, which still radiates from these photographs.

The release of the body in dance went along with dress reform and physical culture, both of which were adopted widely in schools and fashion by the end of World War I. Bodies, especially women's bodies, took on a new strength and articulateness; they became energized for quick response and flexibility. But the new dancers justified their work as more than novel displays of physical prowess. It was to be aesthetic, if not Art—uplifting, inspiring, at the very least a notch above recreation or exercise, and certainly more beneficial to the viewer's mind and spirit than a trip to the music hall. "Physical culture," in the words of Duncan scholar Ann Daly, "accepted the body only as a transparent representation, or 'expression,' of the soul. Body-building thus was another form of character-building."[2]

Duncan and St. Denis, the most important progenitors of the modern dance, insisted above all on dancing as a serious and respectable art. However much their private lives may have contradicted it, their dancing was to be morally impeccable, a purifying flame to scourge the sins of the past. They may not have been any more economically secure than the nineteenth-century ballet girls whose survival depended on the acquisition of wealthy lovers. Indeed, St. Denis plied the hated commercial stage to pay her bills, and Duncan had a generous paramour in Paris Singer. But their dancing, their attitude toward their dancing, was altruistic.

Philosophy and form were both put to work in the service of elevating dance practice from the taint of decadence. Dancing, or perhaps any physical activity that does not result in a product, has always been suspect in Western culture. But the stigma attached to doing something for pure pleasure could be lessened by rationalizing physical practice into systematic processes leading to the dancer's higher evolution.

François Delsarte, the French teacher of rhetorical gesture, had devised an elaborate system linking life (vitality, emotions), mind, and soul in a triune scheme that was applied to the parts of the body, the way body parts combine in movement, and the directions movement goes in space. Delsarte training spread widely, undergoing shifts and extensions from its beginnings in the mid–nineteenth century, but keeping its tightly logical, Christian ethic. It promised that orators could be convincing, actors could be moving, stage tableaux could project emotional states as well as three-dimensional pictures. Genevieve Stebbins, a principal exponent in America, reported that a basic configuration of Delsartism—the Ninefold Accord—was even considered "the key of the universe" by one of the master's early students.[3]

Delsartism (in America this meant a system of exercises based on breathing and conscious activation of specific parts and zones of the body to convey specific expressive information) found its way into ladies' literary recitals, patriotic pageantry, and emulation of Greek statuary. It was a major item in the curriculum of the Denishawn School. Delsartian gesture undoubtedly underlay the movement in much Denishawn dancing, since both St. Denis and her partner, Ted Shawn, were devoted to the Delsartian ideal equating movement with spiritual and mental harmony. Perhaps the widespread practice of Delsartian "statue posing" inspired St. Denis to imitate other iconography, to put painted or carved East Asian goddesses and dancing girls into motion. It wasn't only that St. Denis was trying to re-create particular dance forms; she wanted to merge with the sacred or profane personas they suggested. She would *become* Kuan Yin or Radha—or the simple devotee of *The Incense*, the Yogi, the nautch dancer—by assuming and then animating their body positions. Denishawn dance flowered out of the effort not merely to look like Greek or Indian or Siamese, Japanese, Burmese, or Arabian dancers, but to *be* those figures, to take on their physicality, and so to dance them.

Isadora Duncan's Hellenism floated on an even more idealistic plane. Surely she saw the Greek marbles in the British Museum, danced in the moonlight at the Theater of Dionysos. Surely she draped her body with the tunic and the Phidian curve. But she did not try to dance like a sculpture come to life, regardless of how many adoring witnesses called her statuesque, heroic, monumental. Many disciples have recorded and interpreted Duncan's teachings, but the way she transformed her notions of body use and development into stage apparitions that stunned a generation has never been explained. Her effects remain shrouded in mystique.

Perhaps she was merely an intuitive dancer responding to the rise and fall of her musical accompaniment. But even her writings reflect the need to synthesize individual experience with a larger continuum. In 1903 she compared her ideal dance to the rhythms of nature: "we must try to create beautiful movements significant of cultured man—a movement which, without spurning the laws of gravitation, sets itself in harmony with the motion of the universe."[4] Her followers codified a technique from this credo, and it is echoed in one of the most influential books on art theory to come from the early twentieth century, Robert Henri's *The Art Spirit*. In 1915 Henri wrote, "It is not too much to say that art is the noting of the existence of order throughout the world, and so, order stirs imagination and inspires one to reproduce this beautiful relationship existing in the universe, as best one can. Everywhere I find that the moment order in nature is understood and freely shown, the result is nobility."[5]

Duncan seems to have rejected the most important approach to musical analysis of her time, the eurhythmics of Emile Jaques-Dalcroze. Although this was not primarily a system of physical training, the Dalcroze exercises, like Duncan's, were based on a full activation of the torso through coordinated breathing, and asked little of the lower body in the way of intricate footwork. So pervasive were the ideas of holistic, "natural" movement, and the vision of ancient Greece as a source of a purer, more elevated life, that the photographs in the Dalcroze manuals could almost be interchangeable with those of the Duncanites in Arnold Genthe's book.

Dalcroze used the whole body to develop the most sophisticated rhythmic sensitivity, but neither personal interpretation nor formal composition was a major goal of his training. He felt the true realization of the artist would come through a unity of mind and body, asserting in the preface to the first volume of his Méthode Jaques-Dalcroze that these exercises "clearly indicate our intention of establishing through our rhythmic studies an intimate alliance between the physical and artistic faculties, and of making music, in its infinite dynamic and temporal nuances, serve the education of this musical instrument par excellence which is the human body."[6]

What Duncan, St. Denis, and Dalcroze had in common was a stripping down of movement to "motions familiar to all races, such as walking, running, skipping, jumping, kneeling, reclining and rising," as Irma Duncan characterized the vocabulary of Isadora's technique.[7] In effect, this basic locomotor lexicon also pervaded the many systems of gymnastic and body training long established in schools, colleges, and recreational clubs. Resembling calisthenics in the abstract repetitiveness of their movement routines, these programs often used music to help students integrate moving with healthful breathing. Music also lent a degree of aesthetic sheen to what quickly became an activity attractive to women. Rhythmic gymnastics, much of it imported from Scandinavia and Germany, built strength in the arms and back, often through the use of clubs, balls, and other quasi-sporting devices. It might incorporate ballet positions and even steps, it might be adapted from folk dance forms, and it might promise an improvement of social graces, but rhythmic gymnastics was not intended to train girls for the stage. The mission was health and beauty.[8] Elizabeth Selden, the first to articulate the principles of the new dance as a genre in itself, saw the link between recreation, physical training, and dancing: "With the advent of barefoot dancing, the Dance has once more advanced to the rank of an educational subject . . . and it will lie with the dancers themselves to establish it as an art."[9]

The passage from physical education to modern dancing was not a big step. Proponents of rhythmic gymnastics, aesthetic dancing, and other physical training for young ladies were eager for new inspiration. Mary Wood Hinman, Doris Humphrey's teacher, for many years traveled to Europe during summer vacations to study folk dances and sought out new developments such as the Dalcroze system. It seems that on their perpetual quest for respectability, dancers would embrace anything with a formal structure or a program of development. They explored the systematic teachings of the German modern dancers, with origins before World War I in Rudolf Laban's experiments. Nor did the performing expertise of the Germans go unnoticed in the emerging world of American concert dance. Harald Kreutzberg made his first U.S. tour in 1927, and Mary Wigman made hers in 1930, both to huge acclaim. Ronny Johansson, a Swedish practitioner of the "free dance," taught at Denishawn as well as at the Cornish School in Seattle. Ted Shawn worked with Margarethe Wallmann in Germany and later brought her to give modern classes in New York City at the relocated Denishawn.

All this was in the air when Dorothy Bird, a shy girl from British Columbia with a doubtful dance education and a love of performing, arrived at the Cornish School in 1930. The domesticated Delsarte she had been exposed to was like a folk art, a device for making amateur theatricals, certainly not the codified and high-minded philosophy imparted to Martha Graham around the same time at the Denishawn School. The casual folk and recreational dances that Dorothy had studied suggested nothing in the way of a future to her, and certainly nothing she had experienced resembled in any way the professional atmosphere she encountered at Cornish.

The school was founded in 1914 by Nellie Cornish, a remarkable Seattle woman who was determined that her native city must not suffer culturally from its location on the western edge of the continent. Convinced of the interrelatedness of the arts, she brought top practitioners of the most progressive methods onto the faculty. Besides the inclusion of Dalcroze eurhythmics as a staple of the dance training, the rotating dance staff included Adolf Bolm, Dalcrozian and Orientalist Michio Ito, and Wigman dancer Lore Deja in the late 1920s and early 1930s. Martha Graham gave the first of several summer courses there in 1930, and a spellbound Dorothy Bird followed her to New York without pursuing the curriculum at Cornish any further.

Bird's first teacher at Cornish, Ronny Johansson, offered a challenging, rigorous regimen, but Bird didn't take to it. One extraordinary thing about these new dance ideas is that they were inherently personal. They depended on something besides the rapport between teacher and student; each system required a re-siting of the body, an investiture of breath, balance, and bones, a particular response to time, an arranging of limbs in unfamiliar ways. If it fit your body, you would want to master it; if it felt alien, you might push your body into its forms with fanatical discipline and never really learn it. Bird's first response to Martha Graham was electric, almost mystical. The assurance and relief of her words, "I knew I was in the right place at the right time after all," have been echoed by countless modern dancers who were lucky enough to meet the teacher and the style that their bodies needed.

Graham, who became her teacher, director, and lodestar, had by that time emphatically distanced herself from her own mentors, Ruth St. Denis and Ted Shawn, and from the contemporaries who had also set out to remake dancing, Doris Humphrey, Charles Weidman, and the other pioneers of the German and American modern dance. Graham was undoubtedly a singular performing presence, but it was not charisma alone that attracted Bird. Indeed, this timid creature would never have presumed to emulate a star like Graham or, for that matter, like her first dance idol, Anna Pavlova.

From Bird's detailed account, and from the witness of others in Graham's thrall at the time, we can begin to understand why her new disciple felt that "In one stroke she quietly closed the door on all that had gone before." For other dancers and spectators, Humphrey, or Mary Wigman, or some other artist could have been similarly compelling. Graham and the other modern dancers held out something that had not been in the hand of the aesthetic dancers, the Dalcrozians, the Delsartians, the rhythmic gymnasts, or even the glamorous eclectics of Denishawn. They offered the possibility of power and autonomy through physicality.

No stage dancing up to that time had shown so forcibly what women were capable of doing on their own, independent of music, stories, tricks, and sex appeal. Barbara Morgan's earliest photographs of Graham reveal a woman of self-possession in the most intimate sense.[10] What she does in *Frontier, Lamentation, Harlequinade, Imperial Gesture,* is meant to be looked at, but it would not be taking place at all if it were meant only for the audience. What we look at in Graham is not a woman showing herself but a woman experiencing something, not a woman miming or exaggerating experience but a woman who moves through an experience and is transfigured.

In the early 1930s Graham taught actors as well as dancers at the Neighborhood Playhouse, and many of the images Dorothy Bird describes recall the Stanislavskian sense-memory work that was integral to actor training at the time. Expressive acting and movement was produced not from actually grieving, for instance, but from triggering off grieving behavior. Graham would have dancers shout or scream and observe the effect this had on their bodies. Later, they would only have to activate their bodies to feel the emotion. The exercises Graham used to stimulate the five senses—so meticulously described by Bird—testify to the forces Graham brought to bear on this crucial matter.

It is also interesting to imagine the effect this intense inner concentration would have had on young women who came from sheltered, often puritanical families. Here they were, engaging in a sensual exploration of their own bodies, but not for the purpose of seducing an audience. The sense of removal, of masking, demanded by Graham allowed the mover to feel without exploiting her feelings. The Morgan photos frequently show Graham in an inward-focused state; the pleasure or the pain is secretly felt though publicly displayed. Another way we can see this is in the many reports from dancers, Bird included, that the thrust of the energy was to be held in, intensified, never totally given out. The dancers were to start a movement but cut it off, to "trigger the audience to continue the percussive movement in their mind's eye," in a kind of kinesthetic transference.

The movement must have felt good to many students, with its stretches and explosive contractions, its leaps with whiplash midair changes of direction. It must have been thrilling to pound the floor, to launch oneself demonically into the air, to twist the spine, to make a fist and strike out. This movement wasn't ladylike and it wasn't sexy, in ways the Graham movement of the 1980s and 1990s is, but ". . . vital, sturdy, urgent" as Bird describes it, and neither feminine nor masculine. This new body image both protected the adolescent girls in the company and gave them confidence. It proclaimed that these women were to be taken seriously. People used drastic words to describe it at the time: *abrupt, heroic, tense, angular, robust, aggressive.*

Martha Graham wasn't the only one reinventing the female dancing body at that time. Powerful forces in the modern dance were working to bring these sometimes contending personalities into public awareness, and to fashion pedagogical models from their idiosyncratic movement styles. While the founders of the modern dance were still neophytes, Margaret H'Doubler had been teaching educational and creative dance at the University of Wisconsin for years. She published her classic textbook, *The Dance and Its Place in Education,* in 1925. H'Doubler's program at Wisconsin became a prototype for dance departments that supplied dancers and choreographers to the emerging field. Although a tacit dichotomy has always existed between the educational and the theatrical branches of the dance field, one could, in fact, trace a mutually supportive relationship looping continuously from university physical education and dance programs to the training practices of concert dancers, and back again, with periodic informational detours to pull in the audience.

Mabel Elsworth Todd at Teachers College, Columbia University, had developed her physical training along holistic lines, maintaining in one of her early writings that "any study of posture . . . must be approached through an application of psychological and mechanical principles."[11] Two of Todd's important concepts influenced the modern dancers. Rather than objectifying the body as a shifting site of specialized skills, she saw movement as a play of balancing and counterbalancing forces, to which the body continuously makes small adjustments. The flux of moving parts is given coherence by a self-image that the mover may have acquired without being aware of it. In her 1920 article, Todd began to verbalize and connect this rich psychological source with the ways people carry themselves, breathe, and accommodate to the stresses of physical function. Todd's use of imagery to stimulate healthier movement patterns became the practice of ideokinesis; its relevance to the expressive goals of the modern dancers was obvious.

Two of Graham's early company members, Martha Hill and Bessie Schonberg, developed the first modern dance fundamentals courses, beginning in 1934 at the Bennington School of Dance. These courses, carried back to the colleges and universities by the many teachers who attended the Bennington School, were not confined exclusively to Graham or Humphrey-Weidman technique, but comprised an amalgam of basic elements that could be put to use in any creative work. Graham's partner, Louis Horst, exerted a formal influence on her choreography but also, as a musician, constructed ways of teaching dance composition derived from long-established musicological practice. Horst's Modern Dance Forms and Pre-Classic Forms became fixtures in the university dance curriculum.

Critic John Martin promoted the modern dancers in his columns at the *New York Times*, and, through his lecture series at the New School and elsewhere, put a certain pressure on them to organize their thinking. The lecture-demonstration format—whereby the choreographer would present his or her philosophy or aesthetic ideas, demonstrate technical work, show and discuss finished dances or works in progress, and answer questions—became almost an art form in the 1930s. As a strategy for introducing the public to new work, the lecture-demonstration developed the first audiences for modern dance around the country, and it has persisted as a useful conduit from dancers to the public.

In a way, it was the dancers and their most intimate advocates—musicians, teachers, critics—who accounted for what they were doing. Modern dance still is a largely self-validated art form. The most persuasive information we have about the early work is dancers' descriptions of what they did in the studio. They could not see what they were doing on the stage as a whole theatrical event, and that phenomenon was perhaps less comprehensible to them, less intense, than the day-to-day ritual of studio work. Even disinterested observers tended to focus on the visceral effects of the movement and of the performing rather than the choreography or the choreographic style. Elizabeth Selden, one unusually perceptive commentator who was also a teacher, not only wrote of the basics of the free dance and of the individual dancers' qualities but detailed the distinctive choreographic imprint of several major figures.[12] Her view of Graham has not been acknowledged by later dance scholars, though it has the priceless advantage of immediacy.

Graham has often been associated with modernist and primitivist trends in visual art, but contemporary viewers who make this analogy have concentrated on her movement style, not her choreography. Selden identifies typical choreographic devices that support this situating of Graham's work within cultural history. Perhaps these elements became softened or overshadowed by the narrative emphasis in her later dances, the Greek works of the postwar period, which captivated the imagination of intellectuals. In the period covered by Selden, which is also the period of Dorothy Bird's association with Graham, the choreography as well as the studio practice was searing, dionysian, not pretty. Interestingly, Nellie Cornish thought "Her work of that period was perhaps more understandable to the layman than later."[13]

Selden notes the heaping up of disconnected details to drive home an idea in the early pieces, the leaping from climax to climax. She remarks on poses generated by arrested gestures rather than completed ones, and on a sense of "artificial resistance," a moving against gravity or pushing off balance while anchored to the floor; both of these concepts Dorothy Bird verifies in the studio work. Selden sees Graham's distortions of time, space, and intensity as modernist strategies, designed not to idealize reality but to show it without "lovely or serene" details. It seems that in scouring her motifs of decoration and everything that would make the dance flow easily for the viewer, Graham achieved a sort of choreographic cubism.

Selden also compares Graham to the pre-Renaissance painter Giotto. She sees Graham's figures as blocklike forms or gestures cut away from the background. Remarking that Graham seemed to have no interest in the background at all, Selden sees groups arrayed in equal but not harmonized motion across an even field of vision. A narrative that might take place over time could be told in simultaneous actions. These observations prefigure the choreographic breakthroughs, a decade later, of Graham's former dancer Merce Cunningham.

Graham's choreography also had resemblances to the German modern dance, choral movement, and experimental theater of the 1920s. The blocklike forms Selden describes, typical of *Lamentation, Heretic,* and *Primitive Mysteries,* are seen repeatedly in photographs of Laban's and Wigman's dances and in the sculptures of Ernst Barlach. They are achieved in Graham through the massing of bodies, flank to flank, the individuals in the group fusing into one shape. These forms literally bonded the individual dancers into one body, a sort of superdancer, with the explosive power of the Graham vocabulary multiplied but still contained, a formidable energy waiting to be released. Photographs are all we have from the time, of course, and they may be deceptive. But even if the movement of these monolithic groups consisted only of held bodies in locomotion, the close physical contact and the need to find a common impulse must have brought the dancers into a communion that transcended ordinary fellowship.

In revivals undertaken while Graham was alive, however, we can see that the group movement was more than a walking wall. In *Celebration,* they jet en masse straight into the air, each erupting body seeming to give more lift to her partners. In *Heretic,* the human barrier splinters for moments as the individuals pivot into a new formation. In *Primitive Mysteries,* small groups reassemble into their original marching files by an ingenious economy of single steps. Whenever the solidity breaks up, the group seems irresistibly drawn to cohere again, so the audience must give up tracking persons and concede the group's collective presence as a counterforce to the mercurial but powerful presence of Graham the soloist. The group is a symbol as well as a theatrical element; the abstraction suggests both its literal derivation and concepts, feelings, events we don't see. For the individual dancer, this choreography meant not just naturalistic self-expression, but a self more potent, more grand, yet severely concise.

So Graham gave to these early dancers the gift of power through body image. She gave them, too, an almost sacred sharing in what—for all her genius as a dancer—she could not have realized without them. Together they made the dance, and together they were certain they were dancing serious and significant ideas. In return she enlisted them in an absolute matriarchy. Dance mythology tells of how they were not allowed to study with other teachers, even to talk to dancers of other sects. As with all cultists, they followed willingly, gratefully. They might be dismayed later on to find, as Dorothy Bird did, that they had become intimidated. Bird relates the troubling moment when she felt she had to

withdraw from the concert stage because she couldn't choreograph any movement that wasn't "copying" Graham; even as a teacher she couldn't deviate or
make variations on Graham's exercises because she felt Graham owned them.

Bird's sensible response was to turn to Broadway dancing, and later to teaching what Graham had taught her. She did not share her mentor's disdain for
commercial work, and in any case she needed to earn a living. When she admits
that one reason she liked dancing in Broadway shows was that she was a dancer,
not a choreographer, she reveals a seldom acknowledged distinction. Modern
dancers—often unrealistically—expect to become talented choreographers. Bird
recognized that she didn't need or want the burdens of choreographing. She
loved simply dancing. Her account of life in these forbidden stages opens a
whole chapter in American dancing that has been disapproved and nearly erased.
Perhaps dancing in the early Graham group, knowing you were one essential
unit in a powerful machine, actually prepared her for dancing in the chorus of
Broadway shows. She was open-minded enough not to feel demeaned by it.
Indeed, Dorothy Bird's narrative of the shows is as generous and welcome as her
account of Graham's formative work. Taking part in both seemed fulfillment
enough to her; she didn't need to be a star, and it is precisely as a worker that she
has so much to tell us.

By the end of the twentieth century, modern dance has become assimilated into
the cultural mainstream. Although debates still rage about whether "classical"
dancing is endangered by political, multicultural, and media diversity, the legit-
imacy of theatrical dancing is settled, as is its distinctness as a professional activity. But for the first decades, dancers struggled with a tangled complex of
questions. Where did physical culture end and dancing begin? How could
dancers establish themselves as professionals when no one except members of
ballet troupes received a salary? Could a dancer go on the popular stage and
preserve her dignity? What was the difference between studio and university
training in terms of creative goals and performing expectations? How to separate
the idea of dance technique identified with fiercely individual choreographers
from the fundamental training of any dancer?

Martha Graham's summers at the Cornish School are sparsely documented.
She herself claimed to have forgotten when she went there, and in a note of trib-

ute to Nellie Cornish she speaks only of a solo concert she gave with Louis Horst as accompanist, the spring before her first summer session.[14] None of the books on Graham gives a program of the group concerts she prepared in the summer of 1930; few even mention these performances. Perhaps in the momentum of Graham's long career, interludes such as Cornish are significant only as laboratory situations where choreography could be prepared for a "real" premiere in New York, or where important members of her company and teachers of her technique first encountered her.

Today, however, Graham's technique is far more widely known than her repertory. It was in the studios—and with the indispensable collaboration of Louis Horst and intelligent dancers like Anna Sokolow, Bonnie Bird, Dorothy Bird, Bessie Schonberg, Martha Hill, Ethel Butler, Sophie Maslow, Gertrude Shurr, and Jane Dudley—that Graham's creative ideas resulted in choreographic form and a workable pedagogy. This germinal process, the discovery of movement and the shaping of impulse, will, and ego into theatrical sense, is what Dorothy Bird narrates so carefully and lovingly here. Her participation in the process fed her whole life as performer and teacher and enabled her to give this generation in turn some of the passion and the wonder.

The Act of Appreciation

When I took tea with my friend Milly Johnstone in the beautiful Japanese tea-house in her New York City apartment, the two of us would occasionally take time for the traditional Act of Appreciation. After tasting the sweet biscuit and savoring the last drops of bitter green tea, Milly would point out how exquisitely each utensil had been crafted. I held the teabowl in my hands and turned it this way and that, looking for the side that had the most beautiful portion of the design. I then placed the teabowl with that side facing Milly, in accordance with the custom.

Milly once told me of a trip she had made to a pottery studio in a remote part of Japan. It was the day that John F. Kennedy was assassinated. As she left the train, each passenger stood up quietly and bowed to her, saying "So sorry." At the potter's studio, Milly was presented with an exquisite antique teabowl, which she brought home to New York. This treasured teabowl eventually broke, and she took it to a restorer who repaired it beautifully, placing threads of gold in the cracks. When Milly served tea in the restored teabowl to a revered tea master, he examined the bowl carefully and said, "This teabowl is even more valuable now, because it has lived." That teabowl was my favorite. Holding it comforted me and gave me courage when certain events shattered my life.

The Act of Appreciation is a special experience, in which you share the value of something truly beautiful. Time is taken not only to experience sensorily and relish small details, but also to ask questions and listen to answers. Writing this book has been my Act of Appreciation for those who enriched my life with their presence. In preparing the text, I have turned over in my mind all that has happened, as I would turn over a teabowl when contemplating its history and beauty. Then, as is done at the close of the tea ceremony, I bow gently to my parents, Amy Ethel Holley and Claude Cecil Bird; my brothers, Windham, Jack, David, and Mike; my late husband, Paul; and my many friends and associates in the world of theater and dance. Most especially of all, I bow to Martha Graham, who generously opened up to me the world of the arts and gave me a skill that has served me well all my life.

Until I came to New York City in 1930 to be with Martha Graham, I never had thought much about the role of women in society. Much later in life, I learned that it was bold, courageous, independent, spirited women who were in the forefront, leading the way in what came to be called modern dance. Each in their own way broke new ground, tearing off the restraints that had been so tightly clamped on them in a male-dominated, puritanical society.

The first American woman dancer to strike out in her own original direction was Loie Fuller (1862–1928?). She costumed herself in a short straight shift and sandals when she danced. Her hair flowed loosely upon her shoulders. She created magical illusions by manipulating vast amounts of lightweight fabric, illuminated by the newly invented, many-colored electric lights. People flocked to her performances, and enthusiasm for this new entertainment reached wildfire proportions. Her influence was felt everywhere, being especially evident in art and in the deco lamps of Tiffany and others.

Isadora Duncan, born in 1878 in California, was both idealistic and romantic. A rebel in both private and public life, she freed the body by breaking the bonds of corsets and petticoats. Instead of these symbols of enforced imprisonment, which had made life almost unbearable for preceding generations of women, Isadora dressed herself and her dancers in softly flowing Greek drapes, revealing bare legs and feet. Curt Sachs wrote that Isadora "breathes life into the statues of the Greeks. She frees the old Hellenic dance from the rigidity of sculpture from its sleep in the museums."[1] Isadora had excellent musical taste and chose to dance to classical masterpieces. Some say she improvised to the music, dancing as the spirit moved her, but those associated with her claim everything was carefully choreographed. Her first great success was in Paris in 1900.

Isadora died tragically in 1927, three years before I arrived in New York City. I hated the motion picture *Isadora*, starring Vanessa Redgrave. It was pandering and degrading as it focused on Isadora's downfall and not on her contribution, completely missing the value of her tragic life. Isadora was a rebel for all women, but the film made her out to be a self-destructive rebel for herself alone. In reality it was Isadora, the free spirit, who found a way through dance to symbolically tear off the fetters holding women back, and who paved the way for the dancers who were to follow. Isadora was superb, a symbol of proud, fearless, independent womanhood.

Ruth St. Denis (1877?–1968) was a great beauty, an actress, a dancer, and a genius with costumes. When at an early age her dark hair had turned white, her manager, David Belasco, suggested she change her given name from Ruth Dennis to Ruth St. Denis. Dancers have always referred to her as "Miss Ruth," which perhaps indicates that, although she was a truly independent soul, she was not much of a rebel. Miss Ruth was fascinated by the mystical and spiritual concepts rooted in the Orient, and she translated these ideas into successful and highly profitable theatrical interpretations presented on worldwide vaudeville tours. She was completely down-to-earth, practical, witty, and she possessed a legendary sense of humor. Her walk was marvelous, with a flow of movement extending through her back that made people think she had an extra vertebra in her spine. When asked about it, she would say, "I move like a yard of spit." This was particularly startling because she projected the image of such intense spirituality. Under the protection of religious dance, and by putting herself on a pedestal, she dealt well with the expectations set by powerful men for women of her day. She could thus avoid the confrontation faced so fearlessly by Isadora. Ruth St. Denis and her husband, Ted Shawn, founded Denishawn, a school that became the seedbed of American modern dance.

At Denishawn, the most likely to find a home were slim, delicate, sylphlike young girls or exotic, fragile, flowerlike ladies with a flavor of the Far East. Luckily for Denishawn student Martha Graham, she could never have fitted into the mold. She left the fold of Denishawn after working in the school and being on tour with Ted Shawn for a fairly short period. Perhaps because Denishawn required that anyone wishing to teach their technique had to be licensed (and pay the astronomical fee of five hundred dollars for the privilege), Martha set out to create her own way of moving. For the uniform she wanted her students to wear in the classroom, she stripped off the Greek drape worn at Denishawn and replaced it with a homemade leotard.

Martha was joined two years later by Louis Horst, who had been musical director at Denishawn. Having learned from the example of Isadora's tragic ending, Louis insisted on the strictest discipline as he guided and goaded Martha to strip away all artificialities and to progress in her own way parallel to the revolutionary movements of modern art and modern music. In the 1920s vaudeville was fading, and Martha had found it personally humiliating to work on Broadway. Instead of commercial show business, she chose the dignity of the concert world. With the solid backing of the Neighborhood Playhouse providing a basic core of financial support, Martha and Louis created concerts to please themselves.

In the 1930s, Gertrude Hoffman described to me a satire called *Rewolt* that had been performed by singer comedienne Fanny Brice.[2] Gertrude said it had been presented by Miss Brice's husband, Billy Rose, at one of his nightclubs. Miss Brice wore a red mop on her head and performed an exaggerated satire of modern dancers. Many were hostile to modern dance, and especially to women being so independent. It must have delighted the powerful men in the audience, who loved the putdown and laughed loudly. Men adored the dancers when they were young and beautiful, but when the women aged and were no longer so appealing, the men's hostility came to the fore. It was, however, too late to stop the movement toward women's liberation and a totally new form of dance.

Acknowledgments

As far back as the 1960s, when I was trying to explain the roots of the early Graham experience to my adult students in a class in Merrick, Long Island, one student in particular—Joyce Greenberg—told me repeatedly that what I was saying was valuable from a historical point of view. Joyce would question me, and in response to her prodding and evident interest, long-forgotten details popped back into my mind. At first I would recall fragments, which I sometimes wrote down in bits and pieces, but Joyce forced me to be more detailed and specific.

It became very exciting as we dug ever deeper into my memory, searching to uncover buried treasure. Genevieve Oswald contributed further to awakening in me an awareness of the importance of this material with her recognition, in the form of an archive in the Dance Collection of the New York Public Library for the Performing Arts at Lincoln Center. Genevieve insisted that my memories must not be lost, and she repeated emphatically, "You must write it down!"

Seven years ago, Joyce and I began in earnest to organize the material that has now resulted in this work. I asked my friend Dina Bengal, an editor at Behrman House, to give her opinion of an early draft. Dina urged me to make Martha Graham "more colorful, because that is what people expect." With her close friend, Sophie Maslow, Dina had often seen Martha perform but did not really know her. I tried to embellish things as Dina suggested, but I found I couldn't. Martha always dressed in drab colors. She was theatrical only on stage. In attempting to follow Dina's advice, I came to understand that my writing would be valuable only if I gave precise, honest details of what I recalled witnessing.

As Joyce and I wearily neared completion of the manuscript, Francis Mason, editor of *Ballet Review*, energized me with constant encouragement (verging on hypnosis). The unflagging enthusiasm of the late Harry Edelson kept me pressing forward. We are indebted to Maryann Chach, Reagan Fletcher, and Mark Swartz of the Shubert Archive for their many kindnesses and warm personal attention. Rita Waldren and the staff at the Dance Collection of the New York

Public Library for the Performing Arts at Lincoln Center, as well as Marty Jacobs of the Theatre Collection of the Museum of the City of New York, cooperated in every way as we researched photograph files. Special words of deep gratitude must go to Genevieve Oswald and the late Agnes de Mille, who read the working manuscript and contributed many valuable editorial suggestions. Practical advice offered by Pauline Tish, Shelley Gillenson, and Sylvia and Terry Page was most welcome.

I profoundly thank Dr. Miles Galen for preserving my eyesight long enough to complete this manuscript. Supportive friends who have assisted in countless and diverse ways include Lulla and Pearlie Adler, Peter and Susan Bernard, Ruth Birnkranz, June Cone, Betsy Dickerson, Hansi and Leo Frome, Bernie Kaapcke, Dena Levitt, Ruth Wolfert, and Muriel, Herbert, and Ronalda Whitman. Heartfelt appreciation is extended to Marc and Bertha Weinstein for their extraordinary efforts, and to Carole and Wes Richards who have taken neighborliness to the level of high art. My late husband, Paul, and Joyce's husband, Roy, each deserve recognition for retaining a sense of humor, patience, and understanding as we immersed ourselves in this project.

Bird's Eye View

One

Background, Family, and a Pioneering Lifestyle

WHEN DIANE GRAY, director of the Martha Graham School of Contemporary Dance in New York City, invited me to teach two workshops for the advanced students in 1987, I knew instantly what it was she wanted from me. It certainly was not to teach a technique class, but rather to share with the students examples of Martha Graham's "early work." Jane Dudley, whom I had coached when she first arrived in the Graham studio, referred to herself as a master of what she laughingly dubbed the Prehistoric Period of the Graham work, dating from the late 1930s through the 1940s. This prompted me to label myself privately as master of the Neanderthal Period, referring to the remarkable summer of 1930, when Martha taught at the Cornish School in Seattle, and the years immediately following.

At about noon on May 14, 1987, I completed teaching the first workshop at the Graham Studio. In it I had attempted to open the door, if only a crack, for a whiff of the heady stuff that had transpired during the early 1930s, when Martha was in her early thirties and was ceaselessly searching for high levels of energy, combined with a startling and compelling sense of power. That pioneering work was to become a source of inspiration for many leading dancers and choreographers, including Mikhail Baryshnikov, Merce Cunningham, Erick Hawkins, Rudolf Nureyev, Paul Taylor, and Twyla Tharp. As the students and staff teachers who had been observing the workshop applauded long and enthusiastically, I began to feel uncomfortable. I raised my hand for them to stop.

"You do know that it is Martha you are applauding, not me," I said.

"We are applauding you, too, for the way you shared this with us," Pearl Lang graciously replied.

The intense interest of those present awakened me to the realization that the information I had held close to my heart and had cherished for so long was now unfamiliar to dancers of today. I was elated. I felt I was passing along hidden, nearly forgotten, family treasures to the younger generations.

When my husband, Paul, and I were leaving the studio, we saw Martha Graham sitting in the waiting room. As we walked toward her, I was struck by how tiny she was. It broke my heart, for in my memory are vivid pictures of her, seeming so tall and strong, as she commanded the stage with tremendous force and vigor.

Paul reached out to give her a big hug, as he had always done ever since they first met, and said, "Martha, it's so wonderful for Dorothy to be working for you in your studio again. It's really full circle for her, isn't it—1930 to 1987."

Martha looked at me and smiled softly. "You know, Paul," she said. "Dorothy was a total innocent when she first came to me." Then she paused before adding, "And she still is." I protested, laughing, but Martha insisted, "If you once have the quality of innocence, you always have it." There was a moment of silence, then she said, "I am sorry I arrived late. I wanted to see you teach."

I was definitely relieved. It would have been difficult—perhaps even impossible—for me to take on the role of teacher with her watching. As we parted, I whispered to Martha something I had never before managed to say to her but had always truly felt, "I love you, you know."

She warmly responded, "I love you, too."

Over the years, friends and colleagues have urged me to write of my experiences in dance and theater, but I had never truly been motivated until that special day, when I saw Martha at her studio and was struck by the fragility of life. And too, there was the painful, nagging memory of a disturbing conversation I had once with John Martin, the first dance critic on the *New York Times*.

One summer I had gone to the big old house where John Martin and Zachary Solov lived in Saratoga, New York. My purpose was to consult with John concerning a dance history course I was preparing to teach at the Board of Cooperative Educational Services (BOCES) Performing Arts High School on Long Island. Among my questions was one I felt he alone could answer.

I asked John, "After Louis Horst left Martha's studio, who took over his role? Was there ever anyone else who was able to make her discipline herself? Who guided her artistic life as he had done?"

John reacted with such fury he could hardly speak. "You! You of all people can ask this? Do you mean to tell me you don't KNOW that no one could ever take over Louis's role? that no one could replace him? Don't you realize that without Louis standing there beside her, day in, day out, adamantly refusing to let her improvise, she would have done what Carmalita Maracci did? That Martha, too, would have improvised brilliantly with dazzling skill? That she would have changed the choreography slightly each time she danced it, until finally it became diluted and lost its original fierce fire and character?"

John took a moment to contain his frustration, then he went on to explain more quietly and patiently that it was Louis who had helped Martha learn to strip away all trivialities and nonessentials, to seek and discover deep levels of motivations and emotions, then to refine and develop truly original movement patterns. John concluded, "No one else could possibly have done this for her, and no one else ever did! It was Louis! It was *all* Louis!" John appeared heartbroken, near to tears. He obviously was appalled to think that even with my bird's-eye view, I had failed to understand their professional relationship; and more important, I did not fully appreciate the overall significance of the role Louis Horst had played.

I felt very shaken when I left John. It had been startling, unsettling, to hear him assert that even though I had stood next to Martha, connected to her almost as if I were her shadow, I did not comprehend how Louis had acted as catalyst and how, out of the fire of their constant tangling, battling, and shared laughter, had come genuine progress. John had opened my eyes to perceive the historic view of events I had witnessed.

Haunted by the memory of John's emotional reprimand and the reality of Martha's mortality, it suddenly seemed imperative to share my memories, first of working with Martha, and then also of the many other outstanding personalities who had touched my life, including Agnes de Mille, Bobby Alton, Felicia Sorel, Albertina Rasch, Helen Tamiris, Jack Cole, Jerome Robbins, Doris Humphrey, José Limón, Eugene Loring, Orson Welles, Herbert Ross, and George Balanchine. I must begin my story with the special circumstances of my childhood, for there lay the secret of why I fell so completely under Martha Graham's spell. The influence of my mother, father, brothers, and our pioneering lifestyle formed the loom upon which the colorful weaving of my life would take place.

EVERYONE LOVED my Mother. Wherever she went, she was known as Mother Bird. She was usually followed by a small flock of Bird children. There were five of us, four boys and myself. As we all walked single file behind Mother, I secretly felt as if I were nothing more than a couple of legs on a centipede. It would have been different if I had been a boy; Mother was so proud of her boys. But it was always made quite clear to me that I was not a boy, and I felt I was an outsider.

Mother spent her early years in India, where her English father, Major George Hunt Holley, served in the Munster Fusiliers. While stationed in Ireland, he had fallen in love with a happy-go-lucky Irish Catholic girl who was so lovely they called her Dawn, the Belle of Tralee. In defiance of his strictly Church of England, socially prominent family, the couple eloped to Paris. The Major took Dawn and their three children with him when he was assigned to India in the late 1800s. There he organized, directed, and traveled with an army theatrical company. My mother was only a small child when her father suddenly died. She and her two older brothers were summoned to England by her paternal grandfather; Dawn was left behind in India.

Immediately after meeting the three children at the ship in England, her grandfather arranged for Mother to stay in an orphanage, but he took the boys home with him. Mother was desperately unhappy and frightened at the orphanage. She told me she was starved, beaten, and locked in a dark closet. Finally, when she became severely ill, a kindly old doctor informed the family that they must take her back to their estate and care for her. By this time her brothers were away at boarding school, and Mother was again alone among strangers.

At her grandfather's house there were stringent rules to be obeyed. Dinner was served precisely on the dot of six o'clock, and if Mother arrived one minute late, she was not allowed to eat. There were many servants in the house but only the cook, Mrs. Huckstable, treated her kindly. Mother managed to grow to adulthood without learning much of anything that would be at all useful or practical. Upon reaching the age of emancipation, twenty-one, Mother promptly fled, to avoid an arranged marriage with an older man. She traveled to Vancouver Island, British Columbia, to visit one of her brothers. There she met the man who was to become my father. He was so beguiled by her delightful good humor that he followed her back to England, where they were married in 1908.

Daddy had been educated in Scotland at Edinburgh University. His dream of becoming a physician ended after he observed doctors in the operating room. Seeing the screaming patient with blood spurting out caused him to faint. He felt disgraced and gave up the idea of practicing medicine. Instead, he emigrated to Canada.

He often told my brothers and me stories of the times before he met Mother, when he was a pioneer in Canada in the late 1800s. "First I worked as a hired hand, and saved every cent I could until I had enough money to buy land. I paid one dollar for an acre, and the Canadian government gave me the adjoining acre free, in return for my promise to farm the land. I built a shack for shelter, purchased a plow, two oxen and seed. My lone companion was a cat named Tommy, whom I taught to chew tobacco with me before dinner."

Daddy became an accomplished farmer by avidly reading everything about crops, rotation, fertilizing, and animal husbandry. By the time he married Mother, he had the best farm in the whole Qu'Appelle Valley. My brother Windham was born on that farm. Just one year and one month later on a bitterly cold February day, Mother went into labor with her second child, Jack. When she became pregnant soon again, she was despondent. She convinced Daddy that she could no longer face the hardships of living on the prairie. Daddy sold the farm that had been his pride and joy. There was never any question that

Daddy adored Mother, and she always got her way. He affectionately said she was an original. Her roguish, independent spirit invariably served as an example of down-to-earth blind courage.

The family traveled to Parksville on Vancouver Island, where David was born. They lived in a cottage near a wide sandy beach, where the weather was mild and the land was warmed by the Japanese current as it swept around the shore. Here Mother found friends with whom she had much in common. People led a leisurely life, visiting for afternoon tea, tending beautiful English-style lawns, playing croquet, and attending garden parties. It was like a little bit of Merrye Olde England. One year later, in October 1912, I was born—the fourth child in four years.

I was not yet one year old when Great Britain entered World War I. Daddy, the ultimate idealist, believed the propaganda slogans about "making the world a better, safer place for your children," and "the war to end all wars." He felt he must go "home" to England to volunteer for the army, and he took his family with him. My parents rented a house in Bath. Daddy enlisted and was sent immediately to the front. When Daddy returned home on leave, I did not recognize him. His hair had turned white. He had been gassed by the Germans; nonetheless, he was required to return to fight in the trenches. Nine months later, my little brother Mickey was born.

It must have been a tremendous struggle for Mother to care for us. She did not have much money. Rationing was very strict, and there were shortages of everything, including milk. German planes flew low over our house, dropping leaflets that we picked up as they fluttered from the sky. They contained threats to bomb the civilian population. Fortunately, the Armistice was declared before the bombing could take place. The end of the war meant that our family would return to Canada. Most of Daddy's hard-earned money had been spent, and Daddy suffered lasting physical effects as a result of his service in the army. But they never complained and never looked back.

Mother and Daddy made plans to create their own small Shangri-la on Vancouver Island and bought a nine-acre parcel of land at Mill Bay. We camped out there, near a stream that crossed the property and provided fresh water. In a clearing, Daddy made a fire surrounded by rocks and he fried bacon, scrambled eggs, and made the most delicious bread by twisting dough around a stick. Each of us was assigned chores. I collected small sticks for kindling, while the big boys chopped and sawed wood for the fire. Daddy was meticulously thorough about everything he did. He worked to clear the land and trained the boys to help. The foundations for the house were carefully laid. Tall, straight trees were cut, and Mother cajoled her loving horse, Prince, to haul the timbers to the building site. Prince would not do this for anyone but her. The six families who lived within walking distance volunteered to help raise the main supports, and slowly the house went up, higher and higher.

Eventually Daddy and the boys would dig ditches and install pipes to bring what we called running water into the house from the stream. Neighbors were allowed to tap into the Bird Waterworks also.[1] Before long we acquired a cow, a horse and buggy, goats, and chickens. Daddy built a rose arbor surrounded by Dorothy Perkins roses as my private place to play. It was near Mother's flower garden, which had all sorts of mignonettes, nasturtiums, primroses, fragrant mock orange and lilac, and herbs for both healing and seasoning. The plants came from the gardens of friends or through mail order catalogs. The nearest store was some miles away at Cobble Hill, but we were fairly self-sufficient, except for buying fresh salmon from the local Indians.

Working together at Mill Bay, we could readily understand Daddy's pride and enthusiasm about being a pioneer. It was a productive and happy time, with each day having its own challenges and victories. All of us were kept busy, participating constantly in the work of the farm. We experienced a great feeling of closeness and accomplishment as we watched the fruits ripen on the trees and bushes we had planted, and as we partook of the bounty.

After the chores were done for the day, my brothers and I would often play our own complicated version of follow the leader. Each one had to step exactly in the same spot with the same foot as the person in front of them. We balanced along the trunks of fallen trees, jumped from stone to stone across streams, cartwheeled and somersaulted in the meadows, and darted through the yard as baby goats tried to bunt us. In summer we swam, fished, and played in dugout canoes that Daddy had bought from the Indians. We hunted for robins' eggs and chased butterflies. David and I created a network of tunnels under a field of waist-high bracken ferns by rapidly crawling through them on our hands and knees. We all played hide and seek in the tunnels. When we really wanted to know where the others were hiding, we would open our mouths wide and call out, "Oh! Oh! Oh!" The sound carried far, like a yodel. It was our private call. It kept us together, and we loved it. Daddy had taught us to signal this way. He was always worried about one of us getting lost in the forest.

It must have appeared to people on the outside that we lived an almost utopian existence, cut off from the rest of the world. In actuality this was not quite so. We were fantastically healthy physically, but emotionally we were somewhat crippled. Although ideal in many ways, our upbringing was a poor training ground for life in the outside world. Children at that time were to be seen but not heard. This was not just a saying in our home; it was the rule. We were taught to be utterly unselfish and no trouble to anyone. We were totally obedient in this structured environment almost devoid of social contact.

The imposition of discipline was severe. Whenever somebody misbehaved during the day, Mother would report to Daddy in the evening that so-and-so had done such and such, and they should be punished. It was Daddy who administered the punishment—a whacking. The procedure was that you leaned over his lap, he pulled down your pants, then he spanked you on the behind with the back of a hairbrush. Daddy explained ahead of time that if you wanted him to stop, you had to calm yourself, stop crying, and ask him in a normal voice to "please stop." Perhaps this was the traditional British way of teaching stoicism, to enable us to keep our wits about us in the face of dire trouble. Maybe it was unique to our family. I don't know. Daddy could not have known that by teaching me to stoically push down and deny my feelings, I would in the process lose the ability to discriminate. I learned to squelch all feelings, to the point of being frighteningly out of touch with them.

My clothes were often hand-me-downs from distant cousins in England who attended various private schools. The dresses were always navy blue serge and much, much, much too big. Mother pinned them up in great big tucks, sometimes as many as three, and basted them as best she could. As I grew, Mother would let down the top tuck, and when I grew a little more, the next tuck. This meant I never outgrew those hateful dresses.

Windham, being the oldest son, attended an English-style private boarding school. Once I was invited there to a fancy-dress party. I was costumed as Columbine in a plum-colored cheesecloth tutu made by a neighbor. I had difficulty remembering the name Columbine, so Mother told me that if anyone asked who I was, I should say I was "Little Miss Nobody." The headmaster of the school, Mr. Lonsdale, was a sociable man who taught Windham how to behave in the outside world. None of the rest of us had the slightest idea of how to carry on a conversation, much less make a joke. The closest I ever came to having a mentor was a couple from Victoria who spent weekends in their cottage across the road from us at Mill Bay. The man was a Greek sea captain who had gone to sea at the age of twelve and advanced to become head of the Canadian Pacific Boat Lines. We called him The Skipper, and his warm and caring wife we called Mums. The Skipper had a marvelously hearty, melodic voice. When they drove up to the cottage in their car, he would call out, "Hello! Hello! Where is everyone? Where is our little 'golden bells'?" I'd run to get my hugs, and The Skipper would swing me around in the air as no one else had ever done. He loved to make me laugh, and my ringing laughter was the reason he called me "golden bells." I was bathed in happiness with Mums and The Skipper. They were to me the grandparents I had never known. I felt safe and loved with them, and their house was a haven.

It was Mums who introduced my parents to the mystical world of Rosicrucianism. Daddy eventually became very involved, but Mother less so than he. Mother was quite open-minded about religion and liked to shop around for inspiration. There was a small, shared church not far from Mill Bay. Whenever the spirit moved her, Mother would take us to attend Sunday service. Sometimes we heard a strict Methodist, at other times a Baptist minister. The lady from Unity, however, who included hints on how to make face cream from lamb's fat, was by far the most intriguing.

The required schooling for all of us, except Windham, took place in the one-room Sylvania school, two and a half miles from home. Daddy had impressed upon us the necessity of keen observation to details during our daily walk to school through the woods, yet I would often daydream on the way, or wander off searching for the wildflowers Mother loved—I so longed to please her. Students in each grade level sat one behind the other in a row facing the teacher. I happened to be the only one in my grade and, therefore, the only one in my row. The teacher, Mrs. Ballou, never took time for me in class other than to say, "Read with row so-and-so. Follow along as best you can." Being in school was like an extension of our family life. I was fortunate in that a neighbor had taught me to read and write and do simple arithmetic before I began school. In return for the favor, Mother had taught the neighbor's children a bit of French—open the door, close the door, open the window, close the window, and come with me if you please to buy some chocolate at the store. The last phrase was frustrating because there was no store.

Dancing was a popular form of recreation at Mill Bay. Children were encouraged to join in the line dances with the adults. When we did the Virginia Reel, I looked forward to the part where you go around the outside to meet your partner and slide through under the arch made by the other couples. In the spring we danced around a maypole, and I remember getting all mixed up when braiding the streamers. Someone taught me an Irish jig where I slapped my feet into the floor, arms down motionless at my side, while very concentrated and poker-faced. I "climbed the rope" using the complicated toe-heel foot patterns and rocking steps simulating a rough sea of the sailor's hornpipe. I especially enjoyed doing the polka with my brothers. We flew around the room, rotating as we went, getting wilder and wilder as the room spun faster and faster.

My favorite dance was the Highland Fling, taught to me by a patient neighbor lady. Her husband was a major and had a real sword, which we placed across a sheath outdoors on the ground. It seemed as if I practiced forever before performing it once on a stage in front of the curtains. To the tune of "The Campbells Are Coming, Hoorah! Hoorah!" I marched in carrying a sword over one shoulder. Because I was too little to carry the sword's sheath as well, Mother slid it to me from under the curtain, and I placed the two objects on the floor in the traditional cross. I had been told this dance was designed to teach speed and fast footwork in preparation for battle. I carefully and purposefully performed the steps high on my feet, turning this way and that over the crossed sword. It was very challenging, and when they played the bagpipes, it was exhilarating as everyone cheered me on.

Mother had a friend named Mrs. Oldham, a former actress who had been a student of the Delsarte work.[2] It was very much in vogue at the time, and she showed Mother some of the gestures: "I hear," "I see," "I think," "I feel in my heart," "Hush! Don't speak." Mother arranged small tableaux vivants for the Easter and Christmas shows at school and for parties. She hung bedspreads for curtains, dressed my brothers and me as characters from the Greek legends, and stood us up on boxes. After she opened the curtains, we made one or two gestures, and when the neighbors recognized we were "Cupid and the lovers" or "Narcissus by the pool" and dutifully applauded, Mother closed the curtains. My brothers hated it; I on the other hand loved it.

When I was still quite young, Daddy took me to the theater in Victoria to see Anna Pavlova. At first, I was enchanted by the artificial snowflakes that floated down from high above the stage. Then my attention focused on the dark-eyed woman who, before my eyes, metamorphosed into a dying swan. I could almost feel the soft, white feathers on her breast, as I pictured her forging forward through the water. This swan was real to me. I would always remember the undulating movements, not of her arms, strangely enough, but of her neck, which curved, arched, twisted, and pulsated as she gasped for breath after being shot by the arrow. Daddy was more impressed with Madame Pavlova's performance in *The Gavotte*, where she wore an empire-style dress and a bonnet. Her high-heeled slippers were tied with ribbons that criss-crossed around her slim, beautiful ankles.

We were waiting outside the stage door to see her when Daddy said, "Did you see the way she stepped on the floor, how her feet came down so simply, so precisely and delicately? Did you notice the way she carried her head, so finely, beautifully balanced? There is something about this that I want you to understand. Most people might not appreciate this, but it is important to me that you do. It appears that Anna Pavlova is totally unselfconscious, but actually she is completely aware of what she is doing and knows she is doing it perfectly. That is what I want for you. Even when you know people are watching you or talking about you, you should act in a simple and unaffected way. When you grow up, I don't want you to feel self-conscious or shy or tighten up. The secret is to be absolutely simple and direct." When Anna Pavlova finally came out of the stage door, she placed her hand on my shoulder and steadied me as she bent down and kissed me very softly.

I knew then deep down that one day I, too, would be a dancer on the stage. Although I desperately wanted to please Daddy and be simple, straight forward, unselfconscious, I could see that it was going to be awfully hard for me to accomplish this. Instead, I dreamed of dancing among the snowflakes with my neck curving and turning like that of a beautiful white swan, and of my feet encased in exquisite slippers tied with ribbons, rather than the awful Lecky boots we all wore. These sturdy leather country boots—with little metal hooks up the front, around which we laced the thick leather laces—never wore out. They were handed down as they were outgrown. They were very practical for our way of life, but they did not lend themselves to dancing. After seeing and being touched by Anna Pavlova, I no longer wanted to be one of the boys.

Since there was no high school in the Mill Bay area, when the time came for Windham to enroll, Daddy sold our farm and we moved to Victoria. We rented a house there from Mums and The Skipper. It was a big adjustment for my brothers and me to attend an elementary school with three hundred other students. I entered the third grade, but for three days I was too shy even to put up my hand to acknowledge my name when it was called for attendance. Entering public school in Victoria marked the end of the closeness of communal life for all of us.

Mums used her influence to have me transferred to an all girls school called St. Margaret's, where I did very well scholastically. I was invited to many parties, but before long I realized that the invitation was always the same, "Come, and bring your brothers." St. Margaret's school motto, "Service with a smile," was constantly stressed. This reinforced my training at home to be docile and obedient.

In the evening, Daddy and Mother often went to the Rosicrucian meeting. I was aware that as the daughter of two members, I could play a special role in the ceremonies. At the age of thirteen, I went to Mums, who was the Master of the group, to say that I wanted to become involved also. She talked to me at length, explaining that it was most unusual for someone as young as I to join, and that I must be really serious about devoting time to the studies. I also must promise to be silent about what happened and what I learned.

I was ready and willing to commit myself to becoming a "colombe." For my participation in the ceremonial rituals, Mums taught me to walk quietly and be aware of my breathing. I did this conscientiously and learned to walk smoothly and with dignity as I swung the incense. Mums commented that I obviously did not know much in this life, but perhaps I had carried over knowledge from previous lives. Because she believed in reincarnation and karma, she advanced the idea that I must be an "old soul," and I was permitted to attend meetings on a higher level. I always sat near Mums, and she taught me that it was my responsibility to speak my thoughts as they came to me. This did not occur too often, but it was something in a sea of nothingness. It gave me a most welcome feeling of stature. More important, the seed of a new idea had been planted in my mind —that I might have something to say that was worth hearing.

While my brothers competed in tennis, soccer, and hockey, I attended dance class daily after school. My teacher was Nelle Thacker from the Cornish School in Seattle. I was a devoted and motivated student, and I happily immersed myself in a world of make-believe. I appeared in recitals—as one of the sins that popped out when Pandora opened the box, as a Russian peasant, as Peter Pan. When still in my early teens, I was invited by a local orphanage to teach dance to the children. Since there was no music available, I gave the children animal images and improvisations of birds, snakes, and fish. The children loved it; the administrators did not.

When I was seventeen, Nelle Thacker left Victoria for New York City to pursue her career under the name of Marta Terrazzi. She left her school in my care. I was unprepared to undertake the responsibility, not only for teaching but also for disciplining students and managing a business. Money was a subject that was never discussed at home. It was considered shameful, taboo. We never had an allowance, or a paying job. Although I tried to run the school as best I could, I was utterly bewildered, collecting tuition, paying rent, and attending to other details of operating a business. It did not take long for the school to collapse.

At about that time, an exciting opportunity presented itself—an elocution competition open to young people all across Canada. Here was something I could do to please Mother. It was required that the entrants prepare a recitation and submit a written composition about "What I Want to Do with My Life." Since my father had always been a stickler for correct enunciation, we all had very clear diction. I chose to recite a poem that was popular at the time, "Pippa Passes" by Robert Browning. Mother coached me on the appropriate gestures, drawing on her limited acquaintanceship with the Delsarte method. I spoke the words with complete naïveté, being swept up in the meaning of the poem. My composition was written from my heart, and I was very insulted when the examiners from England asked if Mother had helped me. I credit the fact that I had been a colombe for four years with empowering me to focus myself during the recitation, and enabling me to quite innocently and idealistically express my views on paper. In any case, I won first place.

This honor coincided with my seeing a talking picture for the first time. The film was *Seventh Heaven*. I fell in love with the leading actors, Charles Farrell and Janet Gaynor, and the characters they played. I now secretly nurtured a new dream—to go to Hollywood to become a movie star. Anna Pavlova had made an indelible impression on me, but the idea of becoming a ballerina was out of reach. It was abundantly clear there was no future for me in teaching dance. Most of all, I dreaded the idea of spending my life in Victoria.

I was feeling trapped and hopeless when Jack, who was then studying art at the Cornish School in Seattle, suggested that I go there and ask Miss Cornish to advise me as to what to do. This struck me as being a step in the right direction —a step closer to Hollywood. Mother approved wholeheartedly of Jack's idea. She had always encouraged the boys to follow their dreams with "Nothing ventured, nothing won!" Now it was my turn. With a white cane in her hand to signal to the world that her eyesight was failing, Mother and I boarded the boat destined for Seattle. I admired her fearlessness and her sense of adventure. It made me suppress the guilty feelings I had about not telling her my real motives for wanting to go. Instead, I let surface my excitement at the possibility of entering a new, completely different world, down in the U.S.A.

Two

Martha Graham at the Cornish School, Seattle, 1930

THE CORNISH SCHOOL was a beehive of activity made up of budding artists busily sketching at their easels; music students producing a cacophony of instrumental and vocal sounds throughout the building; drama students rehearsing in studios as well as in the theater; and dancers spinning, soaring, balancing in large, airy studios on the top floor. There were dressing rooms, staffed with matrons, who handed students beautiful white towels for use after showering, and lockers for personal belongings. It was an extraordinary school, bursting with serious and dedicated students.

The director of the school, Miss Nellie Cornish, was a powerful little woman, devoted to both the school and the best interests of the students.[1] She wasted no time in telling me pointedly, "You need to look around you. See what is going on in the outside world." Miss Cornish handed me a photograph and explained, "This famous dancer, Martha Graham, is coming to Seattle this summer to teach the dance of the future at my school."

I was both fascinated and bewildered by the woman in the picture. Her head was turned starkly in profile. Her hair was brushed straight back from her forehead and fell to her shoulders, where it was cut off at a sharp angle that emphasized her jaw and the strong, columnlike tendon extending down the side of her neck. This was a far cry from the image of a dancer I had carried in my heart since I had seen Anna Pavlova in *The Dying Swan*.

"But, Miss Cornish, this does not look like a dancer to me. It looks more like a horse," I gasped in protest. With her long, dark hair worn loose and straight like a mane, and her firm lips covering the strong tooth formation, Martha Graham did indeed look to me more like a spirited horse than a dying swan. I had been brought up around horses, and I loved their velvet noses, strength, and wildness. I especially loved Mother's horse, Prince, who always put his head through the top of the open Dutch door in the kitchen to be near her.

While I sat there staring at the photo, my "Hollywood" money was being handed over to Miss Cornish. Mother registered me for the final two weeks of an introductory six-week course in a new style of dancing with the Swedish dancer Ronny Johansson.[2] This was to be a preparation for twelve weeks of summer study with Martha Graham. Mother expected that by the end of the first six-week session with Martha Graham, which was all that we could afford, I would be ready and willing to return to Victoria and resume teaching dance classes. Although I was upset and felt trapped, there was no way I could oppose either Mother or Miss Cornish. I accepted the situation reluctantly, knowing I would have to make the best of it. I did not for a moment dream that one day I would feel deeply indebted and grateful to the two of them for opening the door to the chance of a lifetime.

Ronny Johansson proved extremely talented and charming in her concert. In class, however, she was cold and somewhat harsh. Miss Johansson's technique consisted of swings, figure eights, head circles that made me queasy, and floor exercises I had done in physical education classes at St. Margaret's School. To me this was not the kind of dancing that would lead to performing, and I had set my heart on being on the stage. I hated everything about Miss Johansson's classes. Just as I had often felt excluded, being the only girl tagging along behind my four brothers, here too I felt a total outsider. A number of the students had been carefully groomed by Caird Leslie, a dedicated ballet teacher at the Cornish School. I was not nearly as accomplished as they. The other dance students wore little Greek tunics, ballet shifts, or gym bloomers, so I really stood out in my Peter Pan outfit—a green tunic over long, baggy, green stockings. Miss Johansson did not like me any more than I liked her, and her voice reeked with irritation as she called out, over and over, "Would the lady in green *please* pay attention. Would the lady in green *please* stop dreaming. Would the lady in green *please* keep the rhythm," and on and on. At last the agonizing two weeks with Ronny Johansson ended, and I found myself standing shyly among students from all parts of the West Coast, awaiting the arrival of this celebrated dancer, Martha Graham. After the experience with Miss Johansson, I was distinctly unhappy and apprehensive about being there. It seemed we waited forever for the stranger from New York City.

On arriving at the Cornish School, Martha Graham must have heard the students calling out in the halls, "Where is Miss Aunt Nellie?" "Tell Miss Aunt Nellie . . .," "Ask Miss Aunt Nellie . . ." This must have been as startling to Martha Graham as it was to everyone on their first visit to the school. The title "Miss Aunt" was unique; it had been bestowed on Miss Cornish by a small child. Children of that time never thought of addressing an adult by their first name. All female unmarried friends of the family were called "Aunt" and their first name. Others were called "Miss" and their family name. To say "Miss Cornish" would have seemed cold and formal to a child, so with due affection the child had added both "Miss" and "Aunt" to the first name. Thus Miss Cornish became known far and wide as "Miss Aunt Nellie."

As we waited in the studio, the nervous tension was so great it seemed the building actually trembled when Martha Graham finally walked through the dressing room door, followed by a portly, white-haired gentleman. She had entered very quietly, but with a tremendous sense of dedication and purpose. There was something about this woman that struck a deep chord in me. Where had I seen this kind of quiet intensity, this integrated sense of power and determination before? At first I could not place it; then my heart started to pound as I remembered how Anna Pavlova had come through that stage door long ago. I had never forgotten her—the diminutive yet authoritative stature, the radiant eyes, the dark hair combed back off her face and pinned into a small bun at the nape of her neck. The similarity in manner was startling. I could scarcely breathe. I kept staring, and wondering, Was it the way they walked, placing the feet deliberately on the floor? Was it the imperial carriage of the head that communicated such a powerful presence? I did not know. As I thought of how Anna Pavlova had put out her hand to steady me as she placed a light kiss on my forehead, I knew there would be nothing like that from Martha Graham. Nevertheless, I secretly felt close to her. The feeling came over me suddenly that if my father had been there, he would have smiled and nodded his head in approval, saying, "She is the one you were destined to meet." I sighed with relief. I knew I was in the right place at the right time after all.

Under Martha Graham's cool, quiet exterior, I sensed a fiery volcano ready to erupt. No one could distract her or deflect her, not even Miss Aunt Nellie, who had bustled into the room behind the portly gentleman, proudly prepared to introduce this already distinguished and controversial young dancer to the class. Clearly, Martha Graham chose to short-circuit any chance of being called either "Miss Martha" or "Miss Aunt Martha" as she quickly brushed aside Miss Aunt Nellie and her planned introduction and spoke to us directly.

"Because we have crucially important work we are going to be doing together this summer, we have no time to waste on artificial manners and formalities," she said, urgently. "You may call me Martha, and you may call this gentleman, my musical director, Louis Horst, Louis. The work we will be doing in this classroom will be preparation for the Greek chorus in the play *Seven Against Thebes*. A group of students will be chosen from these classes to be in the production at the end of summer."

In order for us to accomplish so much in such a short time, we were to act at all times in the studio as if we were onstage. The work would be paramount. No marking would be allowed.[3] Strict simplicity and discipline would color our entire lives. Martha underscored these rules with "There will be no greetings, no farewells, no trivialities permitted. There will be only a total concentrated focus on the work we do together."

The excitement in the studio mounted as Martha moved closer to us. Then, as if confiding a secret, she said quietly, "Before we begin, I want to share with you something that I only recently discovered when dancing the role of the girl chosen to be the sacrificial virgin in the ballet *Le Sacré du Printemps*. We were in New York City on the great stage of the Metropolitan Opera House, with a full orchestra, a famous conductor, and many dancers. I had to stand on the stage and be absolutely still for a very long time."

She paused. We waited expectantly, and then she continued, "I discovered that I could command the stage while standing absolutely still. I could make an audience actually long for me to move. I could in fact steal the audience away from everyone else on the stage! Here in this class I am determined that I will teach you how to command the stage without your even making a move. But first you must forget everything you have ever learned before."

This was no problem for me. I did not have too much to forget. Memories of Scottish sword dancing, the Delsarte tableaux vivants, and even my beloved ballet, all vanished under the magic spell woven by Martha Graham. In one stroke, she quietly closed the door on all that had gone before, quite simply and completely erasing turnout, toe shoes, tutus, crowns, and little white wings.

Beginning with that first day, Martha kept her promise to teach us how to command the stage while standing absolutely still. Each subsequent day she built upon the work of the previous day, always with the understanding that everything we did was a preparation for performing onstage. As we gradually accomplished the first phase of the work, I learned how to appear absolutely still, yet be filled with trapped energy, ready to explode into action. In looking back to that time in 1930, I now more fully appreciate the crucial importance of her achievement and wish to share at least a portion of what we experienced in those remarkable classes. Martha presented five categories of potent images we could rely upon to energize every movement we made. Although I am presenting these categories as a unit of cardinal principles, it must be understood that Martha interspersed them within the class work, to sensitize and enrich movement, throughout the entire first six-week session. I think of these basics as equivalent to the Golden Rule that guided my brothers and me as we were growing up.

The first of these principles was to "Feel." Martha awakened us to the potential for energy in "Feel" by directing us to take off our ballet shoes and stand with our bare feet placed three inches apart in a precisely parallel position. The toes and the balls of our feet were to carry the weight. Our heels pointed back but only touched the floor lightly. Martha had us align our feet along the parallel boards of the floor.

"Think of railroad tracks going off into the far distance," she suggested. "The tracks go on and on. They do not converge. Now imagine you are looking over mountains, across rivers, prairies, and plains of America. You are going to learn to think and act like pioneers in the wide open spaces." I was full of pride when she said this, having actually been part of a true pioneering family.

Martha told us to close our eyes and picture in our minds the uneven surface of earth under our feet. The realm of creative imagination that Martha spoke about was unfamiliar and unknown to me, yet I felt my feet respond. My ten toes adapted to the imaginary ground by gripping and pressing. Then she asked us to imagine the nails of the toes turning into long talons, reaching out and retracting again and again. By exploring the feeling of clawing, my feet felt vital and alive. With my eyes still closed, I observed my breathing. I followed Martha's directives: as we breathed in, we might feel the arches of our feet curving and rising like a bridge over water; as we exhaled, we might feel our feet pressing down into the ground and the arches flattening out.

Martha keyed us into the body's balance mechanism in the ears; she urged us to feel how our balance depends on unseen, but constant adjustments of weight. She asked us to lean out an infinitesimal amount one way, return to center, then lean out into another direction. Each time we were to feel all the many adjustments being made inside the body to bring us back into balance. With my head balanced delicately on the top vertebra of the spine (Martha called it the atlas), I tried to find my center of balance by almost losing it, then recovering it. I kept the movement hidden and as minutely small as possible, almost turning, almost tipping. I fought to resist the impulse to move. In my mind I pictured a balancing scale, like the one in the symbol of Justice.

As Martha introduced us to the action of the hip hinge, she touched on the wonderful design inherent in that part of the body. She wanted us to feel the hip almost hinging, as the torso subtly swayed on the legs. We observed the hinges in the ankles and the knees and saw how they long to work like a spring. Martha said we must not allow this to happen.

"Hold in the movement. Contain it. Rein yourself in, like a spirited horse," she commanded. I felt at home with the image of reining in the horse and understood at once, that we were to stand still yet be prepared to burst forth into a wild gallop. "To the audience you appear to be still, but you are never still until you die," Martha stated, as she guided us in becoming aware of the miracle of the human body, with its intricate sense of balance and its tremendous hunger for movement.

With Martha we carefully examined the role of each muscle, one after another, until she had created a total picture of how they held the human bone structure upright. She used the image of a skyscraper, towering floor above floor above floor, high into the air. She compared the bones to support beams, and the muscles to long steel cables that held each floor in position, stacked one upon the other. The cables of this imaginary skyscraper had the ability to pull slightly or let go a trifle, to resist the wind and keep the building upright. She explained that the brain of this miraculous human building had a mechanism resembling a telephone system, in that it received messages when the body was in danger of toppling over and sent out lightning-fast responses to warn certain muscles to lengthen and others to shorten to enable the skyscraper to find center again. The body was engaged in a never-ending battle, with constant warnings about the approaching crisis of being off balance.

Martha enlarged on the skyscraper image by suggesting that we feel the hip bones as parallel sides of a tall building. "Press them apart," she said, "and feel yourself rising up out of the hips, like smoke. Feel the shoulders balancing like a crossbar on the spine, and moving in opposition to an imaginary crossbar in the hips. Feel like a skyscraper swaying in the wind. You are not rigid. You are balancing. Feel the arms hanging easily from the shoulders. Imagine the armpits open and airy, not cramped and frightened. Feel your breasts held high." Even though it was in style for women to bind their breasts like the flappers, Martha did not condone this practice. She told me to be proud of my ample breasts.

Martha moved quickly on, suggesting a variety of images: Imagine that you are a cat purring gently within. Feel as if you have whiskers that enable you to judge your body's width as you move through a narrow place. Feel as if your arms are covered with huge, strong feathers, like the wings of an eagle, longing to spread out and take flight. Feel that you are a snake moving secretly, ever so subtly, inside your skin. After we experienced each example, Martha instructed us, "Absorb these images. Compress them and store the concentrated essence of the image in the notebook of your mind." Each image left me with a residue of feeling that had been extracted.

This essence would be ready to be made vivid at a moment's notice at some future time, in whatever part of the body would be most effective. Martha likened the process of transferring the concentrated essence of an image to a game of hide-and-seek that you can play with an audience. I remember her saying, "It's like teasing them. You don't just hand them something on a platter or stuff it down their throats. You give them little leads, and entice them. Each person will find a different meaning, and it will be their own." She said we should challenge the audience to grasp the feeling and seek the message we are sending. By not being too obvious, we would be inviting them to participate as active partners. Gradually, I came to wonder if the process Martha proposed was actually more like a duel with the audience than a game.

When the time came to present the second principle, "See," Martha came up with a series of astonishing notions. She told us that onstage we would project the *idea* of seeing through an imaginary "third eye," located at the indentation at the base of the front of the throat. Symbolic gestures of seeing—such as shading the eyes with a hand or blinking or straining the eyes—were ridiculous, she said, comparable to placing your hand by your ear to express hearing, or lifting your nose into the air to communicate sniffing the air for scents. Martha stated firmly, "These are examples of indicating, and indicating cannot be tolerated."

Martha pointed out that, because peripheral vision is essential to an animal for self-preservation, many animals have eyes placed more to the sides of the face than ours. We worked to develop peripheral vision by relaxing the eyes with lids slightly lowered, facing the eyes straight forward, yet at the same time seeing as wide an arc in front and to both sides of the face, extending as far back as possible. Using this strangely wide, unfocused gaze, we explored the images of a deer, motionless in assessing danger, yet seeing all around; an eagle as predator surveying the scene far below; an owl, all eyes, waiting; an old cat flattening itself into the grass with eyes focusing and changing as it waits, shivering with excitement, preparing to pounce.

As another way to "See," Martha established the concept of thinking of the face as a mask, with strong bone structure, cheekbones, forehead, and jawline. "Each change of position communicates to the audience your active response to what you are seeing. You can question, reject, threaten, tease, and so on," she explained, after showing how the mask of the face can be turned, tipped, lifted, projected out, pulled back in. I saw that projecting the mask with the chin up and out might suggest enforcing your will. Tipping the mask sideways could imply questioning, thinking, or just waiting. The impassive mask of the face could also be mysteriously eloquent, whereas a smile, a scowl, a raised eyebrow might easily become superficial or false.

"*Smiling is absolutely out,*" Martha said emphatically. "It is so often done to please, to indicate subservience or overeagerness. You are to be proud and aloof." With this, she sternly eliminated all outward facial expressions. We danced with impassive faces.

When Martha saw that we had learned to use the face as a mask, and fully comprehended "See," we gave our full attention to the third principle, "Hear." Martha suggested we close our eyes and focus on hearing with one ear at a time. We trembled with the intensity of listening, but our faces remained impassive. We imagined the ear turning, reaching up and out for sounds, for the vibrations of sounds, for the melody of sounds. She had us fine-tune our hearing, observe how much we could hear and actually identify, and report to her as we attempted to distinguish far-off sounds. When Martha said, "Stretch up one ear and turn it to catch the sound as a deer does when it senses danger," I did it as if my life depended on it. I was familiar with the plight of a deer being stalked, and I identified with it, as I recalled how my father and brothers had hunted for food for the family.

Martha asked us to shut out feeling, sight, and sound, in order to focus on the fourth principle, "Smell." She cultivated in us the capacity to distinguish and identify remembered scents, pleasant or unpleasant, reminiscent perhaps of honeysuckle, fresh-baked bread, stale fish, or skunk cabbage. When she asked us to open our nostrils and test the wind like an animal for any scent of predator, I breathed in deeply and found myself thinking instead of the scent of my rose arbor.

But when she said, "Snort like a racehorse. Become a racehorse," I did as I was told. Picturing Prince in my mind, I nuzzled, neighed, and pawed the ground. The hackles rose on the back of my neck as I tossed my long hair like a mane. My feet and ankles arched and flexed in readiness for the gallop. Under Martha's spell, this shy, tentative dance student was transformed into a wild and powerful racehorse. Martha had to forcefully rein me in.

The fifth and last category of these potent images, or principles, involved

"Taste." First we talked about the inside of the mouth—the aliveness of the tongue, how the juices flowed around it, the bone structure of the jaws, and how the teeth crush food to release the flavor. Martha invited us to shut down Feel, See, Hear, and Smell in order to focus solely on Taste. We tried to recall tastes —sweet, sour, spicy, bitter. We bit into imaginary food and savored the sensation remembered on our tongues. We experienced the pleasure of these flavors or rejected with great distaste those that had not pleased us. I thought of the delicious sweetness of fresh-picked blackberries, and the hateful taste of goat's milk.

Each of the many images used by Martha was explored carefully and then emphatically discarded. I began to feel as if I could see through my elbow, feel through the side of my thigh, and hear through my fingertips. Every image included the return to appearing absolutely still. The purpose was to color the stillness and make it come alive. The dynamic sense of stillness Martha was demanding from us, based on these potent experiments, was experienced not only while standing, but also when crouching, sitting, kneeling, lying on the floor, and even as we moved through the air. Martha made it clear that we were to retain and use only the essence of the image that had been translated into muscular memory. "We use the images as you would use a pitcher of water to prime a well," she insisted, "but then they must be dropped."

On the first day of class, Martha explained to us the reason for sitting on the floor for the warm-up exercises. "Dancers do this not only for the purpose of loosening up the muscles around the hip hinge, but also to develop a centered spine, which we might picture as a perfectly balanced Greek column." To feel how one vertebra is positioned on top of the next in perfect alignment, I would think of a stack of children's wooden blocks. To help us feel how the spine must come up from the floor in a straight line, Martha suggested we imagine a floodlight focused on the spinal column. I had the feeling of rising up out of the floor, of absolutely centering myself. This afforded a clear sense of pinpoint balance, in readiness, and became the norm that we would later be able to distort. Martha called it a "centered release."

We did everything Martha requested to the best of our ability, but if anyone had trouble understanding or accomplishing something, she was always able to help. Martha often told us, "I will not tolerate anything less than absolute clarity and precision." To assist those students having difficulty establishing a perfectly centered upright spine when sitting on the floor, Martha had us sit one be-hind the other. Then we did what brought back memories for me of the laying on of hands. Each of us took turns observing our partner's spine, then we gently touched and pressed the vertebra that needed to be straightened. This provided a quick, effective way to get in touch with a part of the body we could not see for ourselves. We did not rely on mirrors.

In class we did not waste a moment of precious time. While working on standing still and initiating movement with explosive energy, we were also ex-ploring walking, with the object being to prepare us not only for walking, but also for moving slowly "with presence." Martha described how she, and all the Denishawn dancers, were in awe of Miss Ruth because of the beautiful way she walked. Martha wanted each of us to develop such an impressive walk. "Your feet must function more like hands," she began by saying.

"Kneel down and reach out your hands to feel the shape of the imaginary ground. First softly press down on the floor each of your five fingers, then the heel of the hand. Feel the adjustments that would have to be made if you were walking on pebbles or rough ground. Now release your hands from the floor, and see if you can sense the floor in your fingertips before they actually touch it again. That is so you can anticipate in advance any small adjustments you might need to make."

I felt challenged as I reached down to touch the floor. I paused in midair and felt my fingers tingling. "Was this what she meant?" I wondered. It was certainly a revelation to me to think that the human foot was sensitive to shape and tex-ture in the same way as my fingertips, and that my feet had the ability to adapt in a split second as I stepped down upon the floor. I walked with new awareness. I could feel the infinitesimal changes taking place throughout my body as I transferred my weight carefully from one foot to the other and pressed forward. When I was growing up, I had run about barefoot out-of-doors all summer long, and I was suddenly very happy about that. I felt lucky that my feet were strong and pliable. Martha commented that the way my feet worked in walking and running was "just about right."

Martha's use of animal images in the third section of class, when we were re-leased into space, made me ecstatically happy once I finally grasped what she meant about using my memory imaginatively. I felt I was an authority on animals, having lived closely with both domestic and wild animals since childhood. As we sprang into action transforming tiger images to eagle images connected with flight, or as we walked quietly with great dignity like elephants, or rebounded vigorously like gazelles or kangaroos, I felt this was my world.

In my mind is a vivid picture of a day when Martha had us all walk about the studio with stiff legs, stretched taut to make us feel tall. Our arms reached down, down, down, and a little forward toward the floor. Fingers were closed to feel the formation of a hoof. With our necks extended to the maximum height, we nosed about in the air, searching for imaginary leaves in make-believe tall trees that were inaccessible to shorter members of the animal kingdom. That morning we were giraffes searching for a juicy, green breakfast. Martha had chosen the image of this most quiet creature, not for strength or energy, but for the very specific purpose of making us aware of the neck.

"I want each of you to melt down your shoulders and lengthen up your neck," she said. "You must allow the neck to function without interference from the shoulders. If your shoulders are tense, or if they hunch up, you communicate a defensive posture. I want you to be alive to the fact that the prominent tendon extending vertically on each side of your neck is vitally important and expressive. The neck, the throat, can be most eloquent." At once I thought of the beauty I had felt, that had moved me so deeply, when I saw Anna Pavlova dancing *The Dying Swan*. When the swan was struck with an arrow, the expressiveness of her neck—as she thrashed her head from side to side to escape the pain and to reach out for breath—had been heartbreaking. Remembering this, I knew that Martha was right. Facial expression could never surpass the eloquence of the throat.

The stories Martha told us were fascinating. She spoke about the legendary beauty of Helen of Troy, the hypnotic power she had over men, and how the Trojan War began because Helen, the queen of Sparta, had been abducted by a prince of Troy. Martha explained that traditionally in the Greek theater the battles did not take place onstage. It was the custom for a messenger to relay the news from the offstage battlefront to the Greek chorus, which in turn communicated the message to the audience. Martha emphasized that this had to be presented in a stylized rather than a realistic manner. All this was tremendously exciting, but it was at the same time bewildering for me, because often the words Martha used were unfamiliar to me.

Martha was preparing us constantly for the challenges some of us would soon be facing as performers in *Seven Against Thebes*. As a group we all learned the "Greek greeting" that Martha had devised for the solo messenger in the play. We understood that, in performance, the messenger would be standing alone on the empty battlefield in full view of the enemy army. He would raise his arm and hold it high, with the palm of the hand open, to communicate "I come bearing no weapons. I am the messenger of peace." Each of us knew that the gesture must be the embodiment of courage, projecting powerfully into space. We were all horribly nervous as we attempted the movement, because this was the audition and only a few would be chosen to perform.

Martha appeared desperately discouraged as she watched us. She shook her head slowly from side to side, finally saying, "No! No! No! All I can see is anxiety! It is clearly visible in your hunched, tense-looking shoulders. The audience must see the lifted hand, not lifted shoulders!" To avoid raising the shoulder, she suggested that we visualize a child's seesaw, with the shoulder serving as the center support on which the imaginary seesaw would rest. We raised the arm in front by compressing and shortening the muscles in back of the shoulder area, including those far down the back of the torso. Contracting all these muscles acted as a lever to bring the arm up in front and hold it there. Once the arm was up, we slowly released the contraction in the back, allowing the arm to descend gradually in a controlled manner.

Martha was still not satisfied. She explained that since we could not see behind ourselves, we needed to learn to feel the movement muscularly. We took partners and stood one behind the other and focused on the muscles that had to be awakened. When my partner tapped my back to indicate which muscles were needed to activate the lever that brought the arm floating up in front of the body, it suddenly became clear to me. It was also helpful that I already understood how tendons and ligaments worked. One summer I had worked at a chicken farm. After the chickens had been butchered and plucked, we had all chased each other lightheartedly around the yard playing "Attack! Attack!" with the discarded chicken feet, pulling and releasing the sinews that made the feet contract and release. This game was none too aesthetic, but it did make me understand at once what Martha meant by contraction and release.

After we had experimented with contracting and releasing our back muscles, and we still could not achieve the desired result, Martha commented, "The

Greek greeting is a bit more complicated than a simple seesaw, since it involves moving on a breath. The lungs work like a bellows. If you hiss as you exhale, you can feel it. The contraction of the muscles around the rib cage presses the used air out. Then, as the muscle groups relax, fresh new air rushes in. This expansion of the lungs supports the upward floating movement of the arm."

The next day Martha burst into the studio full of energy and enthusiasm and described to us the larger-than-life and overwhelmingly powerful marble figure known as the Winged Victory that had been carved in Greece around 200 B.C. The statue, which presently stands in the Louvre in Paris, suggests a woman, affirmative, triumphant, and brave, projecting power in her wake. I pictured her poised as the figurehead on the prow of a Pilgrim's tall-masted ship, forging ahead with supreme confidence through turbulent waves. I remember Martha telling us how her imagination had been captured by the idea of wings opening to the wind, and the feeling of perfect ease in the open armpits, the shoulders, and what remains of the throat. The idea of powerful wings ready for flight invited us to soar through the air. This was the image, the gift, Martha gave us that day. The feeling of soaring has never left me.

Through the work in the classroom I was gradually released from the vague, undefined fears that had previously imprisoned me. Martha was opening my eyes to the world of the arts. I was mesmerized. Not everyone was totally mesmerized, however. Students sometimes whispered discontentedly to one another that this new style of dancing did not fit into their idea of grace and beauty.

The five cardinal principles were used continuously to introduce us to basic sources of awareness and the feeling of being potent while absolutely still, and Martha was also beginning to teach us to initiate movement with energy. Once again she utilized animal images. She instructed each of us to visualize ourselves as a huge brown bear with small, short-sighted eyes and powerful, long furry arms ending in cruel claws. My bear struck out with menacing swipes that made a generous arc pushing up from the ground into the air, as I stood upright on my rear legs. I was actively reliving the memory of a time when my brothers had come running home, terrified, following an encounter with a big brown bear. In Martha's class, as I imagined the bear terrorizing my brothers, I thrust my feet fiercely down into the floor and felt the energy rebound up through my body as I swung my arms ferociously up and out into space.

This act of rebounding from the floor was emphasized as a crucial factor in initiating all powerful movement. I recall Martha explaining that the hinges in the body are designed for rebound, saying, "Do not focus on up, but instead first beat down, then rebound up out of the floor like a basketball. The more forcefully the ball is hit down, the higher it will go."

As the class progressed, Martha drew our attention to the beauty and symmetry of many Greek sculptured figures. She paid special attention to the way the Greeks understood balance, and the subtle changes that occur in the body when transferring weight from one foot to the other. She called it the "Greek bounce" and explained emphatically, "This must never be consciously arranged. You are only subtly aware that it is occurring. The changing of weight is barely discernible."

We experienced this changing of weight, carefully and slowly, before incorporating rebound into it. Martha would get very upset if anyone faked the body changes or exaggerated them. She related how, when she worked with John Murray Anderson and his showgirls in *The Greenwich Village Follies*, if anyone walked in an affected way, by taking a step and a pose and a step and a pose, he referred to it as "the garbage walk." The subtle centering required in the Greek bounce came easily to me, however, and I could allow the changes to take place without faking them. Like the Greek greeting, the Greek bounce was quickly and quietly dropped, in favor of a less graceful, more primitive, squarer, rebounding jump with feet together.

When moving in space, we began from the back corner of the studio and took turns running diagonally across the floor in pairs. In preparation for takeoff, each couple bounced four times in place with feet together in parallel position. On the fourth count we rebounded explosively up and forward, as if springing off a diving board. We tried to maintain the height of the powerful two-footed takeoff as we broke into a run. I imagined I was a ball, bouncing across the floor.

Then the timing changed, as Martha clapped her hands to give us the double beat of galloping horses' hooves. She divided the class into three groups. While one group clapped, the other two groups galloped freely all over the studio one after the other. We focused on the double beat of galloping hooves. Attention was on sounds, rhythm, and rebound—not on form or position. Then each group took turns moving clockwise in a circle. At first we worked slowly, making a long, lunging push-off with one foot and driving the other knee forward and up to hang suspended for a prolonged instant. When we lunged, the body was in a crouching preparation, and as we suspended, the body arched. I felt like a horse rearing up. We did it faster and faster, with one arm flying forward each time. As the momentum increased, we found ourselves leaping. The transition into a leap had come simply and easily; it was a natural leap.

Martha told us to fill our lungs and hold our breath when we were up in the air. "Freeze up there for an instant if you can," she said. "The audience will remember you up in the air." I felt I was floating, like a kite in the wind. By the end of class we were all practically flying. We had discovered that instead of longing for elevation, we could demand it. The unexpected amount of elevation was so exhilarating that even the ballet students were being gradually won over.

That evening, Bonnie Bird and I went together to the cafeteria in the basement of the Cornish School. Ever since Miss Aunt Nellie had introduced us early in the summer, thinking we might possibly be related, Bonnie and I had become friends. We sat on a table and dangled our legs over the side, because our calf muscles were so sore it was painful even to rest our feet on the floor. We took turns massaging each other's legs with rubbing alcohol, and we agreed that the discomfort was a small price to pay for such an extraordinary experience.

The next morning, it was apparent Martha was getting us ready for something special as she began teaching in a different manner, attacking the work with an almost violent strength. She put up her hand to signal us to wait. I held my breath, hoping this meant she would talk to us. This would give me an opportunity to get inside the movement patterns she was working on, instead of just trying to copy her.

Martha looked around the room and asked, "Has anyone read or heard about Flaming Milka, the amazing young woman who is leading the coal miners in Kentucky to fight for better working conditions?" No one responded. I never read the newspapers. I don't believe many of us did. Martha's frustration was building as she questioned, "None of you? Not even one of you has heard about her?" Martha's voice grew louder as she expounded, "She is magnificent! She is trying to help the coal miners who are worn out, angry, fearful, sick, endlessly hungry, and often miserably cold." Martha paused.

"I want each of you to imagine that *you* are stepping into the shoes of this

courageous woman," she said. "*You* are the one speaking eloquently and hyp-
notically to the crowd of people. *You* are the one stirring their imagination and
rousing them to fight for a better life. You must move with tremendous urgency
and passion and carry them forward with you up the hill, where the crowd can
see you better, and can see where you want them to go. Quickly now, take a partner. One of you will be the active partner. You will lift the other, who represents
the crowd. To be a leader like Flaming Milka, you must be strong enough to lift,
at the very least, one person off the floor. Remember, she is strong enough to
sweep up and carry the whole crowd."

Everyone in class must have glanced guardedly around, searching for someone small to lift and carry. I was not fast enough, and I found myself paired with
a girl who resembled a very tall tree. I struggled mightily to lift her. As I looked
at the other students, I could see that I was actually having an easier time with
my stiff, tall tree than some whose partners were floppy and loose, like balloons
filled with water. "There is to be absolutely no laughing!" Martha declared in a
deadly determined voice.

Then she demonstrated fiercely, with wild strength, how the one doing the
lifting must take a very long stride to convey the feeling of going up the hill; how
she should turn her back on the crowd of people, lean forward, hold her head
high, and focus where she demands the crowd must go. Martha showed how we
were to look back at our partner, reach our arms out to her, and figuratively lift
her up, bearing her on our own back, and carry her forward one more step. As
Martha did this, she said, "This arm gesture must communicate both enormous
willpower and unbelievable physical strength. Each of you must be strong
enough to pull the entire audience with you, and carry them symbolically up
the mountain slope."

Since I had been unable to lift my partner, not knowing quite how or where
to take hold of her, I was not at all optimistic about lifting a crowd of people.
Nevertheless, I was ready and willing to try. I took the long lunging step forward,
focused my gaze upward to establish the goal, looked back over my shoulder,
and reached out to the crowd. I gritted my teeth as I swept my arm forward, as if
against great resistance, summoning the people, showing them the way to go,
and willing them to surge like a great wave up the hill. Martha named this sequence of movement the "Revolutionary Call." Although no one could do it to

Martha's satisfaction, it was an important lesson for me. It gave me the feeling of a solid supporting base. I saw how necessary it was to dig down into the ground before pushing and thrusting up, bearing the weight. The effort involved was akin to digging down into the earth and then levering it up, as I had done when preparing the garden at Mill Bay.

The constant pressure of knowing she had to get us ready to perform at the end of summer must have impelled Martha to move quickly on. She chose to rely on more familiar movements to illustrate initiating movement with energy. We began with the "slingshot." Martha instructed us to visualize our muscles as lengths of elastic. To experience this, we again took partners, faced one another, held both of our partner's hands and assumed a long, lunging stance. At first we pulled one another with all our might, then the stronger of the two allowed herself to be pulled. The studio was filled with laughter as we alternately struggled to move one another. Martha stopped this outburst quickly, reminding us, "The work is all important and requires your serious attention." She paused for a moment. "I want you to observe what is happening in your muscles. Tell me what you are experiencing. What do you feel? Which muscles are working?" We each thoughtfully reported our feelings to Martha.

"Begin again," she said. "Place your hands as before. Now separate them about an inch from the hands of your partner. Remember how it felt before, but this time create the illusion of pulling by drawing on your muscular memory." We also examined the opposite motion of pushing, by first placing our hands palm to palm and pushing one another with all our might. Then we repeated this activity without touching, to be sure we had established the feeling of pushing as different from that of pulling and to be certain we could clearly distinguish between the different muscular memory each move presented.

We explored the muscular memory concept further as we formed two teams and mimed a tug-of-war, using a long imaginary rope, digging our feet into the floor, and fighting for our side to win. This was a group effort where each of us shared in the pulling, yet remained sensitive throughout to all members of the team, even though we did not quite touch. Although we were only miming, we pulled with such intensity that we finally fell laughing into an exhausted heap on the floor. Referring to this whole muscular memory experience as "stylization," Martha pointed out, "You have to learn how to simplify and eliminate all nonessentials and to focus your attention."

Martha then invited us to explore quietly what actually happens when we bend, then straighten, first a knee, then an elbow. She wanted us to notice how, as one set of muscles lengthens and stretches, the opposing group of muscles simultaneously shortens, and vice versa. For example, as the elbow bends, the set of muscles on the inside of the elbow shorten, while those on the outside lengthen. The shortened muscles might tremble, trying to hold the sharp angle, while the lengthened ones could feel dangerously stretched, and both want to return to normal where the arm is neither sharply bent, nor completely straight.

"It is most important to observe how both sets of muscles work in opposition, yet in partnership at all times," Martha pointed out. "You must never allow the more passive muscle group to become lax. To focus exclusively on one element of this partnership will result in either weak or floppy motion, or the opposite, a grimly locked, restricted appearance." Being aware of this duality gave a sense of power to every move I made from then on. When we returned to the image of the slingshot, I was now vividly aware of the elasticity in the opposing muscles as I pulled back slowly to aim. I could experience the energy, first held tightly in and then released explosively as I let go.

Holding energy in then suddenly releasing it was further explored through a foot race. We crouched at the imaginary starting line chanting, "Ready, set, go!" as we first pulled back and then let go like a slingshot projecting ourselves forward into the race with instant energy. Martha invited the more athletic members of the class to demonstrate the surge of energy required in the tennis service, the preparation for the graceful action of a high dive, and the concentrated power of the baseball pitch, until we understood ever more clearly how to initiate movement with a burst of energy.

In talking about sports, and baseball pitchers in particular, Martha compared the movements of a truly talented athlete to a thread moving through a string of tiny beads, without missing a single bead. "Imagine a necklace made up of many different beads," she proposed. "Think of each bead as a way-station through which the thread passes. Since the thread does not actually move, you have to visualize it moving through each of the beads. The majority of people might become aware of a few of the beads, but the truly gifted athlete observes and feels each bead, that is, each body change, and allows each to occur in perfect sequence without losing sight of the goal." This was a clear illustration for me, portraying the basic quality of sustained movement.

Martha built on this idea by quickly moving on to another aspect. "Imagine a little train chugging along the tracks, going up and down a mountain," she suggested. "It stops abruptly. Suddenly, it has to back up. This is very hard for the little engine to do, because it must back up the mountain. The little engine manages to push the first car backward a bit. Then that car pushes the next car, and on and on, with each car pushing the next one in line and getting it started, until the little engine is finally able to push the whole train back up the mountain."

We saw that this example of sustained movement was different from that of the beads because a substantial visible effort was involved. Martha told us that when we move, the audience must feel the muscles thrusting against the resistance of our weight. She warned us not to smooth it over and make it seem easy and facile. We were to value even the smallest changes as they occur, and to enjoy them. She advised us we should always remember that the coordination of the human body must be not only truly and deeply felt, but also treasured.

"When you successfully combine perfect coordination—driven by intense energy—with a clarity of purpose," Martha stated, "you will have achieved truly organic movement." With the images of the string of beads and the little train, Martha was introducing us to radically new and significant concepts. She had awakened in me an awareness of movement itself, as opposed to movement seen only as a series of static poses.

As an example of how Martha regenerated movement that had been brought to us from the Old World into a creation with an American sense of power, freedom, and energy, let me describe how Martha transformed the German-style swings that we had learned in Ronny Johansson's class. A number of students, including Bonnie Bird and Grace Cornell, had been skilled and at home in Miss Johansson's class work. But I, having entered the class late in the session, had not mastered the successive movement that was supposed to come up from the floor and ripple through the entire body, simultaneously with the moving figure-eight designs in the arm pattern.

Martha watched carefully as Bonnie demonstrated these German-style swings. She then quickly proceeded to show us how to look at the bare bones of an arm swing by having us first simply swing one arm forward and back. I pictured the pendulum in an old grandfather clock. Martha developed the idea with her instructions. "Do this in a loose, heavy way. Notice how the swing begins quickly, then slows to a suspended moment at the apex. Observe how the weight of the arm brings it down and back. Now imagine that you are holding something heavy, like a schoolbag, and swing your arm. Feel how the added weight slows the swing as the arm comes up, and adds to the momentum as the arm goes down."

I felt my shoulder muscles roll forward, allowing the arm to rotate inward a little and then rotate out on the backward swing. There was just the barest hint of a figure-eight pattern of movement in the shoulder. But no sooner had I noticed this than we suddenly found ourselves moving away from "swing" toward "whiplash," which we explored by way of the image of first a whip, and then a lasso. I immediately pictured in my mind the beloved vaudeville comedian Will Rogers, wielding a lasso as a prop that symbolically roped in his audience, as he told dry, down-to-earth, satirical jokes. Soon Martha transformed the movement of swinging the arm forward and back by incorporating into it the powerful, lashing, fluid quality of the lasso.

"Now you are really going to challenge yourselves," she warned us. "This time you will combine the whiplash of the arm swings with moving on a breath." Standing with feet parallel, weight forward on the balls of the feet in readiness to initiate the movement, we began the complex preparation for the swings. In the brief time it takes to say "Eight and a . . . ," we rapidly, sequentially exhaled the breath sharply, percussively, and tightened the crouching muscles around the hip hinge to the ultimate degree, to trigger a driving, percussive heel beat that thrust into the floor, which then sent us high up on the balls of the feet with taut, straight knees. As we pressed even more air out of the lungs, tightened the abdominal muscles, and released tension in the back, the spine formed an overcurve that included the head. At this point, the image flashed through my mind of a kitten being carried by its mother to a new, more secret place, suspended securely in the air by the scruff of the neck. Meanwhile, my arms pressed forward, parallel to one another in continuance of the overcurve, suggesting to me an opening umbrella. The three-count preparation was then complete.

"The feeling is like that of a bow forced to curve in readiness before an arrow is shot into the air," Martha emphasized. This exquisite moment of suspension was to be treasured and stretched out in time. At the culmination of this preparation, when the suspension was no longer bearable, I burst into action like a thunderclap, with everything coming together—heels rebounding on the floor, air rushing into the lungs, arms lashing past the thighs, torso arching ecstatically, armpits wide open, and face lifted to the sky. For one moment I hung in the air, the embodiment of Winged Victory, before swinging down sharply into the bowlike curve that would precipitate the forward rebound again. All that might register in the eye of the audience was an explosion of force like the powerful punch of a champion prizefighter.

At first I had practiced the rebounding bounce on the heels tentatively, feeling that the motion would jar my spine. Soon I found that by allowing the contraction and release in the hip hinge to move the body's center of gravity forward and back in space, the impact of the heels on the floor was deflected by the change in the angle of contact. There was no shock at all. As my softly padded heels bounced on the floor, the movement sprang forth from the hip hinge, up into the air like a geyser.

As soon as we had learned to incorporate the whiplash quality of the arms into the swings, Martha introduced a variation. We began by standing in a long narrow stride, with our feet placed one in front of the other along a single board in the floor. We had prepared for this long stance by practicing what Martha called "the Mexican sit," in which we took partners, faced one another, held hands, and squatted down low, without quite sitting on the floor, then rocked a bit forward and backward to increase the elasticity in our Achilles' tendons. For the variation on the basic swing, we crouched low, centering our weight over the back foot. The front leg was straight, ankle sharply flexed, heel on the floor, which gave a strong feeling of the foot being thrust forward as if into the boot of a Russian Cossack dancer. When we let go of the bowlike tension, we sprang forward out of the crouch, arms lashed down past the thighs, torsos flung forward as the arms swung out and up to crown a high-arched, free, wild lunge. The fundamental difference between the two swings was that the basic swing occurred in the down/up dimension, whereas the variation moved in a backward/forward plane. The balance for the variation was precarious, to say the least.

To help us understand the source of energy needed to propel the forward momentum of the variation, Martha pointed to an imaginary spot slightly below the belly button. "This is your center of vitality," she stated. "If you draw back and integrate yourselves fiercely enough, and fling yourselves forward into the lunge with sufficient power, the life force in each of you will burst forth from that magical place. This force is powerful enough to break a large rock!" Then she muttered something like "the walls of Jericho fell down, didn't they?"

The idea that the life force in me was so strong that I could break a big rock and shatter it into pieces was astounding to me. I could scarcely wait to try it out. The opportunity came one morning when Bonnie Bird and I, and two other students from the class, went out soon after dawn to the beautiful Volunteer Park near the Cornish School. We were running barefoot in absolute abandon on the soft green grass, up and down a small hill, when we came to a big rock. We stopped, and we decided we had to test Martha's words. Each of us stood facing the rock from a slightly different angle. We drew our bodies back into the preparatory curve, thrust our heels fiercely into the ground, and shouted, "On your mark, get set, go!" Together we lunged forward explosively, projecting our life forces toward the rock. We waited. We watched. Nothing happened. The rock stood as before. We tried again and again. Finally, exhausted and more than a little disappointed, we gave up. Had we really thought we could shatter the rock? Martha had said we could.

Back at the studio, we told Martha about it, and she smiled. Then she said, "You did learn to initiate movement with powerful energy, didn't you?" Martha was right. We certainly had learned to do this. What was most astonishing was that this dynamic result had come from Martha's creative adaptation of one tiny segment of Ronny Johansson's graceful figure-eight exercise.

Day by day throughout the summer Martha incorporated something new into our strictly followed ritual-like routine. Each move was analyzed minutely and strictly proscribed on findings that came out of the work we were doing. She explored a thousand different ways to find the one way to coax us to leave behind the clichés of the past. Her convictions were fierce and strong. The intensity of her fury at times frightened me. But it was always exhilarating, as Martha swept us forward with her toward an innovative and revolutionary new movement vocabulary.

From the first day, I secretly felt Martha was often focusing her attention on me. She seemed to use terms I could relate to and sometimes checked to be sure

I understood what she was explaining. I felt like a piece of parched ground soaking up her every word as if it were rain. During this first six-week session of the twelve-week summer course, I became much more daring, much more free to be myself. When Martha divided the class into groups for running, galloping, and leaping, I found I just could not wait for my turn, and I ran with all three groups. The others might have been glad to rest, or felt they had to mind which group they were in, but I kept leaving my group to slip back in the circle. Martha didn't seem to mind. Surely she could see that I was almost bursting out of my skin with the joy of it all, and for this she chose not to scold me. Perhaps she sensed this was something I had wanted for so long—to be part of the action, not just a tag-along as I was with my brothers, but a valued member of the group.

Before beginning the second session of the course, we were scheduled to have a long weekend break. As the time came to leave the Cornish School, I approached Louis Horst at the piano to shake hands and say goodbye. We all knew he would not be present for the remaining six weeks; he had a previous commitment in Europe.

"Goodbye, for now," Louis said. "I'll see you in New York City in the fall." I was stunned. I had no idea what he was talking about. Actually, I did not even know where New York City was.

That weekend Jack and I took the boat home to Victoria. As the family sat at the dinner table, I told my parents, "At the end of the summer I will be going to New York City. Louis Horst said he would see me there in the fall, and Martha always says, 'When it comes to any decision to do with dance, Louis has the last word. His word is law.'"

My parents looked first at each other, then at me. With raised eyebrows Mother said, "Oh?" That was all she said. We never did have much conversation at home. I thought I detected a slight gleam of approval in Mother's eyes, and I read this to mean that the door was not completely closed on the idea of my going to New York City. I felt, too, that Mother's lively sense of adventure had been aroused, and she would be on my side.

Three

Martha Graham's *Seven Against Thebes,* 1930

AS THE HOLIDAY weekend drew to a close, I was in my room packing for the return trip to Seattle. Daddy entered and said, "You cannot go to Seattle. Jack is ill, and seventeen-year-old young ladies do not travel alone."

"But I have to go!" I pleaded. "Martha and Miss Cornish have arranged a work scholarship for me." With classes costing four dollars each, I could not possibly afford to attend the rest of the summer without their help. "They are depending on me to report to work tomorrow at the Cornish School."

Daddy had always emphasized responsibility, so he reluctantly agreed to let me travel alone. In the late afternoon, Mother and Daddy escorted me to the pier and watched me embark on the boat. As darkness set in, I was scared. Never before had I been allowed out in the evening without at least one of my brothers at my side. I stood alone on the deck wondering, "Where shall I go? Where shall I sit? What shall I do?"

I looked all around, and through a window I saw Martha Graham sitting alone in the lounge reading a book. I entered hesitantly, walked toward her, half-whispered, "Hello," then turned and fled. I walked briskly around the deck several times trying to keep warm in the cold, breezy evening air. Once more I was drawn near to where Martha was sitting, and she beckoned to me to sit with her. What could I say to her? It was a four-hour trip to Seattle. Could I tell her I had never before been out alone at night? That I was frightened to death?

I need not have worried. Martha carried the conversation totally. "I had a lovely weekend at the Empress Hotel. Victoria is such a beautiful place. The hanging baskets of flowers are so lovely. Are you thinking at all about leaving Victoria?" Before I could answer, she struck me speechless. "Have you considered coming to New York City to work with me when the classes at the Cornish School are finished?" Never had I wanted anything so badly in my whole life. I could not even look at Martha or reply, but my head did move automatically as if it were floating by itself in the water, bobbing down and up, down and up. Although I could not manage a word, I felt the matter was settled completely.

Martha was, as always, utterly practical and suggested a way I might be able to travel to New York City without having to pay for transportation. She told me she had heard that, if I got a job working as a waitress for the Fred Harvey chain of railroad station restaurants and worked for a while, when there was an opening at another of their restaurants in a nearby town they would send me on. Gradually, if I were lucky, I could work my way across the country to the eastern seaboard. The whole idea sounded petrifying to me, and much too slow. Nonetheless, I knew that somehow I would find a way to go to New York City. To think ahead, to discuss and plan, was something I had never experienced. When one does not talk, one does not learn to think ahead.

It was pitch dark when the boat docked in Seattle, and I was wondering how to get to my boardinghouse. Then Martha asked, "Would you like to ride in a taxi with me?"

I practically fainted with relief. "Oh, yes," I replied.

As we rode together, Martha asked, "Would you mind if we stop first at my apartment? There is something I want to get for you. You may keep it for three days, but then you must return it to me. Promise?"

"I promise," I said, without knowing what on earth she was talking about.

The driver stopped at Martha's building, and we walked upstairs to her apartment. Martha found what she was looking for in the bedroom, and when she came out, she placed in my hand an exotic object that appeared to be a necklace. It was made of soft silky tassels in warm, glowing colors of gold, green, peacock blue, crimson. It was threaded together with seeds that moved and rattled mysteriously, and it smelled wonderfully of fragrant spices that made me think of India. I was so engrossed with what Martha had given me, that my family and my loneliness and uncertainty were all banished from my mind.

As I cradled the treasured necklace-like object in my hands, Martha and I walked from her apartment to the door of my boardinghouse nearby. I walked up the stairs alone, but I no longer felt alone. I placed Martha's token next to my cheek on my pillow and drifted promptly and peacefully off to sleep. How did Martha know that this intriguing object would enchant and distract me from the bonds of family? Was she really so perceptive? I don't know, but I did feel quite certain that the time had come for me to emerge from the protective cocoon of my family and try out my fragile wings in an exciting, strange new world. I knew I had found someone I could depend upon. To this day, I still remember how I gave this treasure back to Martha as I had promised. I loved it so. I wonder whatever became of it.

Early the following morning, I walked to the door of Martha's apartment building and waited for her to appear. As we walked together to the Cornish School, she talked about the girls who were in her group in New York City—girls that I felt I would soon be meeting. Martha spoke fondly about Mary Rivoire, describing her as a very handsome, passionate girl, with intensely blue eyes and a big mane of dark hair. Mary was Irish and French, a deeply religious Catholic. On the day of performance, even after being up most of the night working in the dress rehearsal, Mary would get up at dawn to go to early mass before coming to the theater. Martha portrayed Mary's stance as bold, sturdy, independent, and totally unselfconscious; she said that, even when Mary rested, she had a quality of absolute purity. It appeared to me that much of the work in class had been modeled by Martha on the way that Mary stood—quite naturally and with innate dignity.

When we arrived at the Cornish School, I reported directly to work at the cloakroom. The checking procedure must have been explained to me, but somehow I failed to comprehend it. The complaints must have been numerous, because before the day was over, Miss Cornish simply gave me a full scholarship. I was so relieved at not having to work! I instantly and gratefully flew into Martha's classroom.

Before each class, I scurried into the studio to lay claim to a spot as near to Martha as possible. Then I would warm up carefully, in order to be ready when she indicated to the pianist that the class should begin. Each class began in the same way. We performed a set sequence of carefully choreographed warm-up and floor exercises. Even the transitions between each exercise had been worked out, so that they had an air of inevitability about them, as if they could go no other way. Each exercise was one brief fragment, repeated over and over, that would then flow logically into another similarly brief fragment. The rhythm was usually a simple one-two, one-two, or a one-two-three-four, repeated many times. Sometimes a phrase was eight counts long, but only when it was adapted from a dance such as *Rustica* or *Heretic*, or part of the choreography Martha was creating for the entrance in *Seven Against Thebes*.

I learned that the sequence of exercises would be the same for each class and I became confident and secure within this choreographed routine. Occasionally, Martha would notice someone executing a small, accidental way of getting from one segment of the sequence into the next, and she would stop the class and have us watch what that person was doing spontaneously. If Martha thought the movement was more original or interesting than the ones we'd been doing, she would incorporate it into the transition, and we would learn to perform it this new way from then on.

The theme of energy was often explored. First we talked about the basic idea of person-power involved in walking, meaning the pushing forward and transferring of weight from one foot to the other. Martha compared this to the far superior and more complex push-off power of four-legged animals. We accepted the idea of the multiplication of person-power in relation to the formation of the wheel, with each spoke representing a leg taking one step. When Martha spoke of electrical energy, I tried to visualize the mysterious, unseen force moving along wires. This did not seem to be useful to me as a dancer, since there was no movement visible in electricity. It was different, however, when she suggested the image of a steam engine. The memory of clouds of steam puffing from the smokestack, as part of the process propelling the pistons that turned the wheels, was clear in my mind. Playing choo-choo had been a favorite game at Mill Bay, and I could relate the action of the legs to the action of steam-driven pistons.

All these energy concepts were intriguing and useful, but the real stunner came when Martha startled me completely with a new vision of energy so revolutionary and exciting that it was as if branded in fire on my mind. Martha began by telling us of a conversation she had had with a talented painter named Mark Tobey, about a discovery that was rocking the scientific world.[1] Martha's eyes were wide with excitement as she told us that, although previously we had been taught that the smallest particle of matter was the molecule, scientists had recently discovered that within molecules there are even more minuscule particles called atoms. "These atoms seem to be dancing and vibrating in their own rhythmic pattern, as they move on their own path in space, each with a mission or a special role to play in the total choreographic pattern. Can you imagine," inquired Martha, "that even in a rock, which appears to be so hard and solid, myriads of tiny atoms are all dancing according to a plan?"

"Even in our bones, our skin, and our hair?" I asked breathlessly.

"Yes," nodded Martha. "They are everywhere, even in the wind and the rain and everything you eat." So this was what the puzzling stuff called energy was all about. It was not something outside of me; it was inside everything, including me. I was an integral part of this huge world composed of sparkling energy.

This was for me a moment of pure, radiant joy as I grasped eagerly onto the concept that every bit of me—the soft flesh, the hard bones, the life-sustaining oxygen entering my lungs, the heart pumping the fluid blood through my veins—was made up of countless tiny, vibrating specks dancing purposefully in space. Thinking about this ever-ready source of energy reminded me of the exquisite hummingbirds that visited our garden in Mill Bay. In my mind I pictured them humming and hovering in the air, little helicopters, fluttering above the flowers before inserting their slim beaks into each one for nectar to fuel their pounding hearts. The realization that energy is something we all have, from the time of our first breath until our last, made my own heart beat with excitement. I had taken this energy for granted, barely even acknowledging it or noticing it, yet I now saw it as something miraculous.

In the background I heard Martha's words, "Energy is a subtle factor in sustained movement. This is the hardest to do well." I thought to myself that the secret to performing sustained movement would be to internally incorporate the vibratory quality of the hummingbird's wings. But, while I was savoring this idea, Martha was already moving ahead. "Energy can be trapped and held inside, so as to be almost invisible, or it can explode out and be cut off percussively. This is the quality that we will be using in the choreography. I want you to stamp your feet noisily on the floor."

Stamping my feet smacked of disobedience, and I had never been allowed to do this at home. In response to Martha's request, I first hesitated, then I tentatively slapped my foot against the floor. I could stamp my foot quietly, maybe, but surely not loudly. As I struggled with my feelings, Martha urged us to clap our hands together: clap the hands like cymbals, clap softly, cup the hands and clap explosively. She had us start to stamp a foot fiercely but cut off the movement abruptly before the foot contacted the floor. We did the same with clapping. We started the movement but then did not complete it. "Gather together all the power you can muster," Martha said. "Start to strike, or punch, or kick, or clap, or stamp, then suddenly STOP, as if you are driving a car too fast and must jam on the brakes. The objective is to trigger the audience to continue the percussive movement in their mind's eye after it is cut off."

We were to involve the audience, get them to crave for us to complete the movement for them, strive to obtain a reaction on their part. Martha described this as a kinetic response. She called this movement quality "segmented movement." She told us to visualize it as a piece of a pie, removed from the whole pie, a segment that is cut in a sharp angle but yearns to spring back and complete the circle again.

This segmented percussive movement was difficult for me. Strong feelings made me uncomfortable. I had clearly learned to suppress my emotions all too successfully, and this activity was distressing for me. Even so, I could readily see that the percussive quality was important to create a harsh but exciting impact, which projected a feeling of strength of purpose and high energy. At times it seemed that sustained movement, which flowed and suited my temperament, was being established as the norm, as the natural flow, which Martha called "organic movement." But then, when she was choreographing, Martha would distort from this norm to create excitement, to startle, to wake up the audience and make them look and think and want to understand. This was how she would entice them to participate in the process.

I treasured a rare time when Martha stopped working for a few moments to tell us how in the old-time melodramas, before actors had microphones to amplify their voices, they searched constantly for ways to stir up enough energy in themselves to empower the sound of their voices to carry farther than usual. One way they did this was by grasping the metal ladder backstage with both hands, and shaking it vigorously until their whole body was vibrating. Then they would immediately charge out onto the stage to deliver their lines. When they spoke, their voices seemed to tremble with deep emotion, which carried to the furthest row in the balcony.

Another device she described was intended to help actors project their feelings through the dim, flickering light cast by gas footlights. It was the system of learned gestures formulated by François Delsarte. The Delsarte work had been used by singers, orators, and lawyers in the courtroom, who also needed to supplement the voice. It had certainly not been intended for dancers, but Ted Shawn taught it to them with almost fanatic devotion. Having been Ted Shawn's assistant, Martha was well acquainted with the Delsarte system. The way in which the Delsarte work had spread across the United States and Canada, permeating the thinking of the public without anyone even realizing it, was amazing.

Martha explained that this work had become trivialized, and sometimes even laughable, especially in amateur theatricals and in the silent movies. Martha pointed out that silent movies had been filled with a combination of live action, suspense, and pantomime. With the arrival of talking pictures, voices and dialogue suddenly became all-important. She emphasized that everything associated with cliché poses was superficial, affected, and had to be discarded. Martha relegated Delsarte's teachings to the rich soil in the compost pot of history, calling upon them for satiric purposes only.

Dealing with the whole problem of indicating feelings artificially with learned gestures had obviously created a dilemma for Martha, because of her deep devotion to Miss Ruth. One day Martha asked us, "If I were to come onstage and tiptoe through the raindrops, would you respect me or would you laugh at me?" And she proceeded to mimic tiptoeing through the raindrops with satiric fragility, sensitivity, extreme delicacy. Everyone's eyes widened. It was a difficult moment. We laughed in astonishment.

"Now," Martha said, "suppose I chose to perform a dance entitled *Ode to a Dead Bird*." She gave us a short sample. Martha was skillful at *indicating* feelings of sadness, happiness, a wide variety of emotions that were not necessarily valid or appropriate. She had us laughing so hard, we were falling all over each other. Martha joined in and then asked, "Would it have been terribly embarrassing for you if I had been doing this kind of interpretive dancing seriously instead of satirizing it as I did?" We all agreed it would.

"That's right," she explained. "It's because I was acting in an exaggerated, superficial manner. Now, do you comprehend once and for all that mime and dance are separate and completely different mediums? To be in tune with the rest of the world of the arts, especially modern art and modern music, we need to adopt a new, revolutionary way of moving. Everything must be taken apart and re-created in a fresh original way. The dance in America cannot be characterized merely as light entertainment. It must be recognized as a new and emerging art form based on action, initiated from a deep, inarticulate level. In it, we will deal with inexpressible matters of the heart through the eloquence of body language. What can be put into words should be spoken dramatically, or sung, or written in prose or poetry.

"Can't you see that the time for this new, intensely dramatic dance movement is here?" Martha asked, with a tremendous burst of impatience. "The audience of today is ready and waiting. People are clearly bored by dancing that consists of static poses, indicated reactions and feelings alone. What does intrigue and excite an audience is *action*. Action is what dance is all about! Feelings involved with action are acceptable. Sentimental *reactions* are unacceptable. You must think in terms of *verbs*," Martha constantly admonished us. "They are the action words. Adverbs can occasionally be attached to verbs to enhance them and add color. But stay strictly away from nouns and adjectives. They are static, static, *static!*"

She suggested that we ignore all little in-between words, because all they do is clutter things up. "Just remember: NO sentences," she said, in summary. "Only verbs and adverbs. Clean and simple."

I welcomed everything she was saying. Her vital, sturdy, urgent kind of dancing seemed right for me. I embraced the new body image that was being created, not feminine or masculine but a strong, vibrantly active, independent, disciplined human figure.

BONNIE BIRD, Grace Cornell, Nelle Fisher, Bethene Miller, and I were the five students chosen to perform in the Greek chorus in *Seven Against Thebes* by Aeschylus. When Martha began working in earnest on the choreography, she explained that we were to disregard the style depicted in classical Greek statues, which we had attempted unsuccessfully earlier in the summer. Instead, we were to capture the flat, two-dimensional quality of the earlier, more primitive, Greek friezes.

Then Martha clarified what she meant. "When you make your entrance into the theater, you will be flattened out against the side wall. You will advance your feet precisely, one directly in front of the other. To practice this stance, use a narrow board in the floor as a guide, and align your feet along it."

As we moved forward in a line along the single board, I imagined myself confined in a space between two high parallel walls. Martha cautioned, "As you progress, tip your body forward or backward. *Never* allow yourself to tip into the sidewise dimension. When you raise one leg in back, you should resemble the figure of Mercury, but you must flatten and twist to retain the two-dimensional quality."

As we slowly twisted the upper torso in opposition to the lower part of the body, we did not have the security provided by a turned-out foot on the floor for balance. Martha warned us to be careful. We moved in slow motion as we tipped as dangerously far forward and then as far backward as was possible. Arm movements were angular, and restricted to the same two-dimensional plane. Our hands were shaped into flat, spatula-like designs with the thumb sometimes extended separately. Martha wanted us to emphasize the profile of the face as one shoulder came forward directly under a firm, aggressive chin. The movement felt strange and compelling, like a tightly wound spring.

At the same time that Martha worked to prepare us for this intense, almost ominous entrance, she was evolving sharply concentrated two-dimensional exercises in the classroom to feed into the choreography. She remarked that not only in class, but in rehearsal too, she was always watching for "accidents" that might suggest something more unexpected than what she had planned. To know that Martha was always watching for an instinctive muscular response that she could incorporate into her choreography was exciting, but it created a competitive atmosphere.

In rehearsal, if any one of the five of us forgot for an instant to abide by the restrictions of the Greek frieze and allowed an arm or a leg to protrude out of the narrow space permitted us, someone would hiss, "Watch out! You are not allowed to do that."

Martha repeatedly warned us, "You must not for one moment allow the movement to become static!" By picturing the slow movement as the action of gears, linking into the chain of a bicycle when I pressed on the pedals to climb a steep hill, I could achieve a feeling of resistance that enabled me to execute the movement in a powerful, yet sustained way. Martha challenged us further.

"You have to infuse even the smallest movement with fierce energy," she added. "Otherwise, what you are doing will become nothing more than a series of boring little poses. Imagine that your every motion is being restricted by huge elastic ropes. Lean your torso as far forward and down as you possibly can. Make the audience believe you are going to fall forward. Fight to keep your balance. Now rise up, and tip the torso back, back, back, as your foot swings forward and up. If you are *really* approaching the danger point, there will be people in the audience who will want to rescue you, and others who might feel tempted to give you that extra little push that would be your undoing. The goal is always to evoke a kinetic response from the audience."

For the "Dance of Grief" section, Martha needed to stimulate in us a keen sensitivity to variations in rhythms of breathing. She asked us to sit on the floor, with both knees bent comfortably to one side. Then she commanded us to shout the word "NO!" one after another until we each achieved a clear, resounding sound.

"A stifled or weak sound is just not acceptable," she insisted. "Your voice must ring out clearly, like a gong! If you do this correctly, you will find that as you thrust down into the floor, you will rise up and strike out, like an aroused cobra. Those of you who sink back with raised shoulders, or slump down, will find you are able to muster only a muffled sound. This is a negative, neurotic reaction. It is not what I want. The 'NO' occurs on the exhalation of the breath, on the contraction. Notice the percussive rhythm of your breathing when you shout. It is quite different from the even, rhythmic pattern of the breath when you are resting."

Martha next had us explore different rhythms of sobbing. She said it is rare that people want to show they are sobbing. They may turn their face away, or cover it with their arms or hands, in an effort to conceal their feelings. "To begin, you are going to cry, to blubber, like little children who don't try to hide their feelings," Martha instructed us. "If you have to prime the well to get started, you may fake it a little by beginning with 'boo-hoo-hoo, boo-hoo-hoo.'"

Although Daddy had trained me to suppress my sobbing, I soon forgot my inhibitions and was caught up in the experience. While attempting to capture the rhythm of sobbing, we discovered all sorts of ways of covering our faces to conceal our feelings. We bit at the knuckles of our hands, or beat our fists on the floor. We utilized gulping breaths; small, fast staccato inhalations; long sustained wailing breaths; as well as quiet rocking and keening. Martha watched as we magnified the sobbing until she felt we had experienced it thoroughly, then she called out, "Cut!" We stopped instantly.

Martha had previously warned us that our job was to communicate key feelings to the audience, and let them figure things out for themselves. "If you feel it too much, you will come across as self-indulgent," she pointed out. "Only lead them on, and give cues. Don't get carried away." We were to be cool and objective about what we were doing, and I liked that. We repeated the sobbing, this time quite objectively, testing out a variety of possible positions—elbows in, elbows out, stretched arms, clutching around our knees or shoulders, throwing the head back, then inclining the head down. We lashed our bodies in figure-eight patterns, sometimes even spinning around and rolling on the floor.

Suddenly the experiment was over. Finished. We never did it again. We never needed to do it again. Martha had succeeded in getting us to observe and understand so completely the endless possibilities of moving on a sobbing breath. The experience was like that of eating something new. You tasted, swallowed, then digested. The memory was part of you from then on. Even the vaguest hint would be enough to recall it. Less is more. Pare it down. These principles would apply on the stage. Economy was the key word.

"For dessert," said Martha, "we can explore the rhythms of laughing. The Chinese believe laughter is good for you." She described small porcelain figures that sit like buddhas and rock with laughter, making their big stomachs shake as they sway back and forth. Then she asked, "Who here is a giggler?" As everyone in class looked at someone else, Martha pressed on, "Perhaps if you each tickle your own ribs with your fingertips, that will get you started. Go on. Giggle!" One by one, we started to giggle. Martha urged us to make it larger, bigger, then huge. Soon we were reeling with laughter, slapping each other on the back, even somersaulting and falling to the floor like figures in a harvest painting by Brueghel. Martha called out, "Cut!" This time I did not want to stop. It felt so wonderful!

At that point, Martha invited us to attempt some of the robust, laughing falls from *Moment Rustica,* which she had just choreographed for her group. The laughter exploded out of us as we hung in the air, first suspending, then falling, crumpling softly into a ball on the floor, before instantly rebounding up again. But then Martha startled us out of this blissful feeling. "What we have to start working on now is not a laughing matter at all," she announced. "You are all much too polite. You must break this habit of extreme politeness."

Although Martha did not use names, I knew I was one of those overly polite people. At first, Martha resorted to animal images, perhaps because animals were not trained to be polite. I remember becoming a rattlesnake, coiled and rattling, ready to strike out of nowhere. I would shoot out my face with open fangs ready to bite, while imagining my spine whipping and snapping.

Martha surprised us by saying, "Now I am going to teach you how to spit. Take a partner. Imagine you are fishwives at the marketplace, arguing over the price of fish. It is a matter of only a penny, but each penny is desperately important to you, so you must stand your ground. Stand face to face in a wide stride, look each other straight in the eye and alternately take turns saying, 'Yes, you will!' or 'No! I won't!'"

I was relieved when Martha said, "You really don't have to spit in your partner's face, but you must imply this. As you aim to spit, expel your breath toward the ground diagonally in back of you."

I gritted my teeth and, very shyly, faced my partner. At first I whispered the words, "Yes, you will." or "No, I won't." My voice grew progressively louder as I got into the spirit of it. Soon I was laughing, and loving it. This was a game I relished. Martha had given us the shape of the movement, and she watched us fill it with the sound of the words boisterously exploding out of us, followed by the insolent mimed spit. After a full day of this I, for one, was living the part of a fishwife, and even after Martha said "No more fishwives!" the echo of the gypsy-like fishwife remained in my muscles.

A newfound sense of excitement was bursting out of me, and my movement was sharply focused. Martha had achieved what she wanted—a sharp, intensely driving hip thrust; a bold, defined line through the chin and shoulder in profile, with emphasis on the strong column on the side of the neck. The fierce energy Martha sought was finally there. Its liberating surge charged through me. No longer were we graceful little Greek sylphs; we were down-to-earth women with powerful feelings.

The variation that grew out of the fishwife theme was strong enough to underlie the restrained, slow-motion choreography of the two-dimensional entrance in *Seven Against Thebes* and keep it clear-cut and compelling. The residue of conflict and insolence, combined with the strictly contained energy, is something I have never forgotten. No one outside of class would ever know how she had accomplished it. But I certainly believe that it was this stroke of genius that created the barely visible overtones of locked-in energy that contributed so mightily to the strangely awesome mood established for the audience when we made our entrance.

The development of the strong stance of the fishwife improvisation led directly into work on both "dramatic" and "rhapsodic" qualities. Faint remnants of the Delsarte work resurfaced fleetingly when Martha stated that the Mind (designated as the forehead area) was knowing, and the Will (signified by the chin) was strong. She employed a level gaze, incorporating forehead focus with a strong chin, powerful neck and spine. She made it clear that dramatic movement must involve intense energy directed to a purpose. To illustrate this, Martha asked us to imagine that we were so immensely tall and huge that we could stand with one foot on one island and the other foot on another island in the middle of a sea. She described this position as being the stance of the Colossus of Rhodes. As she told us about this ancient statue, everyone was striving to get the feeling of such a domineering stance. We glanced around anxiously checking on one another. No one dared to laugh. Whenever Martha challenged us to try something new, I regarded it as a life-or-death matter.

"Hold this stance," she said, "and rebound down-UP, down-UP. Drive your heels down like drumbeats. Rise up higher than half-toe." This powerful down-UP preparation was followed by a sudden, violent release from the center into a wide aggressive lunge on half-toe with arms stiff and straight like a spear. Impelled by hip thrusts, the movement lurched from one side through center to the other side. Eyes were open wide, chin over the shoulder, forehead strong. The heel kept up its insistent beat on the floor, down-UP, down-UP. This went on and on, relentlessly, frenetically, center-left-center-right, until the brutally heavy, crushing feeling of power was fully established in our muscular memories.

Martha then pointed out that what we had been doing dramatically could also be done rhapsodically. In explaining the meaning of *rhapsodic*, she referred to ancient Greece, and the rhapsodists who told stories in song. She spoke of troubadours, folk singers, town criers, and of how news was carried in times past by word of mouth from town to town and village to village. In terms of verbs, she explained that *dramatic* was action in the present tense, and *rhapsodic* was romanticizing in song or poetry relating to the past tense. To set the mood for an exploration of the rhapsodic quality, Martha had us sit comfortably on the floor. She requested that someone sing softly. It was settled that the song would be one we all knew, the Irish folk tune "Molly Malone." Martha asked us to join in singing very quietly, or to hum along. She encouraged us to rock gently from side to side, allowing the head to sway with the melody. The focus was no longer on the spine, the direct gaze, the visible cord on the side of the neck, or the bold firm chin. Instead, the focus was on feeling the melody of the song and on allowing the neck to loosen, opening the side, the front, and then the back of the throat, while relaxing the eyes, almost letting them close. There was a new feeling of unity in the classroom as we did this.

"Return now to the movement theme we did in the wide stance of the Colossus of Rhodes," said Martha, "but this time we will be moving rhapsodically." The rebounding heel beats in the wide second position remained dramatic. She changed the coloration of the lunges merely by having the head thrown diagonally back, eyes almost closed, and the throat open, as if singing out. It was fascinating to think that just the changed angle of the mask of the face, and the change in the cord on the side of the throat, could send such a different message to an audience. I marveled at how emphasizing the eloquence in the throat could be so startlingly effective. We practiced alternating from dramatic to rhapsodic and back to dramatic in a number of exercises, until it was clear to us all that dramatic movement was appropriate for action, whereas rhapsodic movement was reactive. It was becoming ever clearer to me that Martha was an absolute master of body language.

My appreciation of Martha grew greater every day. I was filled with an almost overwhelming mixture of awe and gratitude. As we began class with the series of basic exercises, each having its own specific purpose, I knew that this was home for me. These same exercises, which in later years would be used by dancers all over the world, were known to us quite simply as "the warm-up." One morning we sat with legs open wide, toes pointed, back straight, head balanced easily on the atlas. We rocked slightly on our sitting bones as we centered ourselves. There was always a moment of complete stillness before beginning each exercise.

We were working on the arms, using the image of powerful eagles' wings. I reveled in the feeling of strong feathers on my wings. My shoulders pressed down to bring up feather-covered elbows, as I imagined myself preparing for flight. I was absorbed in the work when Martha, glancing my way, started laughing. I thought, "Oh dear! What am I doing wrong?" Martha stopped the class.

"I see we have to work on wrists and hands," she said. "Dorothy, your hands are always anticipating shape and texture. When you take hold of a cup or spoon, the hand senses the shape, and prepares to fit the contour, and adjust to the weight before making contact. Today I want you all to override that instinct. I want you to initiate the action." Martha looked straight at me. "Form your hand into a strong, aggressive fist with a firm, powerful wrist. Now, punch like a prizefighter!" I tried, but my thumb had slipped inside my fist. "The thumb," Martha insisted, "must come around outside the fingers, grasp them firmly and hold them together. The thumb acts as a brace for the fist." For the first time in my life I was able to assume a threatening gesture.

Hands became crucially important when Martha began working on what I think of as the "Circle of Pain" segment in *Seven Against Thebes*. Martha began by having us all move on a sobbing breath. We added gestures of grief, including beating with a fist, as we had done in class. It soon became apparent that we would be unable to convey the violent intense grief that Martha envisioned.

She looked at me and shook her head from side to side. "Oh, Dorothy! What are we going to do with your ribbons? Your hand movements are *still* as lyrical and gentle as ribbons floating in the air! This is no way to communicate the powerful feelings of women whose husbands and sons are being maimed and killed on the battlefield."

I was terrified Martha was going to give up on me when she suddenly stopped cold, as if frozen. For what seemed like a long time, she did not move. Then she took a deep breath and spoke decisively.

"I want all five of you to form a circle. Lock your hands tightly together, and *don't let go!*" She had some of us sob over toward the floor, while others turned in toward each other, to give comfort and support. On the opposite side of the circle someone was rising up high, as if crying out in protest. We twisted sharply down one way, then sprang up the other way. Heads flung from side to side, up and back, then over toward the floor. The remembered rhythmic pattern of a sobbing breath silently enriched the movement. Heart-rending, shuddering sobs were torn out of us. We were cautioned always to keep the mask of the face impassive. No pained expressions were allowed. With our hands locked tightly together, we shared in this grief, just as we had once shared in the melody of "Molly Malone."

And to think, all of this was accomplished without anyone making even a single hand gesture! Martha had devised a brilliant way to include me. But that was not all. The most amazing transformation took place in me. By expressing intense feelings through my open throat, head thrown wildly back then deeply bowed, I was releasing my own agonizing suppressed emotions. I could at last express feelings I had never allowed to surface before. Martha had not just disposed of the "ribbon" problem, she had found a way to convert our individual weaknesses into a powerful, massive lamentation. The movement was strictly choreographed, but it retained the appearance of total spontaneity.

The Greek costumes Martha had in mind for us were inspired by an exquisite Fortuny gown she owned. It was made of delicate, wrinkled, twisted silk, which conformed subtly to the contours of her body. In attempting to achieve the clinging effect of the gown, but without incurring the cost, Martha enlisted our help in assembling the costumes. She took me shopping when she bought yards and yards of white cheesecloth and several shades of Tintex dye. Then she invited several of us to her apartment to work with her on the costumes. She told us to be very quiet, because she did not want her landlady to know what was going on in her kitchen. We watched Martha as, one after the other, she mixed the different packages of terra-cotta, red, and sand color dyes in a huge cauldron on the stove. She tested the color and declared, "This will have to do."

The material was divided into five sections, a length for each of us, and then placed in the cauldron of boiling dye. We took turns stirring for a long time, all the while laughing about the witch's brew we were making. We argued back and forth incessantly. "It's done." "No, it's not done." Finally, Martha determined that it had reached the desired shade. We wrung out and then tightly twisted the dyed lengths of cheesecloth and placed them in the oven, hoping to bake in the tiny, uneven pleats. It seemed to take forever to dry. We spent the time anxiously scrubbing the mess on the floor, the stove, the pot, removing all traces of the dye. Martha seemed concerned that the landlady might appear at any moment.

What eventually emerged from the oven did not at all resemble Martha's delicate, form-fitting Fortuny gown. Even though she was disappointed, Martha pushed ahead the next day. She hastily fitted and struggled to pin the stiff, scratchy, wrinkled lengths of cheesecloth with huge safety pins onto the homemade leotards we were wearing. She instructed each of us to take the costume home, sew it up, and bring it back in time for performance the following day.

The only sewing Mother had ever taught me was to sew invisible hems around linen handkerchiefs for Christmas gifts, and I could not do even that to her satisfaction. What to do with the pinned, wrinkled-up cheesecloth was beyond me. Having no notion of what or where to sew, I retreated to my room and went to sleep.

Early the next morning, the long-awaited day of the performance, I ran all the way to the Cornish School carrying my bundled-up, unsewn costume in my arms. As I ran I prayed that somehow I could slip through undetected, safety pins and all. At the school everyone was busy with a thousand last-minute details. I entered the dressing room, trying to be as inconspicuous as possible. Martha came in to personally supervise our makeup. First she had us apply a heavy layer of what she called greasepaint all over our faces and necks. It was creamy pale, almost white, and I found it horribly repellant. I felt like a clown. I was surprised when she said we would wear no rouge, and even more shocked when she told us to draw on bold, dark eyebrows. Then Martha showed us how we must paint two parallel lines to accentuate our eyes. Someone roughly drew them for me—the top line along the edge of the upper eyelids, close to the lashes, and a heavier, longer line below the lower lashes. Both lines extended beyond the outside corner of the eye, with a space between them. We placed a small patch of white between the lines at the outer corner of each eye. Martha said this was important to define the eyes and make them seem larger when seen in profile. To dramatize the eyes when facing the audience, we placed a dot of red paint where the upper and lower lids meet on either side of the bridge of the nose. Martha said this would add life to our eyes.

The most exciting part of the ritual of making up came when Martha showed us how to dress our eyelashes. We lit several candles, and then we melted slender sticks of coal-black wax in the flames. Using delicate little brushes we coated each eyelash with jet black liquid wax, adding layer after layer until our lashes glistened with small black droplets. I watched what was happening in the mirror. My eyelids were taking on the character of window shades that could go up and down! It was fascinating!

When it was time to put on our lipstick, my heart sank, and I felt slightly sick as I looked at the dark crimson color we were to use. I was used to rose-petal-pink lipstick, and that for the stage only. This was much too shocking for me even to attempt. I looked around the room, desperately wanting to escape.

Martha—who never missed anything that was going on with "her girls"—stepped briskly toward me and said to the group, "Look. This is what I want." She picked up the lipstick and firmly drew two wide red lines, one on my upper lip and one on the lower, to shape my mouth into a bold, gashlike, somewhat rectangular shape. I looked into the mirror, and looking out at me was a strange, strong, daring person. No one would ever recognize me. I found this wildly exciting!

When I heard an urgent voice saying, "Hurry! Hurry! Get into your costumes," I knew the crisis moment had finally arrived.

Terrified, I went up to Martha and sheepishly told her, "I did not sew my costume. I did not know how to sew it."

Martha was burning with anger. I knew she would be. She roughly took the costume from me and dragged it down over my head. She put safety pins into her mouth and went to work fiercely yanking the cheesecloth into shape on my body, pinning it here and there onto my leotard. She was hissing and cursing half under her breath. Anger was like fuel for her. I was not afraid. I was just thankful that she was fixing my costume so that I could be in the performance. I vaguely remember some kind of headband being tied around my forehead, just a little above my eyebrows, and I heard whispered protests about "looking like a bunch of Indians." I liked being camouflaged like a chameleon. Being transformed into a stranger from another time and place made me feel safe.

People roughly pushed Bonnie, Grace, Nelle, Bethene, and me into a line, told us to be quiet, and pulled us through a narrow passageway into the back of the pitch-dark auditorium. We took our places at the rear of the side aisle and waited for our cue. Once the music began, I knew exactly what I had to do. The slow chain of sternly disciplined abstract movements had become part of me. I wasted no time reacting to the audience, which by then was becoming aware of us as the lights gradually came up. It must have been a startling, eerie experience for the audience to see these weirdly made-up dancers so close to them in the ominous dim light.

Gradually we progressed in a single line. Each dancer tilted independently forward and over, head bowed toward the floor, then arched precariously up and back, with one hand placed on the heel of the back foot, and face looking up to the far-distant ceiling. It was reminiscent of figures in an ancient, very wild, abandoned bacchanal, but executed in slow motion. We mounted the short flight of steps onto the stage one by one in the same two-dimensional manner, until finally we became part of the action of the play. Although I remember little of the actual performance, I do know that the "Circle of Pain" segment burned with the intensity of a huge bonfire.

At the close of the performance, the five of us bowed in a dignified and appropriate manner, as Martha had carefully coached us. We stood with our heads held high, feet together, arms at our sides. We made a small bow from the hip hinge, then returned to place with heads again held high. We looked from right to left, accepting the applause simply and proudly. It was a formal bow that was quite sexless, and it felt good to me.

After the performance, I felt as if I had climbed a mountain, and I would never be the same as I had been before. I had experienced and learned so much, it would be a long time before I could sort it all out or speak about it to anyone. I carried within me the deep conviction that dance could and should be locked into deep rivers of feelings that cannot and must not be put into words. I looked up to Martha as if she were a figure in the Bible, Moses perhaps. I knew that I was one of the chosen people, and I must follow her wherever she went.

Martha had spent a considerable amount of time talking with me during the second six weeks of the summer session. Perhaps she was lonely with Louis away in Europe, or perhaps she missed New York City and the girls in her group. Whatever the reason, she seemed to welcome me each morning when she came out of the door of her apartment building and found me waiting to walk with her to the Cornish School. She spoke to me about the city—the rhythms, the energy, and the vitality of a growing city. I listened eagerly as she told me about the dancers in her group. Besides Mary Rivoire, she spoke of Ailes Gilmore, the beautiful Japanese American whose brother, Isamu Noguchi, was an extraordinarily talented young sculptor that Martha would soon be working with. She described Louise Creston as a warm, sweet Italian girl, married to a young composer. Martha Hill was pictured as a lively, athletic, outgoing girl from the Midwest, as American as apple pie.

Martha was laughing when she said, "Wait 'til you meet Anna Sokolow! Anna is a true New Yorker. She is fiery and stormy, but her feet are solidly on the ground. Her stance is so combative, she reminds me of a little mountain goat with belligerent horns. Her oval-shaped face is like that of a serene madonna, and her hands with long delicate fingers are very expressive." She spoke of Sophie Maslow, tall and feminine, with a proud, secret way of moving, like a high-flying Russian folk dancer. Smaller and more delicate, but full of fighting spirit, was Lily Mehlman. There was a gentle, lovely, windswept, tearful girl called Ruth White. Gertrude Shurr had a Semitic quality about her and had come from the Denishawn School, as had Martha. Martha explained that some of the girls were Jewish. I had never known anyone who was Jewish. The only person I had ever even read about who was Jewish, aside from Jesus Christ, was Rebecca in *Ivanhoe*.

Martha had described her girls so vividly, I longed to meet them. They sounded so colorful, alive, and down-to-earth. They did not seem to be at all like the people I knew in Victoria, who were most concerned about social standing and polite manners. The magical world of New York City held promise of allowing me to escape from this formal, stifling way of life. As I listened to Martha's stories, I was feeling almost dizzy with anticipation. The thought of entering this new world that Martha was opening up for me was frightening, but not nearly as terrifying as the possibility of being trapped forever in Victoria. In my mind there was no question about my going to New York City. I simply had to go.

At least one classmate, Grace Cornell, would be going to New York City. Bonnie Bird longed to go too, but her family was insisting that she must remain in Seattle to finish high school before she could consider further study with Martha.

Martha Graham was a pioneer like my father in the way she had turned her back on what went before and had started from scratch to create something new and wonderful. I felt the same involvement with her that I had experienced when helping Daddy clear the land, or sharing the chores as he painstakingly prepared the soil for optimum growing conditions. Martha was like a gardener, I thought. She grafted, she watered, she fed, and she watched the movement grow. She weeded, and weeded, and weeded. I rejoiced in being a part of this new process of growth in the dance technique. The constant creativity my father had shown on the farm, and his devotion and care of every growing thing, was being relived in the classroom as Martha molded movement with her bare hands. Being with Martha was like a continuation of our communal life on the farm. A difference between Martha and my father was that Martha never gave up.

Martha had become like a mother to me, in ways that my own mother had never been. Toward the very end of summer, Martha sat me down, fair and square, looked directly into my face, and asked me, "Tell me, Dorothy, what do you know about the facts of life? Do you know how babies are *conceived?*"

"Kissing?" I mumbled, blushing crimson and wishing I were a million miles away.

"You can't come to New York City, Dorothy, without knowing how you can get pregnant! So, if no one else has warned you about this, I guess I will have to!" Martha proceeded to explain precisely how the man's seed enters the woman's womb.

When the summer session at the Cornish School ended, I returned to Victoria. Mother could hardly wait for me to get off the boat to tell me the wonderful news. She had received an inheritance from the estate of one of her aunts in England. She had already persuaded my brothers to give up their shares in order that I might go to New York City. My brothers knew how desperately I wanted to go, and they were glad for me, knowing I would eagerly have done the same for them. By giving up their shares, which would otherwise have been put into a trust fund, my brothers provided the means for Mother to buy a one-way ticket to New York City for me, and a round-trip ticket for herself. She was planning to accompany me to New York City, and from there to go immediately on to Bermuda to visit a dear friend.

It was an exciting time as Mother and I prepared to leave. Everyone who heard the news would pause and say, "Tsk. Tsk. Imagine leaving this little bit of heaven to go and live in a bitterly cold, crowded city like New York!"

When I went to say good-bye to Mums and The Skipper, Mums told me that she, Mother, and Daddy had all been so worried about letting me go, they had contacted the Imperator. I had met him once. Daddy, David, Mickey, and I had visited the Rosicrucian headquarters in San Jose, from which he administered activities throughout Canada and the United States.

"The Imperator has promised to place a white light around you to aid in keeping you safe," Mums said. He had also suggested that whenever my parents thought of me, day or night, they should envision me surrounded by a cloud of white light. The Imperator's assurance that I would be protected in this fashion was a prime factor in my being allowed to go.

Mums had another worry. She wanted me to promise that I would remain a virgin until I was twenty-three. This meant, she said, not only that I would not get married, but also that I would not enter into any close physical relationships until that time. I was so blindly eager to go, that I gladly gave my sacred word. Mother and Daddy simply asked me to promise that I would not do anything that would make them ashamed of me. I promised sincerely. This commitment proved to be crucially important for me, because, being the product of our little utopia, I had developed no basis for making judgments on my own. When faced with making a decision, I would ask myself, "Would they be ashamed of me? or would this make them feel proud of me?" The answer was my guide.

Mother and I boarded the boat to begin our journey. As the boat steamed out of the inlet past the breakwater, I could see David and Mickey shouting and waving goodbye to us. I felt awful about leaving my brothers. On arriving in Vancouver, Mother and I found our way to the Canadian Pacific railroad station. The Skipper had alerted the train conductors to watch out for Mother Bird with her white cane, and they made us feel very comfortable. Before long, I was safely tucked into my narrow upper berth, while Mother settled down in her double berth below for the five-day trip across Canada.

Four

The
Neighborhood
Playhouse,
New York City,
1931

WHEN THE TRAIN finally arrived at Grand Central Terminal in New York City, Mother and I disembarked and searched for a taxi to take us to the St. George Hotel ("for women only"), where Martha had reserved a room for us. Soon after we checked in, Martha called me to say Louis and she would be coming by later to pick me up. When Martha and Louis arrived, they invited me to walk with them along Broadway to Fifty-seventh Street, then across to the Great Northern Hotel where Martha was staying.

It was an evening I would never forget. Martha pointed out all the theaters on the side streets where she had worked. The neon lights dazzled me. When she pointed out the Winter Garden Theater on Broadway, I certainly did not dream that one day I would open there in my first Broadway show. Louis, meanwhile, was pointing out the windows of the lingerie stores displaying scanty black lace and chiffon underwear or pink and purple see-through nighties.

"This is where you'll be shopping when you have a sugar daddy," he explained to me. I did not know what a sugar daddy was, but I sensed Louis was teasing me. Because I was so used to being teased all my life, I interpreted this as a sign of affection. Louis teased Martha all the time. They laughed a lot together.

As we walked, Martha told me that Dini de Remer, who often played the piano for classes, had arranged for me to rent a furnished room for six dollars a week in the house where she had an apartment at 103 West Fifty-sixth Street, in back of Carnegie Hall. The next day, Mother and I put our belongings into a taxi and went to see my room. It was small, over the stairs. I shared a bathroom in the hallway with the male tenant of a larger apartment. As soon as I was settled in, Mother gave me twenty dollars, then popped into a taxi and blithely waved goodbye as she left to visit her friend Kitty in Bermuda. Waving goodbye back to her, I suddenly realized I was now completely, utterly, on my own. The city pressed in on me. So many skyscrapers. So many people — dismal, angry people — pouring out of the subways into tall drab buildings. Suddenly everything seemed gray.

I walked to a corner drugstore located in the Wellington Hotel on Seventh Avenue at Fifty-fifth Street, sat down at the lunch counter, and ordered a lettuce and tomato sandwich. The man behind the counter mimicked my British accent, saying "Lettuce and to-mah-to?" As everyone laughed, I turned red. I quickly ate, then retreated to my room.

That first evening, I went with Dini to Martha's class, where I was happy to see Grace Cornell. Martha introduced both of us to the girls in the group and had us show some of the new work she had been doing in Seattle. I was unprepared for the cold reception we received. I sensed antagonism and resentment in the air. It was understandable. None of them had been lucky enough to be in Seattle and to participate in three intensive daily classes with Martha; nor had they been coached as we had been for the performance of *Seven Against Thebes*. Then, too, they knew Martha was helping me adjust to city life, and because of it, I was receiving a lot of her attention.

After class, Martha remarked quietly, "Maybe it might be better if I don't ask either of you to do any more demonstrating, for a while at least."

The next morning I was very glad to see Martha when she came by, saying, "Come on. I am in a hurry, but I want to take you to the Automat to show you how to get breakfast for fifteen cents."

We both got change, lots of nickels, and I soon found to my great relief that I didn't have to talk to anybody. I served myself. The food was displayed in little glass compartments, and I put nickels in the coin slot to unlock the door so I could take the food out. I could indeed get breakfast for fifteen cents—five cents each for juice, toast, and coffee.

Before Martha left, she warned me, "Don't smile at strangers, particularly men, and *don't talk!* You won't know how to handle it. If someone bothers you, just get right up and go to another table." Then she mumbled something about being "a pigeon."

The Automat was the place for me. I ate there often. At times, men would sit down at the same table with me and try to start up a conversation. I would immediately get up and flee, leaving my meal behind. After this happened a couple of times, I learned to take my tray with me when I moved to another table.

My overriding concern was to plant my feet firmly on the ground, to overcome my frequently recurring nightmares, either of being in a rudderless boat with no oars or of floating helplessly in the air, struggling to reach my feet down to the ground. I welcomed the street noises that assaulted me day and night from all sides. Taxis honked. Sirens screamed on fire trucks and ambulances. Pounding jackhammers, vibrating the muscular men repairing the streets, frightened me. But I forced myself to relax, to listen to the sounds of the city, and let them flood into me. The energy, the discord, the friction in the sounds were what I needed to absorb. I had been told how the city rain poured down in torrents, wind blew people across the streets, and the extremes of heat in summer and cold in winter could be brutal, yet I looked forward to experiencing all of this. I had gladly left behind me the growing flowers, cool breezes, light rains, and most especially, the stiff polite manners of Victoria. I saw that city people had to be tough and down-to-earth. The contradictions of city life astounded me—mink coats and limousines on one hand, breadlines and soup kitchens on the other.

It was clear that I needed a job immediately. Gertrude Shurr offered to take me to the Threefold Vegetarian Restaurant to apply for work. I was hired immediately, given a tray, and told to clear the tables. I eagerly cleared off everything in sight, regardless of what course was being served. It never occurred to me that you don't clear the silverware off the table in the middle of a meal. I was fired.

Later that night, Martha and Louis, with what seemed like parental interest, expressed concern for my safety. Louis suggested that I might protect myself in the city by wearing a hat with a large hat pin in it, and learn to use the pin as a weapon.

I shook my head, "No, No. I'd never be able to do that."

"Maybe you could learn to make a frightful face. You could do that, Dorothy, couldn't you?" Martha asked. I shrugged, but she insisted. "You must learn to do it, as if it's a dance movement."

Martha then showed me how to put my thumbs in the corners of my mouth, and a finger in the outside corner of each of my eyes, and pull outward, popping my eyes, and sticking out my tongue. I must have looked quite hideous. Martha made me practice it over and over, until I could do it instantly. We were laughing all the time, and finally, after many repetitions, it became an automatic reflex that was instantly available to me. I had become like a gargoyle that frightens away bad spirits. I felt very grateful to Martha for giving me armor. I actually did use it a few times, and it was very effective.

With all the stress I was experiencing, my nightmares intensified. Although I did not tell Martha about them, perhaps she sensed it, because she advised me, "Stop job hunting for a while, and I will see what I can arrange for you. In the meantime, why don't you take a ride on the Fifth Avenue bus and see the city?"

I did as I was told and boarded a double-decker bus with the open-air top level. It cost five cents to ride to the end of the line. I practically flew up the curved stairway and found a seat in the front row, just like a box seat at the theater. I was enjoying the view of the city, when suddenly I became aware that taxi drivers traveling in the opposite direction would sometimes stare up at me. Often they whistled and waved at me, especially when the bus stopped for a traffic light. Although I felt safe so high up, it was unnerving to realize that they could tell from all that distance that I was, unmistakably, a country girl. After the ride, I returned to my room and waited and waited for Martha to call. Finally, a message came that she had made an appointment for me to talk to Mrs. Rita Wallach Morgenthau, the administrator of the Neighborhood Playhouse.

I ran all the way to the Playhouse, arriving tongue-tied and trembling with anxiety and anticipation. After Mrs. Morgenthau asked me a few questions, I realized that Martha had arranged the interview for me in application for a scholarship. At the end of the interview, Mrs. Morgenthau told me that if I worked hard and the teachers were pleased with my progress, I would have two years to get used to living in the city without having to worry about earning a living. My scholarship would provide free tuition and fifteen dollars a week for living expenses, rent, food, and carfare.

The relief was so consuming I wanted to cry, but of course I didn't. I would be attending classes every day with Martha, beginning the very next day. After Martha's class first thing each morning, there would be dance composition with Louis or his assistant Anna Sokolow, followed by voice with the remarkable choir director Madame Dessoff, acting with Laura Elliot, and speech. In addition, I would learn about makeup, costumes, stage design, and lighting. Guest professionals from all branches of theater, many of them very distinguished, would talk to us and graciously share their experiences and answer our questions.

The next morning I arrived at the Neighborhood Playhouse bright and early, feeling ecstatic. I sensed how immensely fortunate I was to be once again in the right place at the right time. I felt safe with Martha in her class, but when the door opened and Louis walked into the studio to teach his class, I became a little anxious. I wasn't really scared of him, because I knew that Martha trusted him and relied upon him to advise her. She especially seemed to enjoy his astonishing lack of inhibition and his biting sense of humor. But I did feel uneasy. Louis spoke his mind without the slightest hesitation. He had a scathing, stinging tongue. I had never before met anyone like him.

Louis began the class by telling us about two dances we would be working on. First would be a solemn, stately pavanne, to be followed by a sprightly and dazzling galliard. These court dances, which had been used in earlier times to teach refinement and style, would now serve as our introduction to theme and variation. Every member of the class would be expected to devise an eight-measure movement sample of each court dance. From these samples, Louis would judge if any theme had sufficient merit to warrant further development. Louis was also promoting his firm conviction that dance must once again lead the way, and music must accompany it. Just as music had been composed to fit and accommodate the shapes of the pre-classic dance forms, it could and should now do the same for modern dance.

Louis stressed the crucial role of dance in the royal courts of Europe. He stated that the pavanne was essential to people of all ages who wished to participate in formal ceremonies such as christenings, weddings, funerals, and corona-tions. The galliard was danced by the younger, more agile and daring members of the court. Both these dances demanded great style. A lack of style was not tol-erated. Louis's first assignment was that we learn to perform the pavanne in the grand manner, with a sense of importance placed on every gesture or turn of the head.

"For this dance," Louis said, "you must learn to move as the aristocracy did, like peacocks!"

I was well acquainted with peacocks, and I was ready to attempt the image of a peacock for Louis, but he was not yet finished with his instructions. Louis was requiring that the image be an abstraction. Abstraction? I shrank back. What did that mean? I racked my brain for the Latin root and thought of words like *de-tract, retract, extract. Abstract* must mean to draw out the important part, but how do you do that? And what had this to do with dancing?

"You must walk extremely slowly," Louis detailed. "Acknowledge bows as you proudly approach the royal throne. Present yourselves. Stand still a moment. Then kneel on one knee in a calm ritualistic fashion, as if taking part in a cere-mony where you are being knighted. Bow your head to say, 'I submit. Behead me if you wish.' The monarch will then gesture symbolically with his sword, and you will be dubbed a knight. Rise and withdraw from the monarch's presence, like a peacock, opening up your fanlike tail."

Louis stated that the seed of all the actions of the pavanne must be included in a meticulously counted eight-measure phrase, which we would prepare for class. He established the three ways he wanted us to work. The first was "rhyth-mically," matching a movement to every note. The second was "lyrically," whereby we were to create a dramatic scene while capturing the quality of the music simply as background. This approach seemed to be especially suitable for the acting students. The third was "authentically," utilizing the historical de-scriptions in Arbeau's *Orchésographie*. Arbeau's book was written in French. Fortunately, I had picked up enough French from Mother to work out a few phrases by dint of immense, dogged determination and frequent reference to a French-English dictionary.

Louis selected how each student was to compose the assigned phrase. He stunned me with, "You will compose yours rhythmically."

I had always simply moved so happily to the music, responding to and following the melody. I was able to dance the galliard by singing to myself "God Save Our Gracious Queen," which had the musical accents in just the right places. Although I understood that Louis wanted us to create original movement patterns that demanded certain rhythmic accents, I could not help but resist counting the music. Moving to counts was a whole new concept for me. Fortunately, I had the assistance of Anna Sokolow. Louis depended on Anna to help students prepare the assigned movement samples.

Throughout her growing-up years, Anna had lived on the lower east side of Manhattan, near the Henry Street Settlement House. She had been one of countless children who had participated in classes, workshops, and performances supported by the philanthropy of the Lewisohn family. When the Lewisohn sisters —Miss Irene and Miss Alice—decided to create an uptown workshop, they named it the Neighborhood Playhouse Studio of Arts Related to the Theater. It was their hope that, by creating a pool of young performers who would be well prepared to work together harmoniously at a moment's notice, they would avoid the agony of holding open auditions.

They chose Martha Graham to lead the team of instructors, since she was considered the most innovative figure on the scene at that time. Louis Horst was invited to join the staff to teach principles of dance composition, and to expose the students to the new, modern music. Anna, who had been an outstanding student downtown in Louis's first class, was invited to be his assistant. She played an important role in Louis's work as he began utilizing the pre-classic dance forms. Louis's classes, with all the aristocratic elegance of the ballroom environment, were in direct contrast to Martha's classes. The combination of the two made for a wonderfully rich double life at the Neighborhood Playhouse.

Anna stands out most clearly in my memory of the Neighborhood Playhouse. Martha's description of Anna as being like "a little mountain goat" was just right. She was secure on her feet, so agile, so in balance, and so fast! When Louis assigned me an eight-bar rhythmic study using whole notes, half-notes, quarter-notes, and so on, it fell to Anna to pull it out of me.

She took stock of the situation and advised me, "Just step it out. Go forward, back, and side-together-side. Take one step for each beat."

Anna made up a sequence of steps, which I copied gratefully. Then she went on to help the next person. What both Anna and Louis could never begin to comprehend was that I did not understand what it was I had to divide into halves and quarters. What was a whole note? What size? What length? Who decided? What kept it constant, going on evenly for a period of time? I agonized over this.

In Louis's class I suffered in a frenzy of insecurity as others got up to show their brief studies. I watched as Louis proceeded to demolish almost every one as "unoriginal," or "inappropriate," or "cliché," and on and on. This was not the Louis I knew outside of class. I suddenly felt that the study Anna and I had prepared was utterly inadequate. Days later, when Louis finally called on me, my heart sank. He stared at me intently, while puffing repeatedly on his cigar. Then he took an extra long puff, blew out a stream of smoke, and caustically inquired, "W e l l . . . ," long pause, "Are yuh pregnant yet?"

The whole class exploded in laughter. Blood rushed through me in a hot flush of embarrassment. Every thought was driven out of my mind. I was in a state of total confusion. Desperately, I looked around the room. "Are yuh pregnant yet?" The question reverberated in my ears. My eight-bar study was the last thing on my mind. At Louis's insistence I haltingly began stumbling through the movements I had prepared. I knew it was a total waste of time, and soon Louis put up his hand to stop me. He began explaining sarcastically, as if I were an imbecile and couldn't count, that two half-notes equalled four quarter-notes. His voice droned on and on as he laboriously described the note values, right through thirty-second notes. He was delighting his audience of students, who were only too happy that it was not their turn in the hot seat. I could see that I was being made to pay the price for being Martha's pet of the moment. Louis had everyone howling with laughter. His class had become a torture chamber for me. I was never comfortable after that humiliating day. But I did not buckle under or give in. I prepared every dance form as required, dutifully absorbing everything he told us, relying on my stoicism to get through the ordeal. I valued my scholarship too much to ever miss a single class.

Although Anna was not supposed to do it, she stepped forward to become my ally. Louis had frightened me out of my wits, and I needed and depended on her. Louis's vocabulary of musical terms was unfamiliar to me. His total disdain for clichés was terrifying. Having had no musical training of any kind, I was unable to recognize, much less dismiss, clichés. Anna generously gave me hints and encouragement, by asking the right questions and complimenting me on the way I moved. She had a constant fund of concepts at her fingertips, which she freely shared with me. Anna provided movements that were dissonant, strange, unbalanced, rhythmical, and spatially interesting. Gradually, with her help, I learned that I could fulfill the tasks Louis set for us.

Anna fascinated me. When not in class, she wore a tight, short, black skirt with silk stockings and high-heeled Fifi D'Orsi shoes with ribbons tied in a bow on her instep. She didn't worry a bit about the many runs in her stockings, or the fact that her skirt was so tight the rump was stretched out where she sat. Anna was the epitome of New York City to me. By watching and observing her, I came to see that she always stood up for herself and said exactly what she thought and felt. She was not only cool, tough, and independent, but also direct and down-to-earth.

Miss Irene once asked several of us to make her a leotard like ours. She brought in enough beige jersey tubing to make a dress, and we asked her to disrobe so that we could fit it for her. She wore her corset and stockings as we timidly and loosely wrapped the fabric around her body. Anna courageously took a large pair of shears and cut off the excess material around the legs. Suddenly we realized that Anna had cut through Miss Irene's garters!

"So sorry, Miss Irene. She didn't mean to," we said, as we fled, mumbling various apologies for Anna. I don't know for sure, but I suspect Anna just might have been driven to do it. She was a wild one, refusing to be beholden to anyone. The opportunity may just have been too tempting for her to resist.

Anna had an appetite for drama. I laughed with delight when I heard that, before making her entrance in an acting scene, she irreverently flushed the toilet to suggest the sound effect of trumpets announcing her arrival. Anna was cast as the Virgin Mary in a studio production of a medieval study. Her angelic, oval face tipped to one side, and her delicately shaped hands fell into place with the two center fingers close together. It looked authentic, that is, if you could overlook the black dirt under her fingernails. Her face appeared spiritual and ethereal, her body was costumed exquisitely; but her fingernails gave her away and endeared her to me. She was real. She was everything I wanted to be. She was grounded.

Anna's face was always immobile and strangely pure. Her head rested very objectively on top of her tense little body, which communicated instantly the feeling of distortion. Movements did not flow for Anna as they did for me. In attempting to accomplish what Martha was asking of her in the classroom, Anna seemed to wring movement out of herself, as if battling with her tautly constructed, tiny frame. Martha would caution Anna, "Go easy. Don't force it!"

Soon after Martha took possession of the studio on Ninth Street, I began demonstrating for her in the late afternoon class for members of her group and outside students. The studio ran the entire length of the building, from the back windows to the front ones overlooking Ninth Street. Over the stairway was a closed door that led into Martha's small, private domain. It contained a built-in bed, bookshelves, a night table, and a personal telephone. On one wall of the hallway of the studio, which served as our dressing room, were deep shelves extending almost up to the ceiling. These shelves were covered by heavy monk's cloth curtains, behind which Martha kept everything imaginable. On the other side of the hallway, I hung my belongings on hooks high above a bench to keep everything out of reach of Martha's dachshund, Madel. Ailes Gilmore had warned me about Madel, who had once chosen Ailes's favorite hat as a place to relieve herself.

Memories of the small bathroom in the studio still make me shudder. One day some of us were scrubbing and polishing everything in anticipation of a visit by Martha's mother, who was coming from her beautiful home in Santa Barbara, California. Martha sent someone to buy flowers and assigned me to apply a fresh coat of white enamel paint on the toilet seat. I was very proud of the way it turned out. Shortly after Martha's mother arrived, we heard her voice in the bathroom, first calling softly, "Martha! Martha!" Then she started screaming, then weeping, and finally shrieking. Martha ran into the bathroom. Wails from behind the door were growing louder and louder. Martha sounded distressed. It seemed there was nothing she could do. Her mother was stuck to the paint on the toilet seat.

"Oh, my God," I thought. "It must not have been completely dry. Did I spread the paint on too thick?"

With the protests assailing my ears, I quickly slipped out the door of the studio and flew down the stairs. I was frightened to death, yet at the same time almost exploding with irreverent laughter. Martha's mother reminded me of the ladies in Victoria. When I returned to the studio later that day, everything was calm and quiet. I made sure to keep as inconspicuous as I could. Martha's mother never spoke to me before she left. Later, Martha told me that her mother had been wearing a brand new, very expensive, black lace corset, which had been ruined. I felt somewhat relieved. It could have been worse.

Being around Martha, we never really knew what to expect. One day she lost her temper about something that had occurred at a rehearsal. Furiously she tore into the dressing room as if hunting for something. In her anger and haste, she pulled everything from the shelves, ripping down the monk's cloth curtains, rods and all. It was chaos. I never knew what caused the storm. I only knew we would have to clean up and restore order before we left.

When Martha returned to the studio, she sat on the chaise lounge she always used when teaching or rehearsing and signaled us to get back to work. I was on the floor near her, in some kind of lying position. Out of nowhere, one of the white fur scuffs she wore around the studio whizzed past my ear and slammed into my arm. Startled, I looked up at her. She glared at me. Her eyes widened, but no words were spoken. Just as suddenly as it began, the fury was over. We quickly and quietly went back to work. Work was all that was important. Nothing else mattered.

Whenever I was demonstrating for Martha in the classroom, she had only to utter the words "centered release," and I knew instantly what she wanted. My spine straightened. I rested the weight of my head lightly on the crowning vertebra of my spinal column and looked out squarely and objectively. I turned the mask of my face from front to side as if balancing a small, symbolic crown on top of my head, while allowing air to fill my lungs. When Martha asked for a "high release," I arched my upper back area, then lifted my face to permit me to draw in the last possible speck of fresh air and fill my lungs to almost bursting. Martha called this an "ecstatic body."

The definitive example of this ecstatic body was demonstrated for us by Louis's pet dachshund-mix, Max, who somehow managed to rise up on his hind legs, a feat impossible for the average dachshund, in order to offer his diaphragm area to be scratched. As one of us obliged and scratched, he would arch his body, reaching higher and higher, until he finally toppled over. Max was our model for that moment in a high release when the pinnacle of the ecstatic body was prolonged momentarily. We, like Max, were reaching for pleasure and more pleasure before the exhalation of the breath came explosively and abruptly.

With the exhalation came the inevitable contraction. Contraction was always exciting for me. It meant action. To tighten, to hit, to strike, to shout. Although contraction is a noun, I thought of it as a verb that attracted many adverbs: *violently, suddenly, sharply, hideously, powerfully*. It did not lend itself to adverbs such as *gently, softly, quietly,* or *sensuously*. Contraction was always potent and often dangerous. By having me perform these movements, Martha was opening doors that had previously been locked to me. I was being introduced to a world where one can play out, at least symbolically, what Martha often called "deep matters of the heart."

Martha used the flat, spellbound contraction in the back falls and the hip swings. She privately shared with me a story of how she had devised her wonderful, complex back-fall sequence that required sixteen measures to complete. In April 1930, Miss Irene Lewisohn had cast her as the Virgin Mary in Richard Strauss's *Ein Heldenleben*. Martha had to decide what she, as a dancer, should do when the high point in the music dramatically portrayed the Immaculate Conception, so as not to offend those in the audience who were sensitive to such matters. With the help of Jean Rosenthal, a student at the Playhouse, she experimented with the idea of a pool of light on a dark stage. They decided to beam a pinpoint of light from high up in the first box on the top level to the spot on-stage where Martha stood.

"I let my breath out gradually in a sigh, and fell back slowly, almost imperceptibly, toward the floor," Martha described her movements to me. "Before actually reaching the floor, I felt as if an angel caught me in his arms, and cradled me gently for a moment, before releasing me to drift down to settle on the floor."

Following this slow eight-measure descent to stillness came a sudden, turbulent, whirlwind ascent from the floor. The movement was carefully choreographed, but it appeared tumultuous, abandoned. Demonstrating this fall, which Martha had taught me, evoked in me a feeling of supreme bliss. I rolled, rocked, tipped, spun almost into a somersault, and finally made my ascent straight up from the floor to stand breathless, as if suspended in the sky.

In the fall of 1930, I began attending rehearsals of the Graham Group. I first watched, then understudied *Heretic*, but my movement quality was not ruthless enough for me to perform in this dance. My value to Martha was in demonstrating exercises she had been developing at the Cornish School, particularly those related to falling, tilting, and walking. Martha was constantly working on new and different ways of walking. She claimed that when I walked, she was reminded of Miss Ruth. Of course, no one ever walked quite like Miss Ruth, but I had developed a natural flow of movement from the coaching I had received from Mums. Following Martha's evening class, group rehearsals stretched far into the night. Husbands and friends were kept waiting downstairs on the street, sometimes for hours, until we were finally dismissed. No one was excused early during that winter.

One evening, several of us were in the studio waiting for the rest of the group to assemble for rehearsal, when Martha asked us, "Do you know where the word *arabesque* comes from?" We shook our heads.

"Architecture," she stated. "An arabesque is a very strong, gradual curve used to support a high ceiling."

She explained that the great stonemasons knew precisely how to curve the high walls of a cathedral without having to use crossbeams to create the open vaulted space overhead that is such an important aspect of the religious experience. Martha mentioned that she had choreographed a dance called *Spires*.

"I would like to try to recapture the movement in *Spires*. Three of you stand side-by-side, not too close, and raise your arms. Now, lean toward one another. Press one hand against the hand of the girl next to you."

I was in the middle, and it wasn't easy leaning into two opposite directions. We tried to support each another, while reaching up like the tall walls of a cathedral. It wasn't working.

Martha said to me, "Fall forward."

I looked at her questioningly, as if to say, "How?"

"Fall *forward!*" she said impatiently.

With my arms up, not letting go of my partners hands until the very last minute, I fell forward. My breasts hit the floor first. It was very painful. Tears came to my eyes, but I made no sound.

Martha looked at me rather curiously, before quietly stating, "I see that I will have to be more careful about what I ask you to do in the future."

Another evening, as all of us were resting for a moment, Martha called our attention to Mary Rivoire, whom she always called "my beautiful Maria."

"Just look at her!" Martha chided us, "She is like a poem! Even in repose she is magnificent. Now look at the rest of you, all slumped down and exhausted."

Martha was right. What Mary did was never for effect. She possessed an absolutely natural spontaneity and purity one could only envy, but never resent. Even her hair, which stood up and flared away from her forehead, seemed to be full of life. Martha told me that John Martin had once asked her if she had noticed how Mary was so full of fire onstage that she raised one eyebrow until it actually appeared to be a frame for that eye.

"It is clearly visible from the audience," he had said, "and in fact I find it disturbing."

Perhaps the concept of the masklike, immobile face that Martha was so insistent on our using in Seattle, and again in New York City, may have been something she was devising for Mary Rivoire. I had welcomed the mask as protection, something to hide behind, to cover up how vulnerable I felt. It freed me.

It is well known that, at this time, both Martha and Louis each taught us separately in their respective classes that not one movement from one dance would be acceptable or appropriate in any other dance that was being newly choreographed. This concept that no movement could be transplanted from one dance to another was taken from nature.

Louis told us again and again, "Just as an oak leaf would never be found on a maple tree, because each seed, each acorn, has its own individual growth patterns, so movement must grow organically, naturally and spontaneously from the core of an idea."

So it followed that the specific character of a walk appropriate for a new work, *Primitive Mysteries*, had to be found. The walk was to be the seed of the style. In quiet, unpressured rehearsals with her group, Martha meticulously analyzed the coordination of the body as she searched for the precise dramatic quality that would best communicate to the audience exactly what she had in mind. Her patience was inexhaustible. During countless hours of rehearsal, over a period of months, we walked side by side in groups of three or four, without holding hands but with the knuckles of our cupped hands pressed lightly against the knuckles of the person next to us. Once she placed a broom handle across the backs of our shoulders to hold them flat as we walked in groups of three as a unit. Martha decreed that no one should lead, and no one should follow. With no word cues or sounds of any kind, we progressed from walking to an easy loping run, which developed into a wild, free run, similar to the run of untamed horses, hair flying, like the hair of women running in a painting by Picasso. Then, without an outside cue of any kind, we slowed down, changing smoothly to a walk that gradually became slower and slower until we were almost not moving at all, and finally, gradually, we came to a stop. It was exciting to be absolutely still after the wild run, and to be a part of the trio that moved as one.

Using peripheral vision, we could see our bare, flexed feet come forward and hang in the air for a suspended second before a hushed footfall could be heard as we forged forward. We pushed the ground backward under our feet, and the impetus impelled us boldly forward. There was nothing tentative about it. We went so far as to practice walking in the surf at the newly opened Jones Beach on Long Island. First we pressed just our feet through the water, then up to the knee, then up to the thigh, and finally the whole body. When we returned to the studio we could draw upon the distinct muscular memory we had absorbed through thrusting our whole body forward against the surf, then being dragged back by the undertow. We had rehearsed so much that, even when I walked alone, I felt as if I were being carried forward as one of three, with a feeling of buoyancy combined with a momentous thrust.

After a while, all our differences in size, shape, temperament melted away. The group had become one person, with the feeling extending to Martha as being one of us. It seemed as if we even breathed as one. Each of us carried our own weight, but the whole was stronger than the parts. The walk Martha finally found had in it none of the ruthlessness of *Heretic* nor the laughter and abandon of *Rustica*. This hushed and silent walk, which permeated the fiber of everything we did, became the key to *Primitive Mysteries*. Uncluttered by sets, props, and elaborate music, this enigmatic walk would not only introduce the cast of characters, it would also transport the audience in their imaginations to a different time and place, where they would see something they had never encountered before. The walk was like a piece of cloth onto which the story would be embroidered.[1]

When Martha finally allowed Louis to come into the studio to see what she had created, they decided that all the entrances and exits should be executed in silence. When Louis wrote the melody and it was united with the dance, the release from the intense concentration of the silence swept us into a feeling of joy that burst out of us explosively. The music was not merely decoration, or something we would copy. It was an integral part, an active partner, emphasizing and clarifying each movement. It supported and defined the dance.

The costume Martha created for herself for *Primitive Mysteries* was a master-piece of simplicity. I was alone with her in the studio when she made it. First she took one large section of heavy, stiff white organdy and cut it into two equal squares. I rather think she had been treasuring this organdy for quite some time. She placed a corner of one of the large squares between her breasts, and pinned it to her leotard. As it fell down in a diamond shape toward the floor, she made a decision about how long she wanted this dress to be. I placed a safety pin to mark the length, near her ankles. She unpinned the corner attached to her leo-tard, and placed that large square of white organdy on the floor. While I firmly held the point still, she carefully folded the organdy, first in half, then quarters, then eighths, thus pleating the fabric like a fan that when folded closed was four or five inches across. With a large pair of shears, she quite simply cut a curve across the lower corner where it had been marked for the length. We unfolded the organdy, and again pinned the top corner at a point between her breasts, an-choring the fabric to her brassiere. We did the same thing with the other square, this time pinning it to the back of her leotard. We put two large safety pins down the side seams to close the skirt around. Martha reached down to the floor and picked up the two curved triangular remnants that she had cut from the squares. She placed one triangle on her shoulder, and moved it around until she was able to create a sleeve and something covering her breast, then did the same on the other side. We pinned the pieces in place, and in almost no time at all, it was basted together. Her costume was complete and was never changed.

It was during this period of time, when we were getting ready to perform *Primitive Mysteries*, that an intriguing letter came for me in the mail. My name and address on the envelope were not written in script but instead were printed rather awkwardly in an uneven, labored manner. I was puzzled by this. When I opened the envelope I found a short note, also printed in the same way. As I unfolded the note, a ten dollar bill fell out. This was exciting! The message said, "Dear Dorothy, I hope you will use this money to buy some good, healthy meals. I hear you are not eating properly." It was signed "From an Admirer." There was also a postscript, "I will be sending more money from time to time." How thrilling! An admirer! Dinners cost fifty cents at that time at Alice McAllister's on Eighth Street. Ten dollars would buy a lot of meals.

I immediately showed Martha the letter. She held it in her hands, looked at it carefully, and took out the ten dollars. She was clearly as puzzled as I had been. After a moment or two, she said slowly and rather thoughtfully, "You know, Dorothy, it may be from someone rather strange. It might even be from a lesbian!"

I had only just recently heard this term, and it sounded a bit scary. Martha paused before continuing, "Of course, it would be absolutely wonderful for you to have lots of delicious dinners." Another pause. "But if you did that, then you would be inclined to feel obligated, and I know that you would not want to feel obligated, would you?"

Martha stared first at me, then at the note and remarked, "There's no return address, is there? So we can't send it back, can we?" Then she smiled at me for a moment before saying, "Dorothy, why don't we just use the money to buy the materials we need for the group's costumes for *Primitive Mysteries?* We could do that today. That would be absolutely grand, wouldn't it?" She used those words a lot at that time—"absolutely grand."

I was shocked and a little disappointed by Martha's suggestion, but she was holding fast to my ten dollar bill. It was true that I would not want to feel obligated to anyone "strange," and this way Martha would not have to feel indebted to Louis for money. Louis sometimes said that Martha was reckless about the way she spent the money he was loaning her. I felt it must have been humiliating for Martha to have to ask Louis for money, so it made me glad to agree to give Martha the ten dollars for costumes.

We immediately went downtown together to shop. In keeping with her established rule that costumes for the group could cost no more than one dollar each, Martha headed straight to the remnant tables. Her hands moved over each of the materials, feeling which ones would stretch, which were rough, and which had movement in them. Martha liked jersey. Finally, she settled on some large remnants of tubular jersey, enough for the whole group. It was a color I thought of as Virgin Mary blue.

That evening Martha cut a length of jersey for each of us, and one by one we stepped into our jersey tube. She pinned a pleat over one hip, and carried it up onto the shoulder. The pleat was sewn straight down the front from the shoulder, over the breast, to the hips. There was no fitting in at the waist or under the breast, but it was fitted closely around the rump. The neck was square, the sleeves short, and the skirt was cut off at an awkward length. We looked very solid. I believe she wanted us to look like the little wood carvings or clay figures she had brought back from New Mexico. The one thing that she surely did not want was for us to look graceful or seductive.

The preparation for *Primitive Mysteries* that had taken so many months was to culminate finally in public performances at the Craig Theatre in New York City. There was tremendous pressure as performance time drew near. The stage was available to us for only a very limited amount of time. Looking at what had been prepared in the studio, and then transferred to the stage, was a devastating experience for Martha. There was so little time to clarify and adjust spacing. Martha became a holy terror, tearing everything apart, respacing, and rechoreographing.

She developed the most frightful headache. When we took a break, she and Louis sat together in the audience for consultation. She called out for me to come and rub her neck, and try to relax her knotted muscles with my "healing hands," as she called them. I stood behind her seat, trying to ease the tension for her, while she and Louis immersed themselves in urgent discussion. Together they searched desperately for ways to solve problems as they arose. Louis pressed always for abstraction and purpose. Nothing could be done for decorative effect. I felt privileged to hear Martha and Louis talking freely in front of me, as if I were a member of their family. Louis drove Martha forward and encouraged us to be patient and keep going. He was a bulwark of strength for everyone as we prepared for the premiere.

On the day of a performance, Martha always washed her hair and brushed it for nearly an hour, working Vaseline into it to thoroughly coat it. The Vaseline made it shine and hold together. Her hair was not sticky, but it was heavy. She wore it long and thick and cut off straight across in back, and it would swing out extending her movement range. For *Primitive Mysteries*, the members of the group wore the black hair nets from *Heretic*, so that no hair showed at all. I had to hide my fair hair with two heavy black nets in order not to break the feeling of anonymity.

The audience for modern dance was very limited at that time, but each of Martha's concerts was considered an event. Sculptors, painters, composers, writers, actors, directors, and stage designers all flocked to see what she was up to. The theater was filled with celebrities and patrons of the arts. Many came prepared to give support for perhaps unpopular, but promising and important works. Others came to criticize. No one knew what to expect.

The lights were lowered. The curtain opened. The entrance for *Primitive Mysteries* made a powerful visual statement. The sudden impact of the walk caught the audience off guard and captured their attention. It was important that they first see the One in White walking with the group, all of us moving together in silent unison. Martha's tremendous presence carried us with her. Her white organdy costume instantly established the mood of her character as virginal, angelic, innocent.

With the first note of the flute, the youthful, delicate, vulnerable heart and soul of the dance was revealed. Martha swung her legs out, almost as if skipping in a childlike fashion, then floated softly, running high on her bare feet, from one small group of friends to the other. The members of each group in turn cherished her, supported her, framed her with sharp designs before sending her with loving care, gently but firmly, across the stage to others waiting eagerly to receive her. Gradually, strange and darker sounds began to ring out like church bells. Hints of the Gregorian chants that Louis loved could be heard. As Martha continued the childlike skipping walk back and forth across the stage, she quite clearly was drawing strength, first from one group and then the other, as the music grew more compelling.

My group was seated solidly on the floor, in a line placed squarely across the upstage area. We were like primitive carved stone figures of the ancestors—the generations. When the somber, cathedral-like chords rang out, we rocked fiercely, turned and knelt sharply as we folded ourselves over into the most compact shapes. As the music grew in strength, we rose, rocking to our feet. I felt that in the act of standing we had become part of the present. Now we used a more full-hearted version of the theme walk, moving jubilantly, joyfully, with a singing feeling as we came forward, and back, and forward again to join in the "Hymn to the Virgin."

Because of the discussions I had overheard during rehearsal, to me it was not Martha onstage—it was an echo of Mary, the Mother of Jesus. When Martha walked forward between two lines of dancers, I accepted the idea without hesitation that she was recalling and suggesting the One who walked on water. I shared the memory and cherished it as she did. With each step, she first raised a foot in front of her, then paused a moment before taking the next step. This allowed one of us, starting consecutively from the back of the line, to drop down and reach a cupped hand forward to place it underneath her foot as if ready to support her weight in the air. At the moment someone placed a hand under her foot, Martha would reach out to touch the face of a girl on the other side of her. With this caressing gesture, she distracted the audience from seeing the hand slip away from under her foot as she stepped down and allowed the next hand to come into position. Martha was like a magician, who knows how to capture the eye of the audience and make them see precisely what she wants them to see.

At another point, Martha sat serenely on the floor, her gown spread out to cover her raised knees. Her lap had suddenly become a resting place to receive the body of a dancer who descended gently in a softly spiraling back fall. Martha rocked the dancer back and forth, as if Michelangelo's *Pietà* had come to life. This vision dissolved just as suddenly as it had appeared. The figure in Martha's lap rose to stand behind her in a wide, deep plié, then spread out the fingers of her two hands into a fanlike shape behind Martha's head. To some, this movement may have suggested a circle of light, a halo, or the points of a crown. To others, it might have represented His crown or an illustration of the Virgin Mary as seen in Sunday school. To me, it was a marvelously colored aura.

When the music of the "Hymn to the Virgin" suddenly stopped, the group—with Martha again one of us—calmly, deliberately, silently assembled and made our formal exit. We took a breath, reassembled, and returned to the stage once more in total silence for the second segment of the dance. "Crucifixus" was urgent, close-knit, and staccato. With the first note of the music, our arms and heads were jolted up. They remained in that position, as if frozen with distress, while we focused up toward that imaginary point where a figure had once hung, suspended on a cross. There was one among us whose head was not held high, one who did not, could not, look up. This was the One in White. Her hands were cupped, raised in a gesture that shielded her eyes from the terrible sight that transfixed the rest of us. A tall girl stood on either side of her to guide and support her in her blind horror. The three edged slowly but steadily forward, as if treading water.

Again and again each small group of the rest of us pressed forward, then fell back, to try to see better. This was done first from one angle and then from another, until at last we were all assembled at what I always imagined was the foot of the cross. Our twisted fingers came up in silent empathy, to feel and shape out the crown of thorns. There ensued a still, silent, seemingly endless moment. When at last the One in White flung her arms wide to suddenly uncover her eyes to see, the first of us broke out of our frozen stillness into a huge, massive, deliberately crashing leap. One after another, the dancers joined in a leaping circle around her, everyone crying out silently for her. As we ran, our arms were wrenched up in back of us in a feeling of self-flagellation, our bodies contracted over. I felt my face, as it thrust forward, was a mask of shared agony and horror.

The momentum gathered. The tempo increased furiously. When at last we stopped, abruptly, we had encircled Martha, who was sitting on the floor. We all tipped forward, head to the ground, perhaps paying homage. As we rocked backward, the One in White slowly, effortlessly, ascended straight up in a moment of near levitation. The timing had to be perfect to create the illusion of "the rising" in an obscure, delicate, subtle way. Sophie Maslow once admitted to me, "I give Martha a little push from the back, just to get her started up. It's our secret," and she smiled.

After this quiet ending, we all walked offstage quite simply and took a deep breath. Then we returned for the last small segment, "Hosannah!" Without "the rising," how could we have shared such a joyful, buoyant, radiant finale? As we walked offstage for the last time, there was a pause, and then the sound of shouting and clapping came like an explosion. An extraordinary ovation followed. It was a tremendous embrace for Martha and her dancers, affirming that what we had all felt for a long time was also being experienced by the audience.[2]

There had been another premiere that night, which was overshadowed by *Primitive Mysteries*. It was *Bacchanale*. This dance had materialized out of the rhapsodic work we had been doing in Seattle. Martha employed the basic theme of tilting. Not just tilting; but tilting with wild abandon that led inevitably into tilting falls. Actually, there was nothing wild about it. Every iota was carefully analyzed and practiced. The falls appeared dangerous, but so long as we followed the rule that the fall must be done precisely to the side—not a shade either to the front or to the back—the landing came softly, without our having to use the arm or hand to break the fall. The rhapsodic moment was the arch in the body as the tilt became a fall. Ruth White was outstanding as she hung suspended in the air with a sense of pure ecstasy before falling.

After the performance, Martha paid each of us ten dollars from the money received at the box office. Part of the receipts was used to pay the musicians and stagehands, and what was left went to pay off her debt to Louis. No one had much money in those days. We all shared and exchanged ideas. Few of us could afford to pay for dance classes, and Martha was struggling. Those of us attending the Playhouse scratched around for odd jobs. I walked children home from the Walden School to their apartments all the way uptown on Riverside Drive. I had only a plastic jacket, and it was so cold it was agony for me.

Martha often pointed to Ailes Gilmore as the model for the way we should move our hands. "See how Ailes presses the air down with her hands as she rises. It is as if she carves her own body's shape out of the air, like a Rodin figure emerging from marble." Remembering how Martha had referred to my arms and hands as "ribbons floating in the air," I was eager to learn how to carve space as Ailes was able to do.

Use of the arms and hands to express emotion was demonstrated for us powerfully by a notable guest teacher at the Playhouse, Uday Shankar. He first observed our dance class, and then he taught us how to communicate the feeling of anger. He started by having us vibrate one hand at low level.

Then he said, "Bring your vibrating hand slowly up. See how the level of anger is rising as your arm is rising. At shoulder level the vibration is still under your control. Above the shoulder level, the audience knows you are very angry, and your anger is growing until it is practically out of your control. When your vibrating hand is high, you are ready to strike. To kill!"

Many thoughts went through my mind as I watched Uday Shankar. Did he know about Delsarte? Did Delsarte learn this from an Indian dance master? I was caught up in the magic of Shankar's movements. He was gently seductive, humorous, blending colors, sounds, and textures I had never seen before. He seemed both masculine and feminine in one beautifully coordinated body, subtly suggesting rage or love and all those emotions that I had never allowed myself to experience.

To bring dancers together, and to inform the public, John Martin hosted a series of lecture demonstrations in which outstanding representatives of each new branch of creative dance would informally present their works-in-progress, speak briefly, and answer questions from the audience. The series took place in a new, hexagon-shaped dance studio in the basement area of the New School for Social

Research in New York City. The performing space was circular, with two or three steps leading up to a raised area where a limited number of people could sit on folding chairs. It was a beautiful space for dance, but there was inadequate lighting, no curtain, no crossover space, and barely any dressing area.

Louis had worked with John in planning the series, and I recall hearing heated discussions between John, Louis, and Martha. John was bitterly opposed to the use of the name "modern dance," saying, "That name will so soon become inappropriate."

I remember Martha making a huge scene with Louis about wanting to cancel her scheduled appearance. She adamantly refused to dance without a proper stage, she hated the idea of being questioned, and she particularly did not like having to share her ideas with anyone. Louis insisted that it was important for her to be represented. As a compromise, he persuaded her to let the group members do the dancing, and she would only speak. At the last possible moment before the performance, Martha assigned the roles. She cast me in her part in *Heretic*. I was puzzled. Why me? Why had she not chosen Mary Rivoire or Anna Sokolow? Either one of them would have been much more appropriate than I.

After John Martin introduced Martha, she first had the group demonstrate moving on a breath, as it had been used in the Greek greeting in Seattle. But for this performance, we allowed the out breath to carry us forward quite freely into space. We were all laughing as we barely managed to avoid crashing into one another. Did Martha choose this example because she had already discarded it as useless? The Greek greeting was followed by *Bacchanale*, in which we were all tilting furiously back and forth, suspending, then falling onto the floor, spinning and rocking. Martha had not prepared us for the circular space, and we had a traffic problem. Some of us became disoriented and lost the sense of front. Martha stopped the dance and pointed out that each of the walls in the hexagonal room was painted a different color. She identified which color was to be front, and we started again. This time we performed it accurately.

Just before I was to go on in *Heretic*, Martha hurried me into her costume, a tunic of off-white monk's cloth, and gave me last minute instructions. "Take four long walking steps and lunge. The group will lunge toward you. Hinge back. Rise and challenge them. Then take eight long steps, lunge, and hinge back almost into a back fall," and so on. Martha gave me a map of where to go.

I anxiously asked, "Which foot do I step out on?" as if that mattered. I had seen the dance and had been a substitute in the group in rehearsal, but in no way was I prepared to dance Martha's role.

I felt like a stand-in on a movie set as I tentatively dashed this way, then that way, obediently lunging and backing up. In my mind was no thought at all of the courageous character of Joan of Arc facing the persecutors, who were locked shoulder to shoulder blocking her way. I was thankful that the dance was brief, and I put my anxiety behind me as I rushed to change into my costume for *Primitive Mysteries*.

Martha whispered to me afterward that John Martin had commented to her privately on my performance in *Heretic*, saying that he felt like telling the group, "You had better just stop that, you old meanies."

From the expression on Martha's face, it was plain to see she was quite satisfied. I sensed I was seeing a side of Martha's personality that I had deep down always known existed but that had not been clearly revealed to me before.

During the question and answer part of one of these lecture demonstrations, a bald man in a dark business suit stood up and aggressively questioned Martha about the "improvisation" at the beginning of the evening, and he mimicked the way we lifted our arm in the Greek greeting. Martha tried to brush him off, but he persisted. Why couldn't we simply lift the arm up? Why all the fuss about the breathing and the shoulder? I felt he was pressing her, and I thought Martha was trying hard to control her temper. She explained patiently, in terms that any layman might understand, that when lifting the arm to reach a book on a high shelf it is necessary to press down the shoulder muscles in back to cause the arm to rise in front. She compared the motion to that of a seesaw and added that, in the process, the lungs fill with breath. She seemed almost triumphant for having broken it down so clearly for him.

The man burlesqued what she had shown him, moving his arm this way and that, as if he were trying to crank up an old Model T Ford. People laughed. Martha was livid. He baited Martha maliciously, retorting, "If I go to a high shelf to pick up a book, I most certainly do not lift MY shoulder and then drop it," and he lifted his shoulder in a very bizarre way, then jerked it down. Throughout this exchange, the dancers, including me, were seated on the curved steps that led down to the studio floor. John Martin was behind us. He whispered urgently for someone to tell Martha that the man was the great Russian choreographer

Michel Fokine. I reached out, and tugged gingerly on Martha's skirt, but she was so wildly angry by now that she paid no attention to me.

Finally, John stood up to fulfill his duty as moderator, deftly closed the subject, and moved on. When Martha finally learned that the man in the audience was Michel Fokine, she was shocked and upset. She protested, "But he was wearing a suit! He looked like a Wall Street banker to me."[3] Years later, Michel Fokine wrote about the incident. He described Martha's work, and all of us, as grotesque. He even used the words "the Graham girls were like barking dogs." Could it have been that he, whose own work had been considered so new and original, had felt threatened by Martha?

When the school semester ended, I returned to Victoria to spend the summer with my family. Bonnie Bird came up from Seattle at the end of summer vacation so that she could travel to New York City with me. She had finished school; and her parents, thinking that I would be watching out for her, were permitting Bonnie to attend the Neighborhood Playhouse and work with Martha. The Skipper arranged for Bonnie and me to receive special care on the Canadian Pacific Railway. We were even allowed to ride in the locomotive and watch the crew shovel coal to fire the engine. We rang the bells and blew whistles at railroad crossings, trying to scare wandering cows off the track. At night, porters from the dining car gave us treats, and each morning we would help them make up the berths. One morning we slept late and awoke to find notes like, "Let sleeping dogs lie," pinned all over the curtain of our berth.

Our first night in New York City was spent at the same hotel where Mother and I had stayed the year before. The next day Bonnie and I found a room on Forty-ninth Street, east of Park Avenue, convenient to the new location of the Neighborhood Playhouse on Madison Avenue. No sooner had we settled in than Martha took me aside privately and defined exactly how things were going to be.

"I have given it some thought, and I have decided that all the small matters that you have been attending to by yourself should now be divided evenly between you and Bonnie. You will decide between yourselves who will walk the dogs, or do the errands. By sharing, and taking turns, one of you will always be available to answer the studio telephone." She explained to me that by doing this I was "learning to be a professional." I had to decide which fun things with Martha and which errands to give up to Bonnie.

It was easy to share the duties of caring for Martha's two miserably undisciplined dogs. These creatures were a tremendous burden. Not only were they impossible to deal with on the street, running and barking and yanking their leashes every which way, but they were also not even properly housebroken. The dogs had accidents at the most inopportune times in the studio, and I was expected to clean up. Martha laughed as she said she had recently heard that pets often take on the personality of their owner. Martha was also inclined to be tempestuous and unruly.

The hard part of the new arrangement was having to give up half of the demonstrating. After a while, as Bonnie and I shared in demonstrating, chores, and accompanying Martha, I began to realize that I was never alone—and most certainly never alone with Martha, or with Martha and Louis. Martha still made me feel special, and she would say, "You *know* I love you best." It soon became clear to everyone that Bonnie was much more capable, practical, and outgoing than I was. By having us share the duties, Martha had us both available whenever she needed us, and she had effectively freed herself of the burden of being responsible for me.

In her classes at the Playhouse that fall, Martha was talking quite a lot about primitive people. She described the wonderful posture they had, and how they carried large bundles and pots of water on their heads. The loads that they carried did not bump up and down but, rather, moved in a straight line through space. The body swayed slightly from side to side, as one foot took over and the other one released. The whole body—not just the hips, but also the shoulders—balanced underneath the load and constantly readjusted. The head, bearing the weight, remained centered. This made for a lateral walk with a strong drive forward. Martha encouraged us to practice walking with two or three encyclopedias on our head, and to experience going up and down stairs without losing our books. Bonnie and I walked proudly with books on our heads from our room near Third Avenue, underneath the "L," and past the Waldorf Astoria to the Playhouse.

At the beginning of the semester, Mrs. Morgenthau laid down the law that the work at the Playhouse must come first—ahead of work with Martha at her studio. She felt we were all much too tired from lengthy rehearsals to take advantage of the class work at the Playhouse, and that anyone who studied there may not be in Martha's group until after graduation. Even though Mrs. Morgenthau was firm in her reprimand, we all knew she was devoted to Martha and Louis, and she never interfered in artistic matters. I continued to go to many of the rehearsals at

Martha's studio and I learned the dances but did not perform. It was doubly frustrating for me, first to have to share my special privileges with Bonnie and then to suddenly be put on hold as far as being in the group was concerned.

All through my second year at the Neighborhood Playhouse, Louis still teased me at every opportunity. Whenever we would give demonstrations of his work at the Playhouse or in colleges, he always picked me to illustrate the dissonant quality of movement. This was somewhat sadistic of him, because anyone else in the class would have been more comfortable with it than I. Others thrived on the vigorous, exciting city sounds that made me flinch. To get into an appropriate mood for performance, I would silently hiss under my breath, "Rats! Mice! Rats! Mice!" as I tensed, winced, and shuddered, all bent over. The image in my mind was of a time on a chicken farm when I carried a lantern for my brothers as they went rat hunting at night in the pitch dark henhouse. The boys wore long pants and heavy work boots, but I had on a skirt, sandals, and bare legs. The boys lifted the cover on the chicken food in the trough, and rats leaped out and ran across my feet. The boys jumped up and down trying to squish as many rats as they could. I was screaming the whole time. It was my idea of total horror, worse by far than any city sounds. While this was not really an accurate image for dissonance, Louis was satisfied. He insisted that I could not stand up straight for my bow but had to cringe off, exiting all bent over. The audience laughed.

Our acting teacher, Laura Elliot, was terrifying and temperamental, but often wildly stimulating. We did selections with her from *The Book of the Dead*, and a lot of things that had to do with bread. Bread was a big thing at that time. Many people didn't have food, or money for food. They were selling apples on the street and standing in breadlines. In the spring of 1932, Mrs. Elliot insisted that, before graduating, we each must play an emotional scene with her from *Broken Dishes*. In this scene a daughter leaves home against her mother's wishes. The key to the scene was that we must challenge Mrs. Elliot to open the classroom door to allow us to leave. Showing tension in our face or neck muscles as we did this was not permitted. We had to be both cool and highly emotional at one and the same time in order to convince Mrs. Elliot to open that door. Mrs. Elliot praised Anna Sokolow to the skies, saying that only she possessed the knack of being sufficiently objective, while remaining in touch with her feelings.

For the rest of us, Mrs. Elliot suggested that we imagine honey trickling down our upper lip into our mouths while we shouted. In the same way that Martha had us assume a mask, Mrs. Elliot was trying to get us to feel without indicating. Once she directed us to mime playing an imaginary cello with deep feeling, as we created this terribly rebellious scene. The principle was to act, not react; to be objective in a crisis; to consciously allow feelings to fuel the fire, while remaining impersonal and involving ourselves in a secondary activity. I was fascinated, because I had seen Martha do this without being the least bit self-conscious about it. Sometimes Martha did it mischievously with dynamite skill. She would look at me and flick an eyelash, barely giving me a wink when she was making a big scene. Martha had us hang from the barre like monkeys, while reciting Shakespeare. She wanted us to free the voice and have it come forth with a ringing quality. Mrs. Elliot and Martha were both working on the same idea, coming from different directions.

For the final demonstration, I was given a scene from *Liliom* by Molnar. I was to work alone, as Julie, and I had to cry. Mrs. Morgenthau asked my classmate, Mary Tarcai, to help me. Mary fabricated a story in which a phone call had come saying my brother David had died. I was devastated. Then she assured me, "It is not true." My tears flowed as if a dam had broken at the frightful thought of what she had said. The scene was very moving. Louis said he was amazed, and that I was a very good actress. Mrs. Morgenthau excitedly told me that the actress Pauline Lord had been in the audience, and she had said I reminded her of the legendary Ellen Terry.

Mrs. Morgenthau then proposed, "Have you considered auditioning as an actress?"

I felt very complimented, and indeed, the idea of becoming an actress was truly tempting. I immediately told Martha what Mrs. Morgenthau had said, and Martha responded firmly, with a distinct threat in her voice, "Well, you can do whatever you want to do. But you should know that actors are false, always acting. Dancers are real people."

I was not totally convinced that this was true, but I felt instinctively that Martha would have looked upon my auditioning as a betrayal. I thereby allowed Martha to slam the door shut on even the possibility of an acting career for me.

Five

Performing with the Graham Group, 1931–1937

AFTER SPENDING THE summer on the West Coast with our families, Bonnie and I once again traveled by train across Canada to New York City. There we quickly found an apartment just south of Washington Square on Sullivan Street. The landlord took it for granted that Bonnie and I were sisters, since we had the same last name and resembled one another a bit. Lots of people thought we were sisters. Whenever we said "No, we are not sisters," people thought it was odd. It was simpler to nod yes when asked. In fact, Bonnie was like a little sister to me.

Each morning Bonnie went uptown to attend classes at the Playhouse, and I walked to Martha's studio at 66 Fifth Avenue where I would spend the day answering phone calls and doing errands. Martha and Louis often met for breakfast at a restaurant across the street from the studio. Occasionally, Martha invited me to join them. The three of us were like a family. We always had a hilarious time, with Louis mercilessly teasing first Martha, then me. When Martha asked Louis if she could borrow money for bus fare to the Playhouse and back, and for a few phone calls, he would first shake his head and proclaim how extravagant she was, then out came the little black book. He'd make a big show of writing the date and the minuscule amount of the loan. Martha would end up laughing so hard the tears streamed down her cheeks. Then she would get back at him by pointing out his weakness for delicacies like pigs' knuckles, or his preference for ladies wearing ruffled lace petticoats as against the skimpy leotards we wore.

When Martha was working alone in the studio, she insisted on absolute quiet and privacy. She gave me strict orders that "No one, and that means NO ONE, not even Louis," could interrupt her for any reason at all. I was proud of my role, standing guard to see she was not disturbed. Protecting Martha from outsiders made me feel I was in some obscure way involved in the creative process. People who wanted desperately to see what went on behind the studio door would sometimes go so far as to bring me gifts. I steadfastly refused to be manipulated.

"Nobody, not I, nor anyone else can get Martha to do anything she does not want to do." I explained, "Martha needs absolute privacy."

So I was startled one day when Martha invited me into the studio and said, "Sit on the floor with your back to the mirror. And watch."

Martha did not use music or counts. She used sounds. Nearly indescribable, primitive sounds. I remember an insistent tapping noise, like a woodpecker carving out a hole in a tree trunk, that she made by drumming with her fingernails up the wall. She made whirring, vibratory, birdlike sounds to accompany herself as she swung her head and shoulders, first one way and then the other, shivering and pressing through the air. She made sudden, swishing sounds, that reminded me of bats flying in the dark, as her feet skidded along the floor. There were silences, interrupted unexpectedly by jungle-like screeches, then total silence again. Deep, growling sounds seemed to come from the bowels of the earth as her torso slowly curved, and arched, and turned. Hissing sounds built into a loud scream. She would beat with her clenched fists on the floor, then cry out repeatedly "NO! NO! NO!" At times she seemed to be keening, as her Irish ancestors might have done long ago. The startling movement patterns that were evolving came not out of these strange sounds, but out of her articulately alive and animated body. She did not represent or copy anything. These movements, so spontaneously bonded to the sounds she made, rose up inside her and exploded out of her body. I sat there, shaken by the experience of seeing her tapping into a deep, rich source of feelings. Martha laughed. I realized that she had been reading me, as one reads a thermometer to see the temperature, and she was satisfied.

Martha called to Louis, "I am ready for you to come into the studio now." She told me to stay. I sat on the floor, absolutely quiet, trying to disappear into nothingness. I knew Louis would serve as the blast furnace through which all these wild movement patterns had to pass to be processed and refined. I felt myself tensing up as Martha performed for Louis. Then I became anxious, fearing I would never again see what I had seen before. The movements and sounds went together so perfectly; I couldn't imagine them being separated. To me, Louis was acting destructively, by forcing her to count out the dance patterns. The movements' passionate quality was evaporating before my eyes, becoming boxed-in, dull, blunted.

Louis was insistent, stubbornly forcing her to do it over and over again, phrase by phrase. She fought him verbally all the way, but he would not give an inch until the counts were finally set. Louis's passion for self-discipline was being imposed on her—with her permission. It was not easy for her to submit herself to discipline. She battled him, like a scorpion lashing its poisonous tail in the air. Louis was like a big old feather bed. He absorbed all the stings. She battered him with clenched fists, but there was no way he would give up until he had forced her to discipline herself. She respected Louis's objective approach, and in the end, she would always acquiesce. It was clear that she wanted Louis to help and guide her during this period of her life.

There was one person Martha absolutely adored, and that was her sister Geordie. Geordie was as gentle and retiring as Martha was bold and aggressive, but there was a strong physical resemblance. When the three of us were alone at the studio, I watched in amazement as Martha would sometimes treat Geordie as if she were a small child. She playfully pulled Geordie onto her lap, stroked her hair, and talked baby talk to her. Geordie would respond by giggling in the most endearing way. Geordie, who was trying to break into show business as an actress, came by the studio one day on her way to an audition. She was distressed because she didn't have any suitable clothes to wear. Martha proceeded to dress

Geordie in her own clothes, but they were inappropriate. Geordie was very feminine, and Martha's clothes were always severe. Martha was overwhelming Geordie with a thousand instructions, not only on what to do, what to say, what to wear, but even how to flirt. Martha demonstrated how Geordie should dip her chin and gaze up mischievously under her eyelashes, claiming, "I have done it myself and it always works. It makes men feel tall and powerful." Poor Geordie. I could see that it was not easy being Martha's little sister.

Martha wanted Geordie to be in the group, but though Geordie is listed as a participant in *Primitive Mysteries* in 1930, she did not really want any part of modern dance. Geordie had toured the Orient with Denishawn, and Martha coaxed her to show us phrases from the native dances she had studied while in the Far East. Martha would beg until finally Geordie gave in and showed us movements in which her wrists and ankles were sharply flexed. These acute angles gave a startlingly alive look. Geordie's huge hazel-brown eyes were part of the dance. They moved all the time, looking to the sides, opening wide or almost closing. She may have been executing a Javanese dance. It was uncanny how Geordie could lower her body to the floor, then rise up out of it. She was so pliable.

I always felt that Martha tried to incorporate into the floor work some of the feeling of what Geordie had shown us. When we sat on the floor in fourth position, we dug the toes of the front foot into the floor with heel high and ankle flexed to the limit. At the same time, the back heel pressed down into the floor, causing the back knee and toes to flare up from the floor. On the out breath, feet and knees relaxed, resting on the floor. It was easy for me to accomplish this because, like Geordie, I had extremely long Achilles' tendons. I loved doing it, but for many others it was almost impossible. The movement was soon dropped. I felt this was a shame, since it had added a feeling of liveliness and excitement to the floor work.

With love and laughter, Geordie described to us how once each season Miss Ruth called the company members together to describe the new production number she was planning for their upcoming tour on the vaudeville circuit. Miss Ruth, beautifully groomed and gowned, would sit in a thronelike chair flanked by tall lighted candles. The older members of the company stood around her. The younger ones reclined gracefully on the floor, like followers of Isadora

Duncan. With a great sense of drama, Miss Ruth would then set forth in detail the new scenario, the new music, the new decor, the new costumes. One part of the description was apparently a foregone conclusion and was barely discussed at all. Everyone knew the steps of the dance would remain much the same as always.

Louis must have witnessed this scene many times when he was with Denishawn. The minimal attention paid to originality in the choreography must have distressed him terribly. This may have been a reason why, in his class work, Louis was so adamant that no movement could ever be transferred from one dance to another. Louis sternly demanded that we first find a strong, unique concept. Once the theme was chosen, he insisted that it be built on logically, allowing nothing extraneous to interfere. He believed that this was the only way this new dance form could survive and grow.

Martha stated that the movement flow must come first, not the music. She did not want to feel she must slavishly follow the form of the music. What she wanted was for the music to punctuate, frame, and accentuate the movement, just as an exclamation point, a question mark, or a comma between phrases emphasizes the meaning of words. Although some composers may not have been wild about this, a number of them eagerly sought work with Martha.

The talented ballerina Nina Verchinina also wanted to work with Martha. She asked if she might study the technique and join the Martha Graham Group on a temporary basis as an apprentice. Nina Verchinina's name had been mentioned in all the newspapers in recognition of her outstanding performance in the modern ballet *Choreatium*, choreographed by Leonide Massine. Martha excitedly confided in me that she was tempted by the idea of choreographing for Nina, but she decided against it. Martha's reason was that having an outsider, especially one of soloist rank who was accustomed to being paid a salary, would upset the equilibrium of the group.

Martha paired me with Ailes Gilmore in *Chorus of Youth* in 1932. It must have been quite startling to see the contrast between Ailes, the exotic, dark-haired Oriental One, and me, the sunny, fair-haired, Blue-eyed One. We walked and ran softly, side by side, like a team of horses, with our long hair loose, brushed out like manes. After the performance, a number of people came backstage to compliment me on my hair, saying that it looked golden in the lights. I was heartbroken. There was not a word about my dancing. My good friend, the ballerina Muriel Stuart, comforted me.

"It's nice for them to see something beautiful," she said. "So respond generously. You must learn to accept compliments gracefully, and say 'I'm happy you liked it!'" Privately, I felt a keen sense of disappointment. I wanted so much to be part of the heart of the dance, the core of the action, not just a decoration.

In 1932, Roxy (Samuel Rothafel) was preparing for the opening of the theater in the fabulous Radio City complex. He planned to operate the theater as a music hall in the European manner. He persuaded Martha to choreograph a dance especially for the program. Martha created a fierce, wild *Dance of the Furies*, which would later be incorporated into a suite of dances called *Tragic Patterns*. For this dance we ran backward, taking huge steps, with head flung up and torso arched high. We thought of ourselves as members of a Greek chorus, screaming out in protest against the Fates. Our costumes were made of dark brown and off-white woolen material. The skirts were huge, and the bodices were tightly fitted with no zippers. I thought I would never get the costume down over my somewhat ample breasts. When I asked why there were no zippers, I was told "too expensive."

The stage of the Radio City Music Hall had been constructed in movable sections that could go up, down, or sideways. Before we did our dance, the stage had been occupied by horses, and the back third of the stage had been lowered three stories to bring the horses into the basement. As we ran backward upstage, all that was between us and this tremendous cavern was a curtain. In addition, there were turntables in the floor with sharp steel edges that cut our bare feet. The worst part was that Martha seemed absolutely uncaring about our safety.

Ailes told me that Martha had called the box office to reserve seats for opening night for a party of one hundred people "to see the Martha Graham dancers." No one picked up the tickets. Newspapers reported that six thousand people attended opening night. Most of them clearly did not understand our segment of the program. The complete show was far too long; our section was cut out. Because Martha insisted that we all be there, prepared to dance at each show, we were paid.

In May 1933, Martha choreographed *Ekstasis*, a solo for herself, to music by Lehman Engel. *Ekstasis* was earthbound. Her feet barely moved on the floor, but one foot would float up, as first one arm and then the other lifted and turned like a tendril reaching out. She moved softly, as if the air caressed her. Her rib cage turned and twisted and moved to the side away from her hips and legs. Her neck opened first on one side, then the other, and her cheek pressed against the air. *Ekstasis* was unlike any dance Martha had done before—not linear, but sculptural. It was gentle, and I adored it.

With *Ekstasis,* as with *Primitive Mysteries,* the costume and the dance were inextricably entwined. One did not precede the other, nor did they exist separately. I saw how Martha's hands were drawn to one particular length of roughly woven, clay-colored jersey tubing. It appeared to be homespun, perhaps silk or linen. Martha climbed into it. The fabric conformed fairly loosely to the changing shapes of her body. As the spirit moved her, she would watch the image in the mirror as it took on shapes, moving first one way, then another. It was odd and absorbing to see how each time the costume seemed to pull her back. She did not do these explorations with the costumes for the group, only with her own solo dances. Much time and thought went into every detail of each costume. Martha weighed the significance of texture, weight, and color. Once, when she was experimenting with sleeves, she showed me how a long tight sleeve might be elegant or modest, a loose sleeve casual and carefree, a rolled-up sleeve suggesting readiness for work.

At around this time, Bonnie and I moved into a large apartment that we shared with Ethel Butler. It was on the top floor of the building where Louis had a studio. Geordie lived in the apartment below ours. Except for the late night noise of the Greenwich Inn Cafe in the basement, it wasn't bad. The bouncer doorman took it upon himself to see that the nightclub patrons did not follow us up the stairs at night. Since we were so close to Martha's studio, it was inevitable that other members of the group would stay with us when rehearsals ran late. For those times, we had several mattresses scattered on the floor. Kathleen Slagle sometimes missed the last train to her home in Chatham, New Jersey, and she would sleep at our apartment. Another guest was the future wife of Woodie Guthrie, Marjorie Mazia, who commuted from Philadelphia. It was necessary that we all take turns in the bathtub. I would politely defer to the others, so I was usually the last to bathe. One night when my turn finally came, I climbed into the tub and luxuriated in letting the hot water continue to trickle in. It was heavenly peaceful, and I fell blissfully asleep. Geordie, banging loudly on the door, woke us all up. The overflowing water was streaming through the ceiling into her apartment. We mopped up the water, but nobody worried too much about it. The paint was already crumbling.

It was beginning to dawn on me that there was a big world outside of Martha's studio when Ethel Butler introduced Bonnie and me to a group of young men. One was a medical student, another a quiet, studious law student. The one who attached himself to me as my guardian was Mogul, who had a job in the post office. Suddenly there were young men waiting for us downstairs at 66 Fifth Avenue when rehearsals finally ended. The young men were close friends, gentle, good-tempered, and full of fun. Together they owned a ten-passenger convertible touring car. They swept us up in it, and we all went flying off to Philadelphia, or some other outrageously distant spot. Their car was adorned all over with horns, which they blew as we drove through the streets, laughing and singing and alarming everyone we passed. Up until that time, I had experienced no social life at all. I welcomed the safety in numbers. I was not yet ready for a close relationship, even though I was nearing twenty-three. Being with Martha had been like being confined in a convent.

In 1933 Martha choreographed *Celebration*, a marvelously energetic dance suggestive of atoms and molecules rebounding to and fro, being propelled in space. We ran backward with tiny steps on half-toe, knees straight, similar to *bourrées*, which created a feeling of vibratory momentum. I jumped in the center of the group until my legs ached. Others split off like firecrackers spewing out in different directions. The dance was impersonal, yet exciting, and we all loved it. The fact that we danced *Celebration* with impassive faces was puzzling to people in the audience. Martha had expunged smiling long before this.[1]

On the same program with *Celebration* was an uncharacteristic dance, *Four Casual Developments*, which Martha created for Anna Sokolow, Sophie Maslow, and me. In the art world people were using "found objects." Martha was experimenting with the idea of using "found movements" in the dance. The costumes for *Four Casual Developments* were made of organdy, soft pink, lemon-yellow, maybe lime or apricot colored, cut out and constructed in the same way as Martha's *Primitive Mysteries* costume. This time she clipped off many small snippets of organdy while adjusting the hemlines, and just when the costumes seemed complete, she impulsively picked up scraps of material and pinned different colored bits all over our costumes until we resembled decorated Christmas trees. I remember little of the choreography, except for a small tableau in which Anna sat on my lap before rolling over and over sideways along the floor with her body straight. Then she sat up, suddenly, and stared at the audience in surprise. At one point, I ran diagonally downstage in a bucolic manner, with my arms and head flung up.

"Do it, Dorothy, the way you imagine Isadora Duncan might have done it, with great passion and abandon," Martha directed.

The dance was great fun to do, and I think New York City audiences found it wildly hilarious, coming as it did in a serious Graham concert. Perhaps I had caught something of Isadora's feeling for a free and unencumbered body. A number of people said I reminded them of her. Lil Liandre took it upon herself to tell Arnold Genthe, the photographer who had taken such powerful photos of Isadora, about me.

"Bring her in, he replied. "I'll look at her." But when I came to his studio, he seemed so intense and fierce, I became shy and timid. He threw his hands up in the air and said, "Don't waste my time!"

That year Martha also prepared *Integrales*, set to the experimental music of the French composer Edgar Varèse. The music was frightfully difficult to count, with constant changes in tempo. There were measures of 2/4, fast 6/8, and midspeed 3/4. Interspersed every so often were measures that Louis insisted we count "one and two and three and four and-and." Martha devised a great step for us to do on the "four and-and" measure. It consisted of six steps, alternating from side to side, progressing into wider and wider second positions. Then our feet came together very fast as we shot the right arm up and pulled it sharply down on the "four and-and" count. We all privately called it "the diddle step."

We rehearsed endlessly. Louis set the tempo for us with a metronome. On the day of the performance, we discovered that this rather fiendish but terribly attractive man, Varèse, had chosen a distinguished, independent, and somewhat casual conductor. Under his baton, the "one" beat of each measure was frequently empty. The musicians rested, but we had to attack on the "one." As the curtain opened, Martha was standing high up on the backs of a small mountain of dancers, all bent over, waiting for her to step down from one back to another in a descent to the floor. Louis was waiting to coach us from the wings, but we could not see him until after Martha had climbed down, and we came running forward. Soon everyone was doing the diddle step at a different time. It was all quite spontaneous, and I enjoyed that, but it was chaotic. The dance ended with Martha running up our backs to the top of the stack to make a final, victorious tableau. As the curtain fell, we all collapsed with laughter and had to be marshaled quickly together to bow in a disciplined, serious manner. This dance was never repeated.

Those of us who had graduated from the Playhouse would often recall what we had done in Louis's classes and remark how fortunate we had been. One day, Martha said we should be working on our own dances, and she offered us the use of her studio for a series of demonstrations. Louis was pleased and said he would help with the music. Sophie Maslow and I were chosen to be the first to show some solo work in addition to the group pieces. The program opened with all of us in a Passacaglia, with variations on a theme that we had arrived at co-operatively. Sophie assembled our individual sections into a cohesive whole.

When Louis saw my variation, which I had built on the aria section, he commented, "What you have done has a singing quality." This was the only time Louis ever complimented me.

I also presented two small studies, using the titles on the music: *Timid Yearning* and *Nevertheless*. One was similar to Martha's *Adolescence*, a sensitive dance close to my heart that explored space tentatively. The second dance was somewhat bolder, but not much. The movement patterns for my *Icelandic Saga* created the feeling of a glistening out-of-doors world filled with exhilaration and vigor. Martha helped me with my colorfully patterned costume of ice-blue and white cotton. She suggested I perform the dance standing on the platform she used in *Lamentation*. The costume covered the platform, effectively making my iceberg tower.

The evening's finale was a satirical funeral march, a dirge. Since Anna Sokolow was the lightest in weight, she was chosen to be the not-quite-dead corpse. We carried Anna in a prostrate position, stretched out on our backs. Her ankles were flexed, and her long feet stuck up. She had a hard time of it, being jolted about as we argued amongst ourselves about which foot went first. With her eyes wide open, Anna seemed to plead for help as we heaved her up and down. The procession proceeded in an altogether disgraceful fashion. Someone got tired and wanted to sit down. Things got wilder and wilder. Anna's body contracted and released, and at the end we all fell and pulled each other down into the grave. Anna sat up suddenly with a bewildered look on her face. It was very irreverent, and the members of the audience, who had paid thirty-five cents each admission, howled with laughter. The evening was a wonderful success.

After the demonstration, I was receiving a lot of compliments when Martha called me into her private dressing room and delivered a smashing blow.

"Dorothy," she said, "Just because people applauded and complimented you, don't let it turn your head. You are going to have to make up your mind. You could go into show business, and be on Broadway. You are pretty enough, and could be a success. But then, you know, they'd want you to keep on doing the same thing over and over again. You would soon get old, and they'd still want you to be young and pretty and smiling endlessly. Then you'd begin to absolutely hate it! You'd make yourself sick trying to stay young. Do you realize that it takes ten years to become a mature artist—a dancer in the concert field? You would have to work very, very hard and give up all thought of making any money."

Martha went on and on. She quoted Picasso, something about a true artist facing reality and giving up the easy way, and beginning all over again. Soon I began to cry. Tears streamed down my face. I knew I did not want to be a Picasso, or a Martha Graham either. I only knew I wanted to be on the stage. I could see that Martha was angry I had been complimented. This confused me and made me terribly unhappy. Afterward, Martha announced that there would be no more demonstrations.

The era of modern dance in college-level education was about to be ushered in, through the efforts of Martha Hill and the forward-looking administrators of Bennington College in Vermont. A festival for the summer of 1934 was proposed in which Martha Graham, Hanya Holm, Doris Humphrey, Charles Weidman, and others would each be given an opportunity to teach their particular style. To promote interest in this project, it was suggested that physical education instructors from local colleges participate in classes at the various studios. One particular group of these faculty members who came to Martha's classes was dubbed "the Marions and the Marys," since most of them coincidentally bore those names. One evening, as I demonstrated for the class, ripples of muffled laughter arose from the back corner of the studio. I looked anxiously at Martha, expecting her to explode in anger.

Instead, I was amazed to see that although she was perfectly aware of what was going on, she was trying her best to ignore it and keep a straight face. Perhaps Martha knew that these strangers to her dance style had bolstered their courage before entering the studio by stopping for a nip or two at Longchamps. I think only Martha Hill had any previous experience with Martha's work. The others struggled for several weeks with the very intense and subtle movement patterns. Their interest evidently was sparked, and there was a flood of applicants from all across the United States for the summer festival. Everyone was astounded when far more students applied than could be accommodated.

Early that summer, Martha bought a secondhand Model A Ford four-seater convertible for seventy-five dollars. It was immediately christened "Tookie" by the girls in the group because of its rather bountiful and hilariously curved contours when viewed from the rear. Bonnie had a driver's license, and she was happy to be the one who would drive Tookie. Martha, Louis, Bonnie, and I spent a good part of that summer in a house in Pound Ridge, New York. Mrs. Edith Isaacs of *Theatre Arts Magazine* had found the house for Martha. She said that Martha had been working much too hard and needed a rest and a change of scene. The house was called Snake Hill Barn, although it had been converted long before into comfortable living quarters. Bonnie and I stayed there with Martha, and Louis came and went from time to time. Every morning Martha worked out in the living room, while Bonnie and I gave ourselves a class nearby in the foyer. After exercising, we would set out in Tookie to explore the area, or go on a food-shopping spree. Until we got to know the streets, we would constantly get lost, yet somehow we managed to find our way home again. Bonnie and I did most of the chores, but it was Martha who supervised the cooking and taught us to make a sensational pot roast, baked in the oven.

Each day was an adventure, quite different from being in the city with Martha. It was a special time filled with fun. Martha told us stories about when she worked on Broadway for the famous producers Lee and J. J. Shubert in *The Greenwich Village Follies*. My eyes widened as she described how she had danced in an erotic scene, wearing what sounded like a harem costume—long bloomers with slits—that seductively exposed her legs. While she reclined on pillows, the male star made passionate love to her. Martha complained bitterly that when she came offstage, her thighs were covered with his reddish-brown lipstick. This so offended and revolted her, she said she never again wanted to appear in a Broadway show.

Louis told us tall tales about Martha in her younger years, when she was "much wilder and more temperamental." Louis claimed that when he played the piano for her in the studio in Carnegie Hall, she once became so angry that she hurled a bottle of ink at him. He managed to dodge out of the way just in time for the ink bottle to fly out an open window.

"Did it hit anyone down on the street?" I asked anxiously. Louis shrugged. He didn't think so.

"But there was another time," he continued, "when she picked up an iron to throw at me, and luckily it was too heavy to go flying out the window."

He told us how, when Martha was on tour and making a phone call from backstage, she became so frustrated at not getting the answer she wanted, she yanked the pay phone off the wall. Of course, Martha never admitted to any of this. She said he was making it all up. Louis seemed to enjoy talking about the early days with Martha. Bonnie and I both knew how proud of her he was. In class he told everyone, "Martha was my first and my most prized pupil. I have never had another one like her."

Once at lunch at Snake Hill Barn, I felt Louis tentatively tickling my knees under the table. I didn't look at him. Instead I looked perplexedly at Martha, not knowing quite what to do. She rolled her eyes up and down thoughtfully, then rolled them all around. I spluttered out my food as we all shook with muffled laughter. Martha knew Louis, just as he knew her. I never heard her laugh with anyone else the way she laughed with him. They were such good friends. They had shared so much together.

When the time arrived to leave for Bennington, Martha and Louis suddenly decided to go by train, leaving Bonnie and me to take the dogs in the car. As Bonnie drove, the dogs raced endlessly to and fro in great excitement across our laps, barking as we passed other dogs on the road. We had no maps, so we drove from town to town and Bonnie would engage total strangers in conversation and ask for directions. We paused often to let the dogs run, or get gas, or enjoy wonderful old-fashioned homemade ice cream cones and the most delicious homemade blackberry pie à la mode. We were persuaded that since it was getting dark, it would be wise for us to take a room and stay overnight. The next morning we started off once more for Bennington. Along the way we stopped next to a huge field, and while the dogs had a good run I picked armloads of white daisies. To pass the time as Bonnie drove, I wove garlands of daisies for our hair, and for the dogs' necks, and then draped daisy chains all over the car. Everyone waved to us as we drove happily along. Fearful of being thought frivolous, we stripped off all the flowers before arriving at Bennington.

I fell instantly and forever in love with Bennington. An immensely long green lawn was bordered on both sides by white houses. There was the white administration building at one end, and a little white farmhouse diagonally in back of it and up the hill. Behind the farmhouse I found a field of wildflowers. Everything was framed by open blue skies with piles of white clouds moving endlessly. Added to all this were the three meals served us every day. It was heaven. Bonnie reluctantly went back to New York City to mind Martha's studio, teach classes, and care for the dogs.

Martha told me to be in the studio each morning ahead of her to prepare the students, most of whom had no knowledge whatsoever of modern dance. I requested that each student take a spot on the floor for the warm-up. They remained rooted to that exact spot both during the warm-up and throughout the rising from the floor to standing. Then we explored the almost endless possibilities of balancing and moving in place. This coming to standing was like a process of evolution; we progressed from the animalistic relationship to the ground to that of an upright human being. The idea of starting a dance class on the floor instead of at the ballet barre was startling to most of the students. I doubt they had ever experienced dance sitting down (and certainly not sitting down on an ice-cold floor). I could hardly wait to tell Martha about a particular student who got up from her place on the floor one especially chilly morning, came over to me, and whispered, "Dorothy, I have to go to the bathroom. Please, would you save my spot for me? I already warmed it up."

That fall of 1934, we all danced in *American Provincials*, a two-part dance. The first part, "Act of Piety," was a solo; the second, "Act of Judgment," was danced by the group with Martha. I watched Martha working on her costume, experimenting with lowering the waistline more and more, and exploring movement patterns that were distinctly lewd. It made me uneasy. She lowered the waistline of her dress until finally the skirt hung, not from her waist, as ours did, but from her hip hinge at the sides, and from well below her belly button in front. She lengthened her white yoke, like the one we wore, until it became a bold stripe of white extending from her throat down the front of her bodice to the skirt line. This drew attention to the motion of her hips as she swung the heavy, long, full skirt. I felt compelled to avert my eyes as she did the final walk forward, with loose stomach thrust out toward the audience. Martha shocked me by suggesting the possibility of sexual inhibition underlying the puritan character she played. It seemed to me then that Martha, a direct descendant of Miles Standish, was being disloyal to the puritan tradition. At the time I blocked it out of my mind. It is only now that I realize the theme must have had to do with Freudian concepts, which were only just beginning to circulate. But I never could understand why she titled her solo "Act of Piety."

In 1935, Martha gathered all of us together and announced that the entire group was to be in residence at Bennington for the whole summer. She enumerated a number of very specific instructions. Among other things, she told us pointedly, "You are not to mingle with the members of any other dance groups. You are to keep to yourselves and not speak to *anyone.*"

Sophie Maslow, Anna Sokolow, Lily Mehlman, Jane Dudley, and others were outraged. They protested that many of their close friends would be there, and they were looking forward to spending the summer together. Even though the cross-fertilization of ideas, the opportunity to make contacts for the future, the simple enjoyment of being all together were among the stated goals of those who had planned the Bennington program, Martha was unmoved.

Eyebrows really flew up when Martha told the members of the group that for the times we worked out without her, if there was any difference of opinion concerning how the class work should be done, they must all accept my version, "because Dorothy's body coordination is impeccable." I felt complimented beyond belief, but at the same time embarrassed. Gertrude Shurr, who had been Martha's demonstrator at the Playhouse when I first came, was devoted to both Martha and Louis, supporting and assisting them in a thousand ways. Gertrude and I approached movement in opposite ways. Having been trained in physical education, Gertrude analyzed it and taught it in tiny segments. This drove me wild. To me this was static, but for others it was helpful. I was always fighting for the freedom to flow. It would have been only natural under the circumstances for Gertrude to resent me.

Once more, Bonnie and I spent the early part of the summer with Martha. Mrs. Isaacs again arranged for Martha to have a vacation before going to Bennington. This time it was in Silvermine, Connecticut, in a tiny antique house with tiny rooms and tiny furniture. Louis looked at it once and snorted with disgust, "It's a doll's house!" He never returned.

There was a natural pond on the property that served as our source of water. Soon after we arrived, the pond dried up, and we had no water in the house. Country girl that I was, I went to the antique well behind the house thinking I might draw some water. Beside the well, as if on guard, were two tremendous black snakes, coiled, their heads stretching high in the air and eyes glaring at me. That really meant the end of our water supply! No water for dishes. Or washing. Or even flushing the toilet. There was no choice but to go out to the garden when necessary, to squat in a secluded spot. We soon packed up and moved to a converted barn, but for Martha it was too late. She had developed a severe case of poison ivy in an area where it was most crucially important for her to be pain free. She had a solo concert appearance to make! How she was able to perform, we hardly dared ask, but perform she did.

In response to our concerned query "How did you manage?" Martha said, "Oh, well, I made adjustments. After all, it was MY choreography, wasn't it?"

Bonnie and I were together so much at Bennington that summer that John Martin affectionately christened us Boatie and Doatie. Unlike Bonnie, I took Martha's stern commands to heart, remaining detached from the other dancers. Perhaps I secretly welcomed the excuse to steer clear of everyone outside of Martha's group. I never once spoke to Doris Humphrey, Hanya Holm, or Charles Weidman, or to the members of their respective companies, although I had seen them dance and knew all of them by sight. I always carefully lowered my eyes if Doris looked my way, but I did watch her from a distance. With her cloud of curly red-gold hair, cornflower blue eyes, and delicate feminine bearing, Doris presented a total contrast to Martha, whose dark straight hair would always remind me of a wild horse's mane, and whose eyes were veiled by lashes that grew straight down. Doris appeared to me to be a porcelain figure—exquisite, fragile, almost breakable, a Nordic ice maiden. Underneath Martha's puritan exterior, I knew that red-hot coals were always smoldering, ready to explode into flames.

At Bennington that summer we worked on *Panorama*. Martha had agreed to incorporate a large group of mostly inexperienced apprentices. Among the apprentices was my friend Muriel Stuart, who had been Anna Pavlova's protégée. We rehearsed to counts without music until just before the performance. We all counted furiously. Counting went against Muriel's nature, since she was naturally very musical. To her, counting was offensive, disturbing, and distracting. In one section of the dance, Martha had us count the movements up to sixty-four. Then she had us repeat this movement sequence backward. Counting backward from sixty-four was difficult. Muriel kept making faces as if her teeth were all knotted up.

The set for *Panorama* was designed by Arch Lauterer. He made the stage area unusually interesting by utilizing many ramps. The set had been built in an armory, and perhaps it was prepared hurriedly. In performance, I saw a two-inch nail standing on its head, point up. It was the only time I ever took liberties with Martha's choreography. I did a sort of forward arabesque, went down on my knees, and crawled elaborately to the middle of the stage, picked up the nail, then returned to the choreography. I doubt anybody in the audience was aware of my improvisation.

In the audience was a friend and advisor to Franklin D. Roosevelt, the highly respected and distinguished social scientist Edouard Lindeman. He had come to Bennington to visit his daughter, Betty, who was a student dancing in *Panorama*. Mr. Lindeman had been asked by a funding organization to observe Martha as she taught and choreographed, and to render an opinion concerning her application for a grant. The story that eventually reached my ears regarding his conclusions was devastating to me.

Mr. Lindeman had given much credit to Martha for her strikingly original and powerful work, both in the classroom and in her choreography, but he felt he could not possibly endorse her manner of working. Her methods were in direct opposition to his strongly held convictions concerning democracy, women's rights, and human dignity. He was startled by Martha's relationship with the members of her group, concluding that she not only ignored many people's individual rights but actually trampled on them. The idea of supporting such behavior was anathema to him. He felt strongly that whether people worked in a factory or a mine or in the arts, where almost everyone gives their last drop of loyalty and strength with no real thought of remuneration, they should be treated with dignity and consideration. His conclusion was that he could have awarded the money to Martha on artistic merits, but hers was not a democratic organization. He went so far as to say that some members were treated as if they were slaves.

"The tragedy is that slaves don't free themselves," he added. "They need a leader who will lead them out of slavery."

At first I was shocked to hear this. It had never even occurred to me to equate dance and work as being at all similar. Then I felt humiliated. I asked myself the question, "Am I, indeed, a slave?"

When we returned to New York City, I gradually became aware of how Martha exercised control over the girls in the group. Martha was like a hawk, all-seeing, missing nothing. With consummate skill she manipulated the dancers by pairing off certain girls. Bonnie and I had always been joined like Siamese twins. Martha played a seesaw game with Lily Mehlman and Anna Sokolow, who together might have caused a revolution in the group. There were brief stormy moments when Martha would seem to favor one or then the other in the choreography. No one could ever be sure who was in favor; it changed all the time. We were rarely paid in money for what we did but instead were awarded little plums, tiny movements in a new dance. Sometimes Martha would take these movements back and give them to a friend. The competition Martha created between friends was divisive. There was a constant feeling of intrigue in the air during rehearsals, and always the danger of someone new being brought in to be tried out as a replacement. Jealousies built up. One after another, as new dancers came, others left. The group had to be replenished constantly. No one remained Martha's favorite for long, and each time someone new came into the group I found myself feeling threatened. Anxiety was rampant in the studio until things settled down to a new balance.

Each new favorite had their time in the sun, as special talents were uncovered and utilized. My specialties were walking, the ecstatic body, and sustained movement—all qualities that were marvelously useful in the classroom but rarely employed in the choreography. Bonnie's special talents were rebounding and spinning, especially chaînés turns. Martha Hill excelled at the fast, sharp, percussive rebound into the flung movement done so close to the ground in the difficult low-slung hip swings and hinges. Only Martha Hill's student from Oregon, Bessie Schonberg, came close to performing those difficult movements well. After these two left, the low-slung hip swings were soon dropped. Ruth White's delicately vulnerable, flung, abandoned way of moving had seemed not to be in tune with the angular shapes that were beginning to preoccupy Martha by the time I arrived. It saddened me when Ruth left the group. Kathleen Slagle, with her faunlike elevation, caught Martha's eye as a fleet-footed jumper. The narrow, slim, almost boyish form of Lillian Shapero produced taut restricted movements that thoroughly suited Martha's choreography. Ethel Butler's wild abandon and sturdy stance were employed. Sophie Maslow—feminine, proud, aloof, independent—was perhaps the most often used. The very young, tigerish Anita Alvarez added an exciting way of ripping up space, low to the ground. She was so unlike all the others, she did not take away from anyone else. Anita's smoldering temperament contributed a new note.

The fact is, we were all "Johnny-one-notes," and Martha played a tune utilizing each of us in turn. We became confident and proud of our one note. Martha was painstakingly assembling a variety of individual talents that were each unique. She did not press us to expand our own range of movement. She simply exploited whatever came naturally to each of us when it was appropriate for her needs, knowing full well that she was encouraging one-dimensional dancers. In her mind, the choreography was foremost, and we were there to serve her goal. The more secure I was in what I did well, the more insecure I became about the movement qualities in which others excelled. I knew my movement vocabulary was limited, and I eventually came to recognize and accept that Martha was not interested in broadening my skills. People like Anna Sokolow, Sophie Maslow, Louise Creston, and Lily Mehlman, who each had a more extensive life outside the studio, were not as dependent as I. For me, what went on in the studio was my whole life. Because I had been brought up to be unassertive and uncomplaining, I was an easy mark for Martha. All she had to do was flash that marvelous smile and I was hypnotized, devotedly hanging onto her every word. I reveled in being part of something I sensed was new, tremendous, important. This was a lot, and for a long time it was enough. But the experience of observing Martha's genius in manipulating the dancers, and of exploiting the talents of each one for her own ends, eventually began to change me.

Edouard Lindeman's conclusions eventually reached Martha's ears and may have prompted her to tell me, fervently, "You should be proud to be involved in this important work. It is just as important as if you were working for Picasso, helping him, making it possible for him to do the work he does. What I am doing will change the way the world looks at dance, as Picasso is changing the way the world looks at art."

I had always felt proud of what I did for Martha. Her words made me feel content again, for a while. But then I began to look more objectively at the life I was leading. I recognized I was definitely one of the slaves Edouard Lindeman had been talking about. It was finally and painfully becoming clear to me that my desire to please Martha had overshadowed every other aspect of my behavior. I realized I no longer had a mind of my own. At every turn I could hear myself respond to questions by saying, "Well, Martha says . . ." or "Martha does . . ." or "Martha does not. . . ." I even presumed to say, "Martha thinks. . . ."

I had completely lost my sense of self. Heartbroken, I concluded I could not wait for someone to come along and free me. Then and there I made a pact with myself. The thought was shattering. Leave Martha? Leave the security of being included in the excitement surrounding everything she did? Give up being her demonstrator? No longer depend on her to make every decision for me? I did not know which way to turn or what to do. To leave Martha was unthinkable; but to stay was impossible.

I believe Martha continued to use me as her demonstrator because I filled the class work with such a feeling of pleasure, allowing the movement I reveled in to flow blissfully through me in a rather playful way. I so loved having been a part of the process of the development of the technique that each exercise gave me a sense of satisfaction, and this showed as I moved confidently and freely from one exercise to the next. When I demonstrated the centered release, Martha said I was the perfect example of the center from which she was then able to distort. She liked to disrupt the sustained flow of movement in jagged ways, to segment it, break it up rhythmically, in order to startle and wake up her audience. It simply was not in my nature to spontaneously interrupt the flow or abruptly cut it off. Above all, I felt that Martha loved me as a mother loves her wayward child—with very mixed feelings.

For a long time it had seemed unfair to me that, whereas I demonstrated the class work so well for her, Martha invariably chose others, who did not excel in class, for the more important roles in the dances. I never spoke to her about this, nor did I speak to anyone else. I kept it locked inside, and as time passed, I began to feel increasingly miserable. Perhaps Martha sensed this dissatisfaction when she said to me, "What you do is important! The work can't all be distortion, you know. That would be unbearable."

Again I felt comforted, for a moment. But within myself I desperately yearned to be onstage — that sunshine place where I knew I belonged and felt I would be safe. That place where no one could speak to me or bother me. From there I could talk to the audience through body language. I always felt a complete rapport with an audience, in contrast with face-to-face social situations, where I still froze and felt hopelessly inadequate. Secretly I hoped that somehow I would have the opportunity to be an actress, as Mrs. Morgenthau had once told me I could be. I was beginning to hate Martha for keeping me chained to the studio.

The summer before Martha began working on *Horizons*, she, Louis, Bonnie, and I visited the young sculptor Alexander Calder on his farm in Roxbury. Sandy, as we called him, was very playful. He had a big, shaggy, bumbly sheepdog with hair covering his face that he dressed in a football sweater with a big insignia on it. His slim black cat wore a tight, very sexy, black satin skirt. "Like a prostitute," he said. The animals entertained us endlessly by tumbling around together. In the kitchen all the cooking utensils, spoons, pots, and pans were suspended, so that they seemed to wave at us from over the stove. The toilet tissue in the bathroom was on a handmade wire sculpture that had a merry way of rocking as it unrolled. Everything around Sandy Calder moved.

Martha asked Sandy Calder to design a setting of mobiles for *Horizons*. He created big white suspended balls, which could be moved on cue by machinery. I remember Martha searching for movements filled with positive feelings for the "Dance of Rejoicing" section in *Horizons* to contrast with the complaints and protests emanating from the Depression. Martha planned to have us move among the mobile suspended balls. She had the theater for only one Sunday for dress rehearsal and performance, however. The stagehands wound the machinery that moved the mobiles, but they could not manage to coordinate the action. As the day wore on, the stagehands became cranky and uncooperative. The sound of squeaking was outrageous when they wound the pulleys that moved the balls, so Martha instructed them to raise the balls overhead and keep them still as we danced. The original idea might have had a marvelous effect, if only there had been enough time and money to coordinate everything.

A number of choreographers, including Doris Humphrey and Helen Tamiris, were working for the Works Progress Administration. Their dancers were paid twenty-three dollars a week, as compared to the six dollars a week Martha was paying me. People urged me to apply to the WPA, but I felt I could not because I was a Canadian citizen in the United States on a student visa.

When Lily Mehlman came to Martha to tell her she had been offered a job choreographing a project, Martha put her foot down firmly, saying "No! It would interfere far too much with rehearsals."

Tempers flared. A hot and heavy argument ensued between them. Martha slapped Lily, and Lily returned the slap, right across Martha's face. Lily stalked out of the studio.

"And don't you *dare* come back!" Martha shouted after her. That anyone would defy Martha, strike her no less, was really shocking.

In the summer of 1936, Martha prepared us for *Chronicles*.[2] She choreographed a lot of whipping and lashing movements that I associated with slave owners. In places in the choreography where I had to bow my head or tip forward, I interpreted these movements as symbolizing submission. Each time Martha asked us to bow our heads, I gagged. My muscles locked against what I now construed as oppression. By the time *Chronicles* was presented, I found myself feeling more rebellious. I could not endure the sense of shame I was experiencing in the face of what I no longer saw as fulfillment, but rather as utter slavery. Confused and insecure, I did not know where to turn for help.

Over the years, my position as fresh young face from the Northwest had faded considerably. To retain the attention I craved, I took on the role of court jester, with my goal being to make Martha laugh. I primitively caricatured other people's faults. I focused my cruel sarcastic pattern of behavior on new students coming into the special summer classes in which I was the demonstrator. One day I had spotted a girl whose knees swayed a bit backward, and whose elbows were "turned around," making her arms weak. In the privacy of the dressing room, I mimicked these overextensions for Martha's benefit, and she rose to the bait, laughingly saying the student moved "rather like an octopus." Knowing that my parents would never have approved of my actions, I was ashamed, miserable, and demoralized about who I was becoming.

Although I was endlessly indebted to Martha for all she had done for me, I knew by now I had to leave. There was not a single thought of my own left in my mind; I existed only as an extension of Martha. Martha had explained to me how Picasso claimed that an artist first had to be broken of naive habits of thinking in order to make room for new, stronger, more constructive thinking to occur. The idea seemed ruthless, and foreign to my nature. I became deeply depressed.

Martha got wind that I was thinking about leaving. She angrily threatened me, "If that is the case, you may not go on tour to the West Coast. I will give preference to someone who will be staying in the group."

Terrified, I responded, "I am not planning to leave," and silently added the word "yet."

I was desperate to go west to see my family, and there would be no other way for me to get there. I had no money. If it had not been for my beloved brother David who sent me fifteen dollars a month, I would have been unable to keep body and soul together. Mother occasionally helped by sending me a dollar in a letter, or a pair of silk stockings. To supplement the meager pay I received from Martha, I, like most of the girls in the group, occasionally modeled for artists we knew and trusted.

Whereas others in Martha's group pursued outside interests, I remained totally within Martha's sphere. Those dancers who had grown up in the New York City area had established contacts through which they found jobs teaching or performing in small companies. May O'Donnell was choreographing, and she and Gertrude Shurr had opened their own studio at 66 Fifth Avenue. They privately coached students who were new to Martha's work and taught the overflow from Martha's classes, as well as students who were not happy with the strictly professional and sternly impersonal atmosphere. Anna Sokolow was busy working with actors, and performing for Jewish groups. She, Sophie Maslow, and Jane Dudley were active in creating the New Dance Group, a dance center for those who were politically aware.

When Martha Hill requested and received permission from Martha Graham to allow me to commute to Bennington to teach on a weekly basis, I was thrilled. Because of my years of demonstrating for Martha, I felt no one was better qualified to do this than I. Soon I found that teaching and demonstrating are two very different skills. Knowing the routine that Martha taught inside out, being able to break down movement sequences, making the coordinations visible, pointing out corrections, and coaching individual students, all this was a lot, but it was not enough. The technique that was so easy for me was impossible for the once-a-week students to retain. What I lacked was Martha's expertise in motivating the class to want to work.

Another area where I was deficient was in knowing how to direct the accompanist to improvise for class work. I assumed the accompanist would know what to play. In Martha's classes, the established sequence of exercises as well as the transitions were all choreographed, like one huge, endless dance. You could pause to explain something, but then you returned to the sequence of exercises. Martha never had to cue the pianist, who was familiar with the sequence and the transitions. I had never heard Martha speak to her accompanist except to insist that she play only one note over and over again, like a drumbeat.

In teaching at Bennington, I found myself desperately dividing my attention between the pianist and the students—who talked! Discipline in the classroom was something I had always taken for granted. Talking was unheard of in Martha's studio. The students at Bennington had been led to believe they would be doing their own creative work, and I had had no expectations of this. The final blow came with the requirement that I must submit reports and grades. I asked a professor, "What should I write in the reports?" He laughingly replied he had written about one student that she had knitted two sweaters in his class, and one did not fit. Clearly, I was utterly unequipped to go out on my own. Because Martha Hill was openly disappointed with me, I knew that door was definitely closed.

To help me get a perspective on things, I consulted a psychologist friend, Mrs. Keith, about Martha's threat to replace me on the West Coast tour. She pointed out that, because I had worked hard for six years with absolute devotion and received practically no pay, I had earned the right to go on the tour. She said that Martha was being unfair, but that I should keep my plans to myself.

"But I can't lie to Martha," I replied, "and I don't think I can keep this a secret." Mrs. Keith suggested that I envision a large safety pin and use it to pin my mouth shut.

I went with Martha on the West Coast tour. Following a performance of *Primitive Mysteries* in Tacoma, Washington, I was stunned to see my father present. He must have taken a ferry and two buses from Victoria to see me. He was so overcome with emotion in reaction to Martha's performance that he barely greeted me, as he said, "Dorothy! Did you see how she rose into the air in *Primitive Mysteries?* She levitated! She actually levitated! I saw it with my own eyes!"

I understood at once that he was referring to the place at the end of "Crucifixus," where Martha appeared to rise up from the floor. I tried to explain to him how it was done, but he was so overwhelmed he would not listen. I had a lot of work to do, packing costumes, and in a way I did not want to disappoint him by pressing the point that Martha was an expert at illusion.

Going home to visit my family was all-important to me, my overpowering motivation for being so anxious to go on the West Coast tour. There was no other way I could have financed the trip, and I desperately wanted to explain to them privately why I was going to leave Martha. As I was preparing to take the boat from Seattle to Victoria, however, Martha suddenly scheduled an all-day rehearsal on what was to have been our day off.

"You may NOT leave!" she firmly said to me.

I immediately called home and said, "I can't come. I have to rehearse."

Without my knowing it, David and Daddy rushed to the dock in Victoria and boarded the boat to Seattle to come to see me. Meanwhile, Martha changed her mind and canceled the rehearsal.

"You may go home to see your family after all," she told me.

I rushed to the dock and just managed to catch the boat embarking from Seattle to Victoria. Without knowing it my father, David, and I passed each other in the Straits of Juan de Fuca.

In Seattle, Daddy and David had a thoroughly enjoyable visit with Anna, Sophie, and Ethel. They also met Gertrude, May, and some of the other dancers. Daddy was particularly fascinated by Anna, who talked politics with him. Afterward, Daddy and David caught the boat home. Meanwhile, since no one had been at home when I arrived, I boarded the next boat back to Seattle. For the second time, we unwittingly crossed paths in the Straits of Juan de Fuca. The trip had been a disaster for me. I never did find the proper time or circumstances to tell my family I was planning to leave Martha.

A later stop at Carmel, California, was heavenly. I went for a walk by the ocean, where I met an artist, and we had an extended conversation. Perhaps it was the perfume of flowers in the air, or maybe the light, but it was magical. Time was suspended for me. I almost forgot about being in the group. I rushed back late to the theater, missed the spacing run-through, did not have time to iron my costume, and ended up putting on my makeup in haste. I was so ecstatic, Martha laughed at me. I thought she might have been angry, but she wasn't. She might even have been worried about me.

We went onstage to dance *Course*, and when Sophie and I started to step up and down from box to box for our mountain-top explorations, the boxes skated along the floor and kept getting further and further apart. It was like stepping on patches of ice floating in water. Martha ordered the curtains closed. In my hurry to get ready, I had totally forgotten my job to hook the boxes together. This time, we locked the boxes together properly and started the dance again. I loved to dance *Course*. It was jubilant, joyful, full of triplets that rebounded so high on our feet that we skimmed along the floor. As the curtains closed slowly at the end, we flew like racehorses going around and around the track, whipping up a storm, with our whip hands adding to the momentum as they circled through the air.

Although I had no plans for after the tour, I was sure of one thing. I would not and could not go back home, as Bonnie was planning to do. Miss Cornish had asked Martha's permission for Bonnie to take a year's sabbatical to teach in Seattle. Since no one but Bonnie could drive the car for Martha, and Bonnie was leaving, I set my sights on getting my driver's license so I could be the one to drive Martha that summer at Bennington.

I had to practice driving all by myself. In the garage in Connecticut where the car had been stored, I checked out the clutch, brake, gears, and gas pedal. For my first try, Tookie jolted violently forward. I braked. Then stalled.

"Oh, I don't want to break up the garage!" I thought. Nervously and ever more clumsily, I started the car again and again, until the battery went dead. I got a new battery and began again the next day. Tookie and I lurched out of the garage, onto a nearby flattened-out area where the Merritt Parkway was being constructed. I drove forward and back, parked here and there, changed gears, turned, and drove around rocks and trees. So far so good, but I had yet to deal with other cars.

On the day of my driving test, I passed the verbal part, then a kindly examiner sat next to me in Tookie. I started with a jolt, put on the brake, and stalled a few times before we got going. I was still terribly anxious about changing gears and making arm signals.

As we returned from the test ride, the examiner massaged his neck a little as he said, "You will learn to change gears smoothly, won't you, dear?"

I replied, "Yes, sir! I promise!"

He signed the small slip of paper that was my license, and I proudly held this symbol of self-mastery in my hands. The next day I drove to New York City on the Old Boston Post Road, stalling and starting at every light until I finally mastered the shifting of gears.

Martha was pleased that I could drive her to Bennington. When we arrived there, I was given a small bedroom all to myself in the farmhouse. The room had tiny windows and a very low ceiling. It was perfect. All summer I demonstrated in the studio and drove Tookie for Martha and Louis but, otherwise, kept out of sight in my little room. I did not say one word to anyone all summer. My lone companion was Sean, a handsome Irish Setter owned by Arch Lauterer. Sean called for me almost every day at the farmhouse. This amazing animal would pick an apple from one of the trees, or find one on the ground, then drop it repeatedly on the porch floor. The sound of bump, bump, bump, was a gentle hint that it was time for his run. I happily flew down the stairs, and together we ran through fields of blue cornflowers, Queen Anne's lace, buttercups, and daisies. When we returned to the farmhouse, he always stood in what once must have been a small goldfish pool, and I splashed water over him to cool him down. Then I went upstairs to my room to read or write home, happy and contented to have been with my faithful friend. There was no way he could divulge my secret, that shortly I would be leaving Martha.

This was the year that Picasso painted *Guernica*. Many of the people we knew were distressed about the civil war in Spain. We all had friends who volunteered to fight there. Newspapers carried the story of a woman referred to as La Passionaria, whose real name was Dolores Ibarruri. In her rich voice she exhorted the people, "It is better to die standing on your feet than to live on your knees." Martha told us of this woman's concern for the people of Spain, and suddenly everything we did in class was colored with a new feeling of fire and strength that had not been there before.

That summer at Bennington, Martha prepared and presented a fiercely dramatic new solo, *Immediate Tragedy*, with music especially composed by Henry Cowell.[3] Martha created this dance in honor of the women who had fought beside the men in the Spanish Civil War. She was determined to portray a woman as strong, objective, courageous, passionate. The tempestuous, abandoned movement patterns she developed for *Immediate Tragedy* startled me. I saw Martha falling to the floor, twisting this way and that, beating on the floor, rebounding up, flinging herself through space. Here was a dramatically expressed burning anger, fueled by heartbreak and grief. Martha's portrayal of this gallant, militant, fearless woman hid nothing.

For some inexplicable reason, the powerfully dramatic portrayal in *Immediate Tragedy* was not as successful as the rhapsodic study *Lamentation* that Martha had first presented in the spring of 1930. We all knew that Martha had been moved immensely by Käthe Kollwitz's eloquent drawings delineating the hunger and suffering endured by women, children, and old men in Germany during World War I. Martha's resulting masterpiece, *Lamentation*, encapsulated feelings of frustration, helplessness, and utter grief. But in *Lamentation* the grief had been shown as stoically born, communicated through economic movement, performed with an often hidden, always impassive mask of the face. The expressiveness of Martha's open throat and twisting feet was far more effective than any facial expression could ever have been. All other parts of her body were shrouded by a long, unfitted tube of grayish-blue wool jersey that she stretched and twisted violently from within. Her veiled, suppressed feelings constantly pressed through the fabric in this rhapsodic song of grief. The solo figure of a woman, locked to a bench, was sculptural: a Nordic portrayal of a stricken woman's powerlessness in adversity. Seeing Martha perform both *Lamentation* and *Immediate Tragedy*, I recalled how she had worked so hard to communicate to us in the classroom the contrasting concepts of dramatic and rhapsodic movements. The real challenge for me was still to express feelings boldly, directly, dramatically, not looking back and recalling them rhapsodically.

After returning to New York City from Bennington at the end of the summer of 1937, I found myself unable to tell Martha of my intention to leave. Each time I saw her, I thought, "Next time will be the time to tell her," but I could not unpin my mouth. It is possible that the tension was building on Martha's part too, because at a rehearsal of *Primitive Mysteries*, Martha directed a cruel, disparaging remark to me. She then ordered me to sit down. But I ignored her. My heart was broken. I said not one word in rebuttal. I simply continued numbly dancing. I was the supreme stoic, only I could not control the tears that streamed down my cheeks. I knew Martha was distressed. She wanted me to stop, break down, scream. Do something! It must have driven her mad. Perhaps if I had cried openly, she would have comforted me, just as I had seen her comfort Geordie. Instead, she stopped the rehearsal.

The next day I was driving Martha up Fifth Avenue in Tookie when she said, "I have two small, special parts that I think might be right for you."

I said nothing at all. It was far too late for anything to change my mind.

Then she inquired, "Are you planning to stay?" I simply turned my head from side to side.

Martha pressed me, "Are you planning to leave?"

I could not bring myself to speak. I swallowed, and my chin went up and down just once. I stopped the car for a red light at Forty-second Street, just past the public library. I looked at Martha and saw big tears trickling slowly down her cheeks. She opened the car door, got out, and walked through the traffic to the sidewalk. The light turned green. I pressed down on the clutch, changed gears, and Tookie rolled slowly forward with the flow of traffic.

That night there was a photography call for all the dancers in the group. Since Anna and others insisted that I was still part of the group, I went to the Humphrey-Weidman studio where Barbara Morgan was waiting with her camera. Martha instructed Helen Priest to put on my costume and stood her in my place. Helen looked at me as if her heart were breaking for me. It was inconceivable for me not to be dancing in my role. I could not believe that Martha would take this part, that had been created on me, and give it to someone who had never even been at rehearsal. But she did. I left the studio. No one said goodbye.

The slave had freed herself but now did not know where to turn. My first thought was to go to Dr. Nathan Kolodney, who headed the program at the 92nd Street YM-YWHA. For some time I had been teaching two Graham classes there. Perhaps he could help me find additional teaching jobs.

Dr. Kolodney emerged from his office and greeted me with, "I am glad you are here, Dorothy. There is something I have to tell you privately."

I waited until he was free, then entered his office. He said, "Dorothy, I have something very shocking that I feel I must show you. It is this letter. You must read it yourself, because you have got to learn to live in the real world. You must understand what you are up against."

The letter was in Martha's bold handwriting. It was three pages long. She started by telling Dr. Kolodney that if he wished to advertise that the Martha Graham work was being taught at the Y, he must employ an authorized teacher, and since I had left the group, permission was withdrawn for me to represent her. Martha went on to recommend a new teacher. I was startled beyond belief to see that it was none other than the one she had dubbed the "octopus." I was shattered. If I had not seen the letter myself, I would not have believed Martha was capable of such a heartlessly punishing deed.

I was reeling as I handed the letter back to Dr. Kolodney. I thanked him for having shown it to me. He had done me a real service by being so open and frank. This malicious act sealed my break with Martha and made it absolutely final. The door was not just closed, it was bolted and barred behind me.

Major George Hunt Holley.

Riding to hounds at the estate of Mother's grandfather. Amy Ethel Holley, one of the few women permitted to ride with the men, is seated sidesaddle second from left in foreground.

Dorothy's father, Canadian pioneer Claude Cecil Bird, standing in the doorway of the shack where he lived on his farm in the Qu'Appelle Valley at the turn of the century. Dorothy's aunt is at the washing machine.

Claude Cecil Bird wearing
his World War I British Army
uniform.

Dorothy's mother, Amy Ethel Holley.

Bath, England. The Bird children in Sunday "go-to-meeting" clothes. Foreground, David, Mickey, Dorothy; rear, Windham and Jack in Eton hats.

Dorothy Bird demonstrating the "ecstatic" body in the swings. Victoria, B.C., 1931.

Dorothy Bird, 1931. *Paul Hansen, photographer.*

Martha Graham in the late 1920s. *Paul Hansen, photographer.*

Primitive Mysteries. Martha Graham foreground, Dorothy Bird standing. *Paul Hansen, photographer, courtesy the Dance Collection, New York Public Library for the Performing Arts, Astor, Lenox, and Tilden Foundations.*

Primitive Mysteries, "Hymn to the Virgin," part 1. Martha Graham, foreground; Dorothy Bird in Mary Rivoire's role. Early 1930s. *Paul Hansen, photographer.*

Primitive Mysteries. Left to right: May O'Donnell, Dorothy Bird, Lil Liandre, Anna Sokolow *(kneeling)*, Martha Graham, remainder unidentified. *Photo by Thomas Bouchard, copyright Diane Bouchard, courtesy Diane Bouchard and the Dance Collection, New York Public Library for the Performing Arts, Astor, Lenox, and Tilden Foundations.*

Dorothy Bird in *Heretic* costume. *Paul Hansen, photographer.*

Martha Graham at Bennington College, wearing a coat she made herself.

Left to right: Sophie Maslow, Dorothy Bird, and Martha Graham with Tookie.

The Graham Group on tour, 1937. Dorothy is on top of car; Bonnie Bird is second from left. Martha insisted each member wear a coat with one button closed at the top.

Bennington College, 1935.
Left to right: Dorothy Bird, Sean, and Martha Graham, standing in front of the building where Martha taught and Dorothy demonstrated. Martha helped to make the coat of mattress ticking worn by Dorothy.

The Graham Group on tour in New Orleans, late 1930s. *Heretic* in the pool of company member Charlotte Chandler, who is standing posed in Martha's role. Note that the dancers are shoulder-to-shoulder, as it was originally choreographed.

Course by Martha Graham. *Left to right:* Sophie Maslow and Dorothy Bird as the girls in blue, standing on the mountaintop. *Paul Hansen, photographer.*

The opening position of *Three Casual Developments* in the pool with the original cast. *Left to right:* Sophie Maslow, Dorothy Bird, and Anna Sokolow perched on Dorothy's lap.

Chronicles by Martha Graham, "Steps in the Street" section, 1937. *Left to right:* Kathleen Slagle, Gertrude Shurr, Ethel Butler, Dorothy Bird. Sophie Maslow obscured by Dorothy. *Paul Hansen, photographer.*

Six

Dancing

on

Broadway,

1937–1945

WITHOUT MY JOB at the Y, I was totally on my own. I had no choice but to turn to the one place I loved the most, and where I felt safe—the stage. I heard that Charles Weidman was to be the choreographer for a new George M. Cohan show, *I'd Rather Be Right*, and I rushed to the audition. I found my way backstage as a bee finds honey and quickly changed into my practice outfit—the old washed-out, homemade, beige wool leotard, the long wraparound beige wool skirt, and, of course, no shoes. I joined the other girls onstage, where we were all asked to stand in a line. Some were picked to audition; others, myself included, were excused.

I decided to stay for a bit and watch some of the action from the wings. Charles saw me from where he had been sitting in the audience. He approached the footlights and beckoned for me to come close. Glaring at me, he shook his head as he sternly reprimanded, "Look around you! What do you see? Don't *ever* go to another Broadway audition wearing a modern dance leotard with *bare feet!*" I had the feeling Charles wanted to help me, but under the circumstances, he couldn't. I looked at all the girls, especially the ones who had been asked to stay for the audition. They were attractively dressed in ballet tunics, well-fitted dance costumes, or bathing suits. On their feet they wore either high heels, tap shoes, or ballet slippers.

After leaving the theater, I headed directly to Macy's, where I hunted for a remnant of fabric, as I had learned to do with Martha. I purchased about three-quarters of a yard of shocking blue stretchy crepe and a piece of white rope. From the shoe department, I selected a pair of scarlet sandals with four-inch high heels and ankle straps. When I returned to my room, I draped the rope around my neck, with the two ends going down to a very low "V" in back. I attached the ends of the rope to my panties with safety pins, tucked one end of the blue crepe into the rope in front of my neck, pulled the remnant between my legs, and attached it to the two ends of rope in back. It barely reached. I pinned the seams over my hips and basted the costume together, as I had seen Martha do it. I tried on my costume and red shoes and felt satisfied that I was ready to take Broadway by storm.

The following day a friend told me of a newspaper item reporting that Agnes de Mille was arriving from England on the *Queen Mary* that very day to begin work on a show for the Shuberts called *Hooray for What!* I had first met Agnes through Martha and Louis in the early 1930s. Louis had played the piano for Agnes, and he cited her as an example we students should follow. Agnes was the only dancer who insisted on having previews for her concerts. After the preview, she did something that no one else ever did. She asked for feedback. And for criticism. Agnes was down-to-earth, practical, intelligent, and thorough. I had great respect for her and for her professionalism. I found Agnes's number in the phone book and called.

Agnes answered with, "I just walked in the door." In response to my question she said, "Yes, there is an audition at the Winter Garden Theater. I will not be there, but you can go if you want to." She did not hold out a lot of hope for me, but I was determined and excited about trying out.

The doorman at the Winter Garden was taking callback cards from those performers who had already been seen once and had been asked to appear a second time. I, of course, did not have a card, but the doorman must have felt sorry for me and whispered, "Say you forgot it."

Inside was a scene I will never forget, one quite different from my first Broadway audition. Girls, talking as if they all knew each another, were standing around more or less in a semicircle. Some wore black satin swimming suits with silver slippers, and a few even had on silver fox furs. Several sported mink coats draped over their shoulders. (I did not realize, yet, that they could not safely leave their furs in the dressing room.) Many girls wore ankle bracelets, necklaces, and earrings. Some had their hair arranged very elaborately, and bleached. They all wore eye makeup. The young women that I knew did not wear eye makeup offstage—some did not even wear lipstick on the street.

Near the unlit footlights three men in dark suits sat at a table with a work light suspended overhead. They wore hats pushed down over their faces to shield their eyes from the harsh light and talked among themselves, seeming to discuss each of us. One of the men would point to a girl and make a beckoning motion. She would then walk obediently to the table. The theater was quiet, and it was an agonizing time while the men assayed each girl, made comments, and sometimes joked with her. One would question her formally: "What is your name? Have you ever worked for us before? Yes? We hope you will be with us again," or "No? We hope you will perhaps be working for us—this time." As each girl turned away from the table and walked back to her friends in the semicircle, the men debated back and forth as they made their decision. It was quite a bit like an auction; at least they did not ask to see anyone's teeth.

When my turn came, I walked to the table and stated my name. "Have you ever worked for us before?" asked a man.

"No, I haven't," I replied, with a big smile.

As I turned and walked back to my place, I felt I was walking the plank in *Peter Pan*. I could feel their eyes staring at my minuscule, tightly wrapped blue behind, waggling a bit as I staggered on my high-heeled, ankle-strap sandals. This time I was certain I was "in." I bubbled with laughter the whole time, thinking to myself, "I just wish Louis could see me now. This must be Sugar-Daddy Land, and those men with the hats must be the sugar daddies he was talking about as we walked up Broadway the day I arrived in New York City."

Although this was supposed to be a dance audition, we were never asked to dance a single step. The choreographer was not present and had no say whatso-ever in the preliminary selection process. The girls were picked solely on the basis of appearance and demeanor. Later, I realized that throughout the ritual of auditioning, the men would not openly recognize anyone, even if there had ex-isted a long-standing relationship.

Because I knew Agnes would be at the next callback, I wore my old ballet shoes. I never let her see the red high-heeled, ankle-strap sandals. A number of the girls selected had appeared in many shows. Some were friendly and asked if I were an Albertina Rasch girl. I felt complimented, since everyone knew that an Albertina Rasch girl was a good-looking, skilled line dancer. I simply replied, "No, I am not."

I thought it wiser not to mention I was a Martha Graham girl, since I doubted any of them had ever heard of Martha Graham. Some of the girls were openly hostile. Mostly they seemed a happy-go-lucky bunch and had been chosen be-cause they acted as if they relished a good time. Among the girls selected for Agnes was one who was a ball of fire and could dance up a storm, and two who could tap-dance adequately. Most, however, had obviously never seen the inside of a ballet studio. As Agnes asked each of the girls to execute a few steps, she shook her head from side to side and exchanged worried glances with her assis-tant, Mary Green, a beautiful, sophisticated dancer she had brought with her from Hollywood.

Girls who had been out of town came into rehearsal, assuming that they were more or less guaranteed a job. It was almost as if a state of war had been declared between the business managers, who felt they had a perfect right to choose the girls they wanted, and Agnes, who naturally expected she would be the one to select the dancers. There was a customary seven- or eight-day period during which a dancer could be replaced, and each side had their preferences for who should stay and who should go. I was very grateful when I saw Agnes fighting to keep me.

Agnes came to rehearsal wearing the most skillfully crafted leather boots, size three, and she choreographed dainty little foot patterns for us. She first set an all-girl line dance called "In the Shade of the New Apple Tree." Extra special care was being taken with the costumes for this number. The dresses would be pink, apple-green, and yellow organdy with a wide, low, sweetheart neckline, and a soft, full skirt. Wide-brimmed round hats framed our faces. It puzzled me to hear that under the costume, we would be wearing only the briefest, flesh-colored, net G-string-type panty, and no brassiere. But I loved the costume. It was beautifully fitted, with the bodice made in six panels that afforded me all the support I needed. The dresser for the show casually remarked to me, "This dance has been chosen as the display case for the harem. It's a long-standing tradition, you know."

I did not know what she was talking about, nor did I have any idea how revealing the costume would be under the lights. Eventually, I found that many of the girls were accustomed to the idea of being in the harem, and I think they rather liked it. Sometimes it involved big tips.

Hooray for What! was intended by the writer, Yip Harburg, as an antiwar satire. Agnes and Vincent Minnelli, the director, seemed to be the only ones taking the social comment seriously. Right from the start of rehearsals this became the basis of a monumental disagreement between Agnes and the business manager. Agnes's choreography for "In the Shade of the New Apple Tree" required the dancers to face upstage, with their backs to the audience throughout the entire dance. At the very end of the piece we finally turned to face front, revealing to the surprised audience that we were wearing gas masks. Canvas covered our noses and mouths, goggles shielded our eyes, and a huge nozzle attached to a box concealed our chests. Viewed from behind, the wide-brimmed hats served to completely hide from the audience the ghastly sight of gas masks until we turned around. The whole point of the dance was to show that behind the gentle, bucolic country scene lay the specter of war. I felt very uncomfortable and clumsy in the dance and could neither see nor breathe properly. The girls all loathed wearing the gas masks. Some of them regarded Agnes as an intruder who had arrived in their midst from outer space.

When Agnes wasn't struggling with the corps, she worked with soloists Paul Haakon and Ruthanna Boris. I was in the "Hero Ballet" featuring Paul and a group of men dancing with guns. The costumes for the chorus consisted of loose, grey jersey sacks with face-covering hoods that had holes only for our eyes. Again, we could scarcely breathe. We were arranged in grotesque postures like barbed wire fences or frozen, gruesome scarecrows. On cue we moved to new positions in time to prepare for Paul to leap over us as he attacked the enemy.

Comic Ed Wynn, the star of the show, was present each day at rehearsals, accompanied by his beautiful but totally silent young wife. A tiny, delicate, adorable featured singer, Hannah Williams, was always there with her husband, who acted as if he were her bodyguard. The girls whispered to me, "That's Jack Dempsey, you know!" I didn't know.

Costume fittings were under the direction of designer Raoul Pène DuBois, a tall, slim, gentle man. He designed a dream of a costume for me to wear in the "Peace Ball" scene. The dress was pale pink with a satin bodice, and a long skirt of accordion-pleated, light-as-air tulle. With it I wore long pink velvet gloves and silver sandals made expressly for me. The most perfect touch of all was a circlet of soft pink osprey feathers that crowned my flowing hair.

For the out-of-town tryout in Boston, each of us was asked what kind of hotel room we wanted reserved. Rehearsal salary was thirteen dollars a week, plus a few dollars for expenses. I opted to save money by sharing a large room for five at the Touraine Hotel. In the privacy of the big bedroom that we newcomers shared, one young lady whispered excitedly to me that Saks Fifth Avenue in New York City had notified her that a mink coat was waiting for her upon her return from Boston. I was grateful that Louis had wised me up, so I counseled her, as he had advised me, "It's the country girls who get into trouble because they are too innocent and gullible."

My roommates fascinated me. Occasionally, I found on my makeup table what were known as "happy happies"—little tokens of thoughtfulness—a flower, a piece of candy. It was the custom to leave these gifts for each other, and I soon joined in the practice. At night, two of my roommates would kneel and pray aloud, asking for protection. I was too embarrassed to kneel beside them, but I found myself soundlessly saying my prayers, too. I knew by now that I had embarked upon a distinctly dangerous adventure.

During the rehearsal period in Boston a second choreographer—Bobby Alton, whose specialty was tap dancing—was brought in to lighten things up. He went right to work on a new opening number for the show. The first line of the lyrics told the audience what it was all about: "Hi there neighbor, going my way? East or west on the Lincoln Highway?" We were hitchhikers. I watched Bobby like a hawk, catching all the loose-jointed action and shape of the moves he was making, but I was not getting the taps. I struggled madly in my clumsy, thick-soled oxfords to slap the floor and dig in half-toe, but I did have life in the torso and the gesture of a hitchhiker looking for a ride. Bobby came over to me, took me by the hand, and walked me to the front of the line saying, "It doesn't matter if you don't tap. What you are doing is fine. Just lead the line out." They dressed me in bright-colored overalls, tied a kerchief on my hair, put a knapsack on my back, and black Mary Jane shoes on my feet. I came flying out lickety-split to open the show.

One day Bobby asked, "Dorothy, can you do a bump for us?"

Unlike some of the girls who may have worked in burlesque, I had never done a bump. I took a big breath in preparation, lifted my arms, and arched my back. In a flash, I realized that bumps and the Graham contractions that I had done so boldly and innocently had something in common—a great deal in common, in fact. I blushed every color in the rainbow to think that I had never before seen a connection between bumps and contractions.

In Boston I was invited to attend several parties, but I had always refused. Then I was warned, "Dorothy, you will have to go if you don't want to get your notice before we return to New York." So I went. Just once.

It was a party given in Boss Curley's honor, following his release from prison. At that party, the company manager divulged to me that he was the one who had been faced with the disagreeable task of giving Martha's trio their notice in *The Greenwich Village Follies*.

"I felt it would have looked better if they voluntarily resigned, but she refused, and I was forced to fire them," he said. "I really didn't want to. They were such sweet young girls."

I was sipping a glass of champagne, when someone whispered to me, "You had better leave the party now, Dorothy. Quick! It's urgent that you go at once. Very soon we will probably be getting undressed. Ask someone, anyone, to take you back to the hotel."

The first person I saw was a well-known composer of popular songs, and I shyly asked if he would mind taking me to the Hotel Touraine. He smiled broadly and said, "I would be glad to."

In the taxicab I battled like a whirling dervish as his hands crept here and there and everywhere. He had obviously misunderstood! But I was quite strong —especially my legs. As we pulled up to the hotel, I slipped safely out of the taxi.

At a company run-through in practice clothes just before the opening in Boston, we performed "In the Shade of the New Apple Tree." When we all turned to face front for the final tableau, furious shouting and cursing could be heard, followed by people rushing back and forth conferring with each other. Harry Kaufman, Lee Shubert's associate, argued vehemently with Agnes about her choreography. I found the commotion positively terrifying.

Mr. Kaufman seemed to be about four feet high by four feet wide and was known as "the Hirer and Firer." He was so angry, his eyes bulged out of his face like a bullfrog's. Agnes stood right up to him. She was amazing! She would not give in, not one inch, not even when Harry Kaufman and his colleagues surrounded her, trying to intimidate her. Vincent Minnelli interrupted the dispute and sent the dancers along with Agnes to the foyer to work, while the general rehearsal continued onstage. Agnes polished a step or two, and when there was a break, we were called onstage to show the dance again. More violent arguing ensued, and back we went to the foyer. Again and again we went from the foyer to the stage, and back. Agnes would change a few steps, but she continued to have us face upstage throughout the number. For Agnes, it was a matter of principle. The whole company was watching as we ran through the dance.

One daring and impudent dancer, a veteran of many shows, announced in a stage whisper, "He's sitting in his seat playing pocket polo while we dance!" This was a game I had never heard of before. From then on, dancers glanced at one another and snickered each time we repeated the choreography. People must have wondered why they were laughing, being as we were all so worn out.

Management ordered the entire cast to remain in the theater. Doors were locked. No one could leave. Sandwiches and coffee were brought in. We were forced to stay in the theater throughout that night, all the next day, and through yet another night. I slept in a seat from time to time. While other scenes of the show were being rehearsed, we could hear muffled arguments taking place in the aisles. It was whispered that Agnes was to blame for the situation because she was insanely stubborn. When we were called onstage to dance the "Apple Tree" number once again, we could hear shouting and raging in the foyer. Kaufman and various men wearing black hats rushed back and forth. For some reason they were reluctant to fire Agnes. Was it because of her distinguished uncle, Cecil B. de Mille? Did management expect her to buckle under, either quit or submit to their demands, because she was a woman?

In any event, they would not give up, and Agnes would not give in. She was a Joan of Arc figure to me. Watching this drama unfold was terribly frightening for me. I was worried about Agnes, but I need not have been. The granddaughter of social scientist Henry George, Agnes had been raised in a family of fighters who took on unpopular causes. Their high standards drove her to excellence. The management could not possibly have guessed what they would be up against when they hired her.

After forty-eight hours in the theater, most of the cast was exhausted and near hysteria. It must have been Agnes who requested that an Actors' Equity representative come from New York City to witness what was going on. The representative talked quietly with almost all the performers. When a cast member asked if Equity could step in to protect us from this kind of abusive treatment, the representative replied, "We cannot do one thing for you, except get you your fare home if you are fired."

One of the girls told her about the parties—how we had been told that if we refused to go, we would be given notice. Her response was, "I can do nothing to protect you from any kind of harassment."

Before leaving, the representative gave me my first chorus Equity card. From then on I was a member, and the union automatically took dues out of my salary. Performers were obliged to join even though they received so little in return.

The first time we all put on our makeup was for the final dress rehearsal. The other girls were shocked by my white face, the heavy black lines I drew around my eyes, and the dark crimson gash I had painted on my mouth in true Graham fashion. As soon as we returned to our room, they said, "Let's fix Dorothy up. Dorothy could be a showgirl!"

This was their dream—to be a showgirl. They made me shower and wash my hair, then they helped me rinse it with a strawberry blonde color. They insisted on plucking out my eyebrows, like Marlene Dietrich and Greta Garbo. I protested, but one of them sat on me on the bed while another plucked. The rest directed the operation. Using their makeup, they painted my face, with everyone contributing suggestions—"more rouge," "more mascara." They were ecstatic with the result, but I was bewildered. When we got back to the theater, we ran into Raoul Pène DuBois. He looked aghast at me and said, "Oh! No!"

I told him what had happened, and he responded, "They ruined you!" My heart sank even further when I cleaned off the makeup with cold cream and saw my little piggy eyes with no eyebrows. I was in despair. I only hoped my eyebrows would grow back before we returned to New York.

At dress rehearsal, rumors began to fly that Agnes had been fired and had already left for New York City. As we began rehearsing the "Peace Ball" scene, the tanklike Mr. Kaufman suddenly came tearing down the aisle and up the temporary wooden stairs installed for the rehearsal period. He was shouting all the way, "Bird! Bird!"

Alarmed, I thought, "Oh, he wants to take away my beautiful ballgown now that Agnes is not here to stop him, and give it to some girl that he fancies."

Whatever he had been plotting was short-circuited as he tripped on the top step and fell backward into the orchestra pit. The cast ran forward to see, and wild laughter swept through the company as we saw him sprawled on top of a squashed cello.

The stage manager shouted, "Rehearsal is over. Go back to your hotel and wait there to be called."

At the hotel, Mary Green was crying as she told me that Agnes had not even been allowed in the theater to say goodbye to us. I did not see Agnes for a long time, but when I did, she confirmed my intuition that Mr. Kaufman had been coveting my costume. She also acknowledged that her spirited refusal to cave in or to quit had forced the management to fire her. From this terrible experience, Agnes learned she must always insist on a written contract that would protect her rights. Ultimately, her steadfastness proved beneficial for other choreographers as well. Her pioneering efforts prodded the unions to better represent and protect performers. In the short term, the producers may have had their way—the gas masks were abandoned, and the harem was displayed in accordance with their wishes—but in the long run, Agnes would be the victor.[1]

Upon returning to New York City after the out-of-town tryouts, I was informed, "'They' want your company at a dinner to be served between the matinee and evening show. 'They' just want to meet you."

Baccardi cocktails and dinner were served in a private hotel room. Several men and girls were present. Everything seemed to be going nicely as we sat at the dinner table, when suddenly, just as I was drinking my soup, I felt fingers creeping up my leg under my skirt. I thought of Louis tickling me under the table and of Martha, too, as I looked from one girl to the other. We all burst out laughing at once, and soup spluttered out of my mouth into the plate. Occasional explosions of muffled laughter continued to interrupt dinner, after which we returned to the theater. "They" had gotten to know me a little, and I was never again invited to another dinner.

In the spring of 1938 during the run of *Hooray for What!* I was invited by the New Dance Group to share the stage of the Guild Theater in a dance concert with the lovely Miriam Becker and the skillful Si-Lan Chen. At first I was reluctant to participate, but Anna Sokolow and the composer Alex North persuaded me to accept. I planned to do my hitchhiker dance from *Hooray for What!* as a solo. When I asked Denny, the stage manager, if I might be allowed to borrow my costume from the show, he requested permission from Lee Shubert. Denny told me that Lee Shubert's flattering response was, "Let her borrow anything she wants. She's the brightest thing we have in the show."

For the concert, I prepared a modern dance entitled *Credo* to special music composed by Alex North. It was to be a nostalgic study in which I was torn between yearning to move forward, yet looking back. In creating the choreography I felt woefully restricted, remembering how Louis had insisted so adamantly that no movement from one dance could ever be used in any other dance. To copy or steal movements from Martha, or from any other choreographer, was unthinkable. Martha owned every movement I could imagine. I was paralyzed. I, who had just about the highest extensions and the fleetest feet in town, barely moved a muscle in my dance. Everyone who knew me was bewildered, unable to understand why I seemed so inhibited. As usual I could not, and did not, explain. John Martin wrote that I was still young and needed time to mature. Feeling that I did not belong in the world of modern dance, I fled from my obvious inadequacy on the concert stage back to the show.[2]

During the run of *Hooray for What!* Ruthanna Boris and I became good friends. She took me to class at Leon Fokine's studio. He was a small slim man, with a prominent boney bridge to his nose. He thought of himself as ugly. I thought he was sublimely beautiful when he whistled with the music as he demonstrated développé écarté, touching the bridge of his nose to give the direction of the hand as he carried his arm up and out in port de bras. I liked the way he whispered brief jokes to the girls as they worked at the barre. Above all, I relished being in the atmosphere of the ballet class again, for the first time since leaving Victoria.

Toward the end of class, Russian men drifted casually into the classroom, joking with Leon Fokine. Ruthanna told me some of them had been the "wild boys" after the Russian revolution. These "boys" were men now, but they still came together, not to practice or take class but, rather, to compete in a sporting manner. Their goal was the excitement of the height and the width of the jumps, the number of beats and turns. The mirror did not interest them at all. They would whistle and applaud each other, and it was thrilling to watch. Igor Youskevitch often participated. I was amazed how his lazy, bored attitude at the barre during class quickly disappeared, and he came vividly alive, spellbinding, with his combination of innate grace and tremendous athletic skill.

Ruthanna's friend, the ballerina Annabelle Lyons, was asked by Leon one day to demonstrate fouetté turns at the barre, the way his uncle Michel Fokine had taught them to her. Annabelle had long arched feet and very slim delicate ankles. As she performed the passé développé into croisé and then opened into a spiral in the fouetté turn, she was like a lovely delicate rose, whose petals were turning back on themselves as they opened to the sun. Her turns were poetry. Not forced or grimly determined.

Hooray for What! ran for seven wonderful months. I received a salary of thirty-five dollars a week and felt that I was the luckiest person in the world. At every performance I would change costumes quickly so I could stand in the wings to watch Ed Wynn. Although the musicians in the orchestra pit are a rather bored bunch as a rule, they watched him intently, just as I did, to see what new piece of insane business he would bring to each performance. Ed Wynn played a slightly daffy horticulturist named Chuckles. He had taken a correspondence course in chemistry in hopes of perfecting a gas that would destroy the insects that constantly attacked his fruit trees. His gas, it turned out, could also kill humans. Delegates to the League of Nations were eager to acquire the rights to the formula so they could expedite the next war. There was hilarious competition between Ed Wynn attempting to destroy the formula, and delegates intent on obtaining it. After a long pursuit, Chuckles evaded the delegates and saved the world from their evil plans. In one scene he presided over an international peace conference that was absolutely, hilariously madcap. He was warning peace delegates that if they failed to pay installments on the debt, America would own the last war outright. Ed Wynn's bumbling, lisping manner delighted the audience. In one scene he was hugely "ecthited" because he had just thought of a new, inexpensive way to make lace by mating silkworms with moths, but he was still puzzling out the details.

In the years before air conditioning, many people fled the city when the oppressive summer heat set in. Most Broadway shows closed until fall. As I stood in the wings on closing night, May 21, 1938, I knew I would miss Ed Wynn a lot. I would especially miss our white-haired stage manager, Denny, who every night had prodded each of us as we went onstage, saying "Show your teeth. Smile! Teeth! More teeth!" I had always responded to his command with delirious laughter. It seemed so funny to me, like a satire. I still saw everything through Martha's and Louis's eyes.

I had no idea what I would be doing after the show closed, when a young woman approached me. She asked, "Would you like to go out of town for the summer? My name is Elsa Fried, and I'm taking a small group of dancers to a summer resort called the Berkshire Country Club. It's on a lake in Wingdale, New York, not far from New York City. You will receive room and board plus five dollars a week spending money, and you'll be dancing in the shows each week."

"Yes, I'll go!" I quickly said, "I think I might like that."

Before leaving the city, I attended a dance demonstration by Martha Hill's students at New York University. It was the year-end presentation of their class work. Among the many small studies shown was an outstanding blues piece, composed and danced by Lillian Solomon. When I said something complimentary about it to Martha Hill following the performance, she introduced me to Lillian. But first, she whispered to me, "Lillian has just recently lost her mother, and she is desperately unhappy."

Martha Hill then inquired if I would consider asking Elsa Fried for permission to bring Lillian with me to dance at the Berkshire Country Club. Although I was astounded by the request, I did call Elsa on the phone. She was a warmhearted person, and before I knew it everything was arranged.

When Elsa, Lillian, I, and several other dancers arrived at the Berkshire Country Club, we were surprised to find there was no proper rehearsal space available. The only open area was in the social hall, where guest activities took precedence over dance rehearsals. Elsa found these conditions impossible. After about a week, she quit in disgust and returned to New York City, leaving the dancers to fend for themselves. Before long, the other dancers left too. Only Lillian and I stayed.

After talking things over, we decided to put together a duet. Lillian was able to draw on her ballet and character training at Kobeloff's Ballet School, as well as her modern skills. I was grateful that Lillian was musical, since I felt insecure in that area. She suggested we use a popular recording of Morton Gould's *Pavanne*. The word *pavanne* attracted me, bringing to mind the work in Louis's composition classes. Once we found a movement theme we both liked, I was full of ideas and devices. I had the performing experience and knew how to vary movement and make it exciting; Lillian had the practical, educational training. *Pavanne* was the first of a number of small, unpretentious studies we worked out together that summer.

Our dance followed the comic Hank Henry, who came from the world of burlesque. He always seemed to have ice cream in his pockets, and he squirted a seltzer bottle from inside the fly of his pants. The stage was in total disarray when he finished. Before Lillian and I could perform, I mopped the stage so we would be able to dance in our bare feet. The audience loved watching this. Ernie Glucksman, the social director in charge of the shows, thought the contrast between the crude humor of Hank Henry and our wholesome, lighthearted dancing resulted in a balanced program.

One of the other performers was a very handsome man who sang and played the accordion. His name was Paul Villard. He had gorgeous dark curly hair and dazzling blue eyes. I first saw him standing on the porch with a group of showgirls clustered around him. They were fawning over him with rapt adulation, and he obviously was enjoying it. As I walked by, he glanced my way, then started to approach me. I turned and walked away. He was so good-looking that I refused to have anything to do with him. "A conceited man is not for me," I said to myself.

Near the end of summer, my brother David wrote to say that Daddy was ill, but not to come home because everything would be all right. Just two days before I was to leave the Berkshire Country Club to return to New York City, I was notified that Daddy had died. I sent a bouquet of red roses, the symbol of the Rosicrucian Order. It comforted me greatly when David told me later that the roses had lasted an unbelievably long time. After Daddy's death, I felt closer to him than I had since I was a small child. I often sensed his presence around me, and it made me feel safe.

When I returned to my apartment in New York City, I found several wires from Felicia Sorel, asking if I wanted to be in a show she was choreographing called *Everywhere I Roam*. I brought Kathy Slagle to the audition, and we were both hired. Felicia Sorel encouraged the dancers to contribute to the choreography. Inspired by the music of Arnold Sundgaard, the dancing in the first act was vibrant, vigorous, and joyful. The Robert Edmond Jones stage setting—a lovely blue sky created by a curved cyclorama in back of a narrow strip of a wheat field—framed a raised floor in the foreground. It appeared that we were dancing outdoors in a field. The character of Johnny Appleseed was played radiantly by Norman Lloyd.

Everyone agreed that the first act was perfectly beautiful, but problems developed in the second act. Marc Connolly, who was famous for *Green Pastures*, was brought in to take over the direction. To me he appeared patronizing and pretentious. He caricatured everything that had at first been so fresh and captivating. The actors were directed to exaggerate and satirize the characters they played, to make fun of them as country bumpkins. This attempt at comedy was neither quaint nor amusing. Mr. Connolly instructed the scenery crew to make a thousand changes, including "and cut the skyscrapers in half for the second act." Mr. Connolly had meant half as many buildings, but instead, the stagehands sawed the sets so as to be half as high.

"What did they think would go under them?" Mr. Connolly asked vexedly.

Ben Kranz, the stage manager, responded, "I guess, the subway."

Under Marc Connolly's direction, the show began to fall apart completely. Shortly before *Everywhere I Roam* came to its sad but predictable end, I received a phone call from a young man at the Theater Arts Committee (TAC). Lillian had previously introduced me to that group. The dance committee members there had pressed me to come to meetings, but being sensitive to everyone else's point of view, I had found it impossible to take sides. I felt uneasy about what was called agitprop, fearing that it might jeopardize my citizenship. Because I considered myself supremely fortunate, and in no way discontented, I had chosen to refrain from participating in TAC's activities.

The young man from TAC now explained excitedly that a sensational new song had been brought to their attention. "They want you for *Picket Line Priscilla*. It's *really* important."

"I can't do it," I stated, "I am in a show. I can't quit my job for this."

"But you *can* do it," he insisted. "The TAC cabaret is specifically for people who are active in the theater. The show will go on at Chez Fire House, late at night to accommodate performers who are working."

He was very persuasive. I knew that the skits, songs, and dances for the TAC shows were satirical, not particularly appropriate for the commercial stage. I agreed to go to the TAC office to hear the song. When I did, it excited me too. The young man asked if I could gather a group of performers together for *Picket Line Priscilla* and work it out right away.

"I'll try," I replied.

That night at *Everywhere I Roam*, I took the proposition to Phil Brown, a young actor with wild red hair and lots of freckles. He was an activist. "You absolutely must do it! I'll help you," he said.

Phil brought in Bobby Breen and George Jacobson, a filmmaker married to Anita Alvarez. George was not a professional performer, but he had a hilarious quality similar to Jimmy Durante. I spoke to Kathy Slagle, who in turn invited Peggy Anne Holmes to join us. It was established from the first that the TAC people wanted me to play the part of Priscilla.

We made up everything cooperatively, sometimes planning while hanging onto the subway car straps as we rode back and forth from performances of *Everywhere I Roam*. I wasn't really sure what a picket line was, so I went to see one. The people appeared tired, discouraged, and openly demoralized. It was very depressing. We felt our picket line must be even more disheartened than the one I had seen. For ours, one picketer was hunched up as if suffering with a bad cold; two others were arguing; one was sitting down nursing a blister; another dragged himself stoically around and around. The music played through softly at first, without the singing. Our first priority was to come up with a walk that had the jazzy rhythm and vigor of the song. As we listened to the music, Peggy improvised a simple but catchy walk. Kathy picked up on it, and we all added variations to the theme.

With that hurdle out of the way, I focused on my entrance. It would have to be dynamic enough to wake up the picketers and get things going. I thought of the Nijinsky entrance Muriel Stuart had described as "marvelous" in *Spectre de la Rose*, when he bounded from a diving board set up offstage to create the illusion of floating on air like the aroma of rose petals. Instead of using a diving board, I pulled myself back as I had done in Seattle, with Martha, when we prepared for the explosion of energy to initiate the foot race, and I catapulted myself onto the stage. I landed abruptly from a long, low, sliding leap, lifted one foot up in the air, took a huge breath, and came down firmly on the "Pic" of "Picket Line" as Beatrice Kaye sang the lyrics.

Three cops, striding as if wearing big boots and swinging billy clubs, confront Kathy, Peggy, and me. Beatrice sings, "When the cops would see her comin' they would start a mighty hummin'." This is my cue to let loose with the battle cry "Un-fair! Un-fair!"

It had to be explosive. On "Un" I breathed in, dug the top of my head down toward the floor, flung my long hair forward and then back. My arms and body came up, fists fiercely clenched, wrists strong. I nailed the movement on the syncopated double beat with a determined Stamp! Stamp! on "fair!" Beatrice and I hit it solidly together, as the cops leaped forward to join the picket line.

The second confrontation comes as the judge, played by George, waves his arms madly and pounds on the desk. The desk is Phil Brown, who has tipped over to offer a flat back for this purpose. When the judge sees Priscilla and her picket line, he rises up into the air (secretly assisted by Bobby Breen). At the sound of "Unfair! Unfair!" he claws the air as he rushes toward us, eager to join the line. The cast then forms an interlocking miracle of motion, a wild and wonderful Rube Goldberg contraption that represents the Ford assembly line. Each worker is united with the next, lifting, lowering, churning, tipping, turning. Meanwhile, Phil, the "scurrilous scab," skulks behind a barricade created by others standing in an interconnected stance, legs wide apart, arms braced to keep him out. When Phil sees an opening and slips through, I am ready. As Beatrice sings, "Scabs don't live to tell the story," I catch Phil on the chin with a chop that sends him flying sky-high (with a little help from George and Bobby).

Ku Klux Klansmen encircle Priscilla. Using my hair as a lasso, I lash out at each one as they speed by. Beatrice sings, "She could make the vigilantes run like ants was in their panties." In the final tableau, Priscilla, now married to a union organizer, is handed a large white handkerchief by each of the men who together simulate a moving clothesline. Priscilla hangs out the handkerchiefs, representing diapers, on the clothesline, as Beatrice sings, "Now she has to pay the piper; now she sighs with every diaper," and Priscilla resignedly sobs, "Unfair! Unfair!"

Before each performance, I washed my hair and brushed it vigorously with Vaseline to catch the light, as Martha had always done. I practiced swinging it in circles, figure eights, and forward and back so I was in control of this powerful extension of self. I dressed in a borrowed black velvet skating skirt, lined with red, and a tailored silk shirt with rolled-up sleeves in my mother's favorite color, "riding pink." Everyone else wore comfortable colorful clothes.

The success of *Picket Line Priscilla* made me the toast of the town, wooed and pursued by distinguished actors, directors, and (strangely enough) dance band leaders. Rudy Vallee expressed an interest in having me go on the road with his band. I could hardly believe it and did not respond. Billy Rose sent word that he would like me to come to his office. Since talking was still so difficult for me, I invited Phil Brown to join me. I was surprised by Billy Rose's appearance. He was small and plump and wore a tight suit. He sat in a chair facing me.

"Would you like to perform *Picket Line Priscilla* with your group at the Diamond Horse Shoe?" he asked.

"That sounds wonderful to me!" I said, excited. I was finished talking, but Phil was not.

"How much will we be paid?" he said. This made me feel uncomfortable, and Billy Rose was not ready to commit himself. When Phil asked what percentage of the take both the composer and the lyricist would receive, I hid my face. I heard Mr. Rose slap the arms of his chair. I looked up and saw him rise from his seat, snorting and puffing on a big fat cigar as he stalked out of the room without saying another word. It was over. We would never get to dance at the Diamond Horse Shoe.

Soon after this, the phone rang in my apartment, and a voice said, "This is Artie Shaw speaking."

"Who?" I asked. Even though he was just about the biggest attraction next to Sinatra, his name did not ring a bell with me. Artie Shaw said he had seen me in *Picket Line Priscilla* and wanted me to go on tour with his orchestra. He was quite explicit, he did not want the group—only me. He requested that I prepare a solo to a blues number, which he had the orchestra play for me, and he carefully explained the syncopated accent in the music. There was none of the zesty, gutsy punch of *Picket Line Priscilla* in either his music or the sad, wistful dance I prepared. My costume was a black satin dress that would have been better suited for funerals. At the opening of the tour in Newark, Artie suggested I sit in the audience for the first show to watch the band and the live entertainment that was to follow the screen attraction, *National Velvet*. The house was packed with rude, restless teenagers who roamed the aisles, talking and laughing throughout the movie. At the end of the film, as the curtain opened to reveal the orchestra, Artie Shaw played a few notes of his signature number, "Begin the Beguine." Instantly, the music was drowned out by the screams of frenzied teenagers. Some people jumped from the box seats onto the stage and proceeded to pull others up over the footlights from the pit. They tried to pull Artie Shaw's clarinet away from him and yanked at his clothing. It was bedlam.

I tried to go backstage, but the doors were locked. Finally someone let me in and bolted the door after me. Artie Shaw was devastated.

"I worked so hard on the orchestrations," he said, "and no one can hear a note!"

I was shaken to my roots by this phenomenon of wild ecstatic fans. We mutually agreed it was out of the question for me to go on the tour.

One evening, a young man who looked a bit like Cary Grant came backstage to compliment me following a performance of *Picket Line Priscilla*. At first I was no more interested in him than in any other of the men who approached me at the theater, but when I heard that he worked at Intourist, I became intrigued.

Anna Sokolow had urged me to go to the Soviet Union, as she had done, to see all the marvelous dancing. She thought the people there would like me. I felt that the Russians might relate to the theme of *Picket Line Priscilla*. The young man from Intourist was called Jeremy Gury. He was dressed like my father, in an old-fashioned, soft tweedy wool jacket and grey flannel slacks. He even wore gold-rimmed glasses, like Daddy. Jeremy lived with his cat in a quiet apartment with brown beams in the ceiling. He talked about Chaucer and smoked a pipe. He seemed scholarly and safe, like Daddy. When Jeremy came on the scene, I was past twenty-three. My sacred promise to Mums was no longer binding.

With the signing of the Russian-German Pact, Intourist closed overnight. TAC ended. Pink slips were given out to people working on WPA projects. There had been theater projects, including an immensely exciting one involving Orson Welles, and everywhere writers were preserving the history of towns and villages. Dancers were performing in every possible space, and most visible of all were the WPA murals painted in many public buildings. Without the modest but guaranteed salary, all these artists soon would be faced with a terrible struggle to survive. It was the end of a brief but magical time of government sponsorship for the arts.

In the summer of 1939, Ruthanna Boris suggested that I go with her to Camp Tamiment, a resort in the hills of Pennsylvania. New Yorkers were attracted there partly for tennis and lake swimming but mainly for the weekend shows staged by Max Liebman, the camp's social director. Camp Tamiment had become a showcase for Manhattan's brightest aspiring revue talent. I was hired on Ruthanna's recommendation to be part of a group of about thirty performers. The company of ten dancers, both modern and ballet, included Jerome Robbins, William Bales, and Anita Alvarez. We worked both collaboratively and independently, with no official choreographer.

Performances were held in the social hall, which converted to a cabaret on Friday nights. Few of us looked forward to dancing in the cabaret's floor shows. The overworked dance band was required to play for us, and they were not at all enthusiastic about dancers who came to rehearsals with elaborate musical arrangements. The band leader went through the motions of marking repeats, cuts, and bridges for us, but when performance time came we often found to our dismay that the band just played on, forgetting the cues. I particularly remember a solo that ended with me hanging in midair, staring beseechingly at the band, plaintively waiting for the music to end, to release me. I decided it was more practical to learn to work with existing band arrangements of familiar popular songs.

Such embarrassments never happened to Jerry Robbins. In the cabaret environment, he was a spellbinding performer. He was mysteriously confident and outwardly carefree, even casual, about every aspect of his solo work. Jerry was completely prepared for any eventuality that might occur. He choreographed startling, dazzling entrances for himself, certain to capture everyone's attention.

He moved improvisationally from table to table, reaching out to people, before suddenly spinning, leaping, and sliding across the floor to another table. He laughed along with the audience, communicating his extraordinary sense of élan, sensitivity to the music, and joy in dancing. As he heard the climactic moment approaching in the music, he readied himself to execute the most theatrical exit imaginable. He disappeared to thunderous applause, then laughingly returned to bow, always at ease but in total control. Jerry openly loved being in intimate touch with his audience, a vital part of cabaret success. His youthful confidence and zest for life was infectious. Everyone shared in the fun.

In the evening, when we were not performing, we mingled with the waiters and the permanent guests who lived in cottages in Sandyville. The waiters were mostly college students earning money for their education. It seems the waiters had discussed me and agreed that I had no manners. They said that I neither greeted them nor said goodnight, and when I danced with them in the social hall I impolitely walked away without excusing myself. I was shocked. I realized they were right. Up until then, I had not realized that the seven years with Martha had turned me into a person who felt that to be polite and considerate of other people's feelings was unnecessary. I had learned to behave in an arrogant manner, while actually I was timid and defensive. I had unwittingly absorbed Martha's and Louis's intolerance of people in the outside world. The impersonal, nonassertive way of behaving that I had accepted as the norm during the years with Martha, I now saw was rude and ungracious and had effectively cut me off from others.

When the location of the shows was moved from the small social hall cabaret to the newly constructed theater stage, Max Liebman welcomed any small dances that we could devise on our own. As the summer progressed, it became apparent not only that Jerry was a very talented performer but also that he wanted to become a serious choreographer. Max must have felt that Jerry showed real promise, because he provided rehearsal space and scheduled time onstage for Jerry to work with the dancers. Thus Jerry had the opportunity to create his first ballet. Albia Kavan, a former soloist in Ballet Caravan and dedicated Balanchine dancer from the School of American Ballet, was in the company. She, Ruthanna, and I along with a few other dancers took a ballet barre together religiously every morning. All of us were seriously motivated to dance and were prepared to be quiet and respectful at Jerry's rehearsals. There we saw him become a different person—resolute and purposeful.

Jerry was the moving spirit behind a hornpipe trio danced by Anita Alvarez, Jerry, and me. We put it together quite spontaneously using a couple of steps from the traditional hornpipe I had learned at Mill Bay, plus some new steps Jerry devised. It climaxed with split jumps that brought down the house. I sometimes wonder if our little hornpipe trio was the seed of an idea that Jerry first developed into *Fancy Free* and then later into *On the Town*.

Jerry and Anita danced an especially haunting duet to Billie Holiday's recording of "Strange Fruit." The Lewis Allen song goes "Strange fruit hanging from a poplar tree." I had always considered the strange fruit to be, in a horrible image, a young black man, lynched. Jerry and Anita's piece was a variation on that theme. In the middle of the dimly lit stage stood a very tall ladder. Jerry was costumed aristocratically in a dark outfit, with his throat and wrists accented by white ruffles that caught the light. In marked contrast, Anita wore a plain, perhaps even torn, shift of nondescript color. They danced with great intensity. Toward the end, Jerry slowly mounted the ladder. Anita stood motionless. When Jerry approached the top of the ladder, he stopped and looked down. We then became aware that Anita seemed to be hanging, suspended, by her neck. It appeared to snap slightly, as her head toppled over to the side. The moment was understated. *Strange Fruit* was one of the most dramatic and heart-breaking dances I have ever seen—a masterpiece.

The popular team of Mata and Hari were at Camp Tamiment that summer. They could be seen polishing the small details of their act on the first tee of the golf course, early every morning before the golfers arrived. Rehearsal space was at such a premium. Danny Kaye was also a resident performer. He and Sylvia Fine, the staff songwriter who later became his wife, were working together on the fast-patter songs that would make him famous. I had seen him previously in a nightclub, and I simply could not believe the transformation that took place halfway through the summer. Danny replaced the red silk Russian shirt he usually wore with an expensive, beautifully tailored dinner jacket and pants. He became a class act, an absolute spellbinder, in complete control of his audience. *Picket Line Priscilla* was presented that summer, with Danny Kaye singing the lyrics. He was marvelous, making it deliriously rhythmic. Bill Bales took over

George's parts, but it was not the same as it had been with the TAC cabaret. The audience for TAC had been especially receptive. I would never again experience any magic quite like it.

Imogene Coca had already established herself as the leading comedienne at Tamiment. She did not rely on tried-and-true vaudeville routines but created her own original material, with the constant help and support of her husband. Onstage she first appeared very fragile and delicate, but then she would, out of nowhere, suddenly surprise the audience with a flaming streak of resourcefulness that developed into wild recklessness. Audiences adored her. She performed a striptease, wearing a huge camel's hair coat. She would parade up and down, leering seductively at the audience, before opening the top button of her coat and peeking inside. A look of horror and disappointment spread over her face, and she quickly closed the coat. She had every gesture down pat. People in the audience laughed until they cried. As she made her exit, she slipped out of the coat, and left it lying onstage. The applause was huge. When she came out for her bow, she was wearing an identical coat, except that it was much, much smaller. She apparently had been wearing her husband's overcoat on top of her own.

It was Imogene who suggested that I dance to "I Dream of Jeannie with the Light Brown Hair," by Stephen Foster. Max Liebman put an old upright piano on the stage, and the accompanist Glen Bacon played and sang the words softly and wistfully as I moved in the moonlight. It was haunting, and the audience loved it.

A recent graduate of Bennington with a marvelously husky voice did a Carmen Miranda imitation with fruit on her head. Her eyesight was so poor she nearly broke her teeth on the microphone in rehearsal. I liked her very much, but Max Liebman said, "She is to leave after the Saturday night show."

He scheduled her to take a lemon pie in the face a couple of numbers before she was to do her song. When I saw that she had taken great pains with her makeup and was near to tears at the prospect of being smacked with a pie, I felt sorry for her. Since I was finished dancing for the evening, I offered to be the one to take the pie in the face. I just loved lemon meringue pie. I didn't think I'd really mind. Dressed in a robe zipped up high on my neck, and with my hair wrapped in a turban, I entered the scene and stood where she would have stood. The pie landed full in my face. Sticky stuff slid down my neck inside my collar and stuck in my eyes and ears. I couldn't see. I could scarcely breathe. I was calling out, "Somebody, please get me off the stage!" but no one seemed to hear. Many years later, at a dinner honoring Agnes de Mille, I reintroduced myself to that same singer, Carol Channing. She then softly sang a song to me, one that I had danced to that summer long ago at Tamiment.

Jerry Robbins staged a song called "Hometown," by James Shelton. To each member of the cast of ten, Jerry gave clearly delineated character movement. He and Ruthanna danced the roles of the Fowler Kids. James Shelton played the Singer Commentator, and I was My Girl. I walked in from the side to center stage and went forward to the footlights, where I opened my arms and smiled a little. That was the end of the song. Though it was simple, it was effective. Lee Shubert had liked it so much, he would incorporate it as "Our Town" into the 1939 Broadway production of *Straw Hat Review* at the Ambassador Theater.

The group dance featured in the Saturday night revues at Tamiment had often ended up as a battle between modern dance and ballet. For one of these, Jerry danced with us moderns—Bill Bales, Anita Alvarez, and me. The ballet people did turns and more turns while we moderns tore around them. Then, as everyone was forming into a long diagonal line toward the front of the stage, Jerry led with a huge slide forward on his stomach. I followed, going into an incomplete back fall, hinging diagonally back on my knees. Bill and everyone else behind us held themselves at higher and higher levels until Ruthanna took up her position atop someone's shoulders at the end of the line. This ballet, which we created cooperatively, became the "Piano and Lute" dance in the first act of *Straw Hat Revue*. "Crazy Cactus," a solo choreographed and danced by Ruthanna Boris, was also performed on Broadway. Choreography that we had done ourselves was credited to a "name," who was brought in at the last moment. With no legal protection, we had to accept this unfairness. In the case of Jerry Robbins, however, clearly he did ultimately receive the credit and recognition due him.

Jerry did one thing during the last show that summer that tarnished my own self-image and that led me to make a serious error in judgment in the future. As one of three satirical impressions, which included a caricature of Imogene Coca, Jerry did a takeoff of me. Throughout the summer, if a group of girls had walked onstage in single file, I would usually enter last, wearing the pièce de résistance, a distinctive hat or something. In his satire, Jerry entered wearing a special wrap, and he added a slither to the walk as he twinkled knowingly. He had captured just enough of my qualities—juxtaposed with insinuating, earthy ingredients—that the audience recognized it was me. They laughed uproariously.

Before this, I had never for a moment thought of my walk as sensuous. The slow, smooth, deliberate walk that I had practiced under Mum's guidance when I was a colombe was still sacred to me. I treasured the memory of being the one to swing the incense as part of the Rosicrucian ritual. This walk, that I had later perfected with Martha, had been turned by Jerry into the stylized strutting of a stripper. As the audience howled and screamed for him to "take it off," I realized I had unconsciously fallen into the trap of the sexy orientation. Instead of feeling flattered that Jerry would choose to imitate me, I felt cheapened and distinctly soiled. He could not possibly have known how his imitation would inhibit me, causing me to shrink back into my shell. From then on, the walking I had done so lightheartedly in "Hometown" became an ordeal.

As we were preparing for the opening of *Straw Hat Review* in New York City, I was shattered to see Harry Kaufman at rehearsal. He was representing the Shuberts, and Max Liebman was permitting him to supervise the run-through of "our" show. Mr. Kaufman took it upon himself to direct me in how to smile for the "Hometown" segment.

"A little *more*, Bird," he said. I grinned broadly. "No. No. A little *less*."

Each time he had me enter and walk forward, I heard hissing from the wings, "Take it off, Bird! Take it off!" followed by stifled laughter.

Mr. Kaufman glared at me with his ball-bearing eyes and said, "Your smile has to be more spiritual, Bird. More *spiritual*."

What I had been able to do so simply before now became torture. I could not understand why Jerry did not stand up to defend me and his choreography. Self-conscious and confused, I began to feel the stage was no longer such a safe place for me to be.

This ominous feeling was confirmed by my experience with several theatrical agents who called me after reading favorable reviews in the newspaper. In one office, the agent came sidling out from behind his desk with a silly smirk on his face. He took my hand and hinted that if I would be "nice" to him, he could make contacts in Hollywood that would open doors for me. All the agents had rather creepy hands, making me cringe and pull away. I was frightened at the prospect of the price I would have to pay to get work, and I made it clear I was just not that interested in a career.

During the run of *Straw Hat Revue*, Jeremy Gury and I were married by a Justice of the Peace in Westport, Connecticut. Two office workers served as our witnesses. The ceremony was mechanical and a bit of a letdown, but I felt safe and protected. Jeremy found an apartment for us on Madison Avenue. It was quite modern, with floor-to-ceiling windows in the bedroom, and an outside staircase leading down to a small garden, which I loved. Jeremy chose every decorating touch, every detail for our apartment. He selected expensive ensembles for me to wear, with matching shoes, hats, handbags, and jewelry. He said I needed to be fashionably dressed when we attended cocktail parties. I had neither cared about clothes nor attended cocktail parties before this, and I realized before too long that it was never going to be comfortable for me to function in the world of advertising executives.

In 1939, Martha Graham sent a message to me saying that she wanted me to come back.[3] She told me she had promised the organizers of the opening celebration of the World's Fair that she "would provide a beautiful Broadway dancer" to represent the Figure of Peace. What could I say? No? I returned to Martha's studio for a meeting the day prior to the performance. She said I was to wear a white gown, a laurel wreath in my hair, and carry the banner of peace. She instructed me to hold the banner high as I followed President Roosevelt after the opening ceremony. Trumpets would be sounded from nearby rooftops. Then I was to wait quietly as the president was helped from the dais into his car, at which time I would lead the dancers in a procession behind the car.

At the World's Fair the next day, Erick Hawkins was there carrying a soft blanket over his arm, and a thermos and sandwiches for Martha. She was obviously spellbound by Erick; she forgot to bring my wreath. Luckily, I had brought a bunch of violets and made a wreath for my head from the leaves. Martha was visibly melting as Erick attended to her every need. She suddenly decided that Erick, not I, should carry the banner of peace, and I should walk behind him. Erick took off his shirt and stood bare-chested, posing this way and that for Martha as he held the banner aloft. Erick strode off in solitary splendor with the banner while I remained to lead the group behind President Roosevelt's car as originally planned. I was angry with Martha and disgusted with myself for having let her use me. But what upset me even more was to see Martha so docile. Erick was the one who was all-powerful, Martha was enslaved. I could scarcely believe my eyes.[4]

That summer, a number of us from the cast of *Straw Hat Revue* returned to Tamiment. I began working together with Nelson Barclift, a happy-go-lucky lighthearted dancer. I felt comfortable with Nelson. He was very proud of his American Indian heritage. Tall and loose-limbed, with arms that made large sweeping gestures, Nelson was open and generous in his movements. Audiences responded to his vivid zest for life. We joyfully and speedily worked up an act, posed for publicity photographs, and contacted an agent.

Nelson and I auditioned for *Lady in the Dark*. We showed the dances we had prepared for our act to the show's choreographer, Albertina K. Rasch, and she hired us. Before long it became quite clear, however, that what she especially liked about us was a dance we had put together to Duke Ellington's "In My Solitude," plus a bit of the "Mooch." Albertina liked this dance so much she simply appropriated it, without even asking our permission. She directed us to perform our choreography in front of the other dancers and instructed them, "Just follow along, and copy every move they make."

Aside from adding an entrance, the only change she made was in the music. Instead of dancing to the sustained Ellington song, we were abruptly expected to adapt our choreography to a lively beguine that got progressively faster and faster. It must have been difficult for the rest of the dancers, because the choreography was never reshaped to fit the new music. Appropriating choreography was a rather common practice at the time. Nelson and I were so delighted to be in the show, it never occurred to us to protest.

The dazzling and legendary Gertrude Lawrence, from the impeccable Noel Coward world of musical comedy, had been summoned from England to be the star of *Lady in the Dark*. She announced that it would be a total waste of her time to attend dance rehearsals, so a lovely dancer named Betty Lowe was hired to be her stand-in. When Miss Lawrence finally did attend a dance rehearsal, she watched Betty Lowe dance her part twice through. Then she stepped in to do it herself, and she remembered everything! She was like quicksilver. We all stood back in total amazement, spellbound.

From the first time I sat in the audience during rehearsal watching the show come together, there was never any doubt that *Lady in the Dark* was going to be a smashing success. It was the ultimate musical of that time. The marvelous music was by Kurt Weill, who demanded absolute discipline and precision, and also saw to it that the polish never lessened. The script by Moss Hart, "Mr. Show Business," was smart, sharp, and very contemporary.

The show was elegant, glamorous, glittering. Turntables within turntables spun in different directions on either side of the stage, while dancers wearing dazzling costumes flew on and off stage. For the female performers in the beguine that Nelson and I had choreographed, Irene Sharoff designed the first of the strapless gowns. In performance, as we rushed madly to and fro, the steel corset wands sewn into the bodice seams sliced through the fabric and speared us in various body parts. The costumes and the choreography were in constant conflict. Early on I realized that I had better approach the fast, high-arched, tilting backbends very conservatively. As the music progressed to breakneck speed, and dancers got caught up with it, breasts would occasionally slip out of bodices but were usually popped quickly back in by sympathetic partners. All the girls wore identical blonde, upswept wigs. The wigs often went askew when the hair nets securing the curls got caught on the young mens' sleeve buttons as the girls spun under their linked elbows. One day in performance, my wig became hopelessly entangled in the buttons of Nelson's sleeve. The wig fell off, allowing my own long hair to come tumbling down.

Following this incident, our distinguished producer, Hassard Short, called a company meeting and declared, "This was the most humiliating thing that has ever occurred in my entire career."

He said that he had worked with Ziegfeld star Marilyn Miller for years, and her wig never fell off. Then he vigorously accused me of tampering with the wig. I adamantly insisted I had not done anything of the sort. I desperately wanted to counterattack: How would *you* like to wear heavy green glass pendant earrings attached with wires around your ears? How would *you* cope with the matching necklace sporting six rows of heavy, green dangling stones, the size of walnuts, that bounce up and down and smack you in the mouth each time you change direction? Would you fear for your teeth, as I had to, locking my lips closed in defense? How would *you* react if Gertrude Lawrence practically screamed from the wings, "The show is dying without me onstage! Play the music faster! *Faster!*" How would *you* fare, Mr. Short, on that elegant, black, highly polished linoleum floor wearing high-heeled shoes with slippery plastic soles, racing from side to side, sliding this way and that, in the dance that Nelson and I had designed to perform with great intensity in soft, flat sandals? . . . But no, instead I kept quiet throughout the reprimand. (Later, however, I recalled I actually had done a little trimming of the net at the hairline of the wig.)

Through it all, Nelson always remained carefree. In our dance, when we separated to opposite sides of the stage, he would call across to me, "Come on, Tiger Lily!" and as I came spinning under his arm before falling to the floor in a Graham back fall, he would catch me and whip me up, hissing the word "Savage" into my ear, gritting his teeth and doing birdcalls. I responded by making the secret sounds my brothers and I had used to signal where we were hiding in our underground tunnels crisscrossing the bracken at Mill Bay. I loved dancing with Nelson.

Movie star Victor Mature was Gertrude Lawrence's partner for the song "This Is New." As he entered the stage in his skintight white polo outfit, we could hear women in the audience gasp—especially at the matinee performances. Poor Victor. Gertrude danced circles around him, as if he were a bumbling good-natured sheepdog barking helplessly at a firefly. In a dreamlike scene, the female dancers were all identical reflections of Miss Lawrence. We wore red wigs and Hattie Carnegie lavender-colored chiffon gowns with sweet peas decorating brassiere-less breasts. Each girl danced with her partner, then one by one slipped offstage, leaving the men behind. Miss Lawrence danced ecstatically with each of the men in succession, performing a series of lifts that she clearly adored. The men surrounding Miss Lawrence throughout the show were constantly being upstaged by her. Gertrude Lawrence, with her flighty, glamorous, greedy, needy ways, dealt with the men clustered around her with total charm and fiendish skill. She was without mercy. One after another the men quit the show. The only exception was one man who had come from England. In accordance with Equity regulations, he was not permitted to quit and work again during that same year in the United States.

The shoes Miss Lawrence wore intrigued me. They appeared to be glass slippers but were actually made of clear plastic. I watched her endlessly. Her heels would hardly ever touch the floor. When she turned a door handle, or saw someone she liked, she rose up on her tiptoes. There was something about the way she used her feet that was extraordinarily sexy. With knees together, she would flip her skirt and raise one foot in back, like water splashing up from the ground. She was outrageously flirtatious. The audience was enchanted by her.

In rehearsal, Danny Kaye had always appeared submissive and bashful. He often came to me, appearing ever so modest and anxious to please, asking "How'm I doing? Am I doing all right?"

I tried to reassure him by saying, "You're doing just fine, Danny, just fine."

Having seen Danny perform at Tamiment and in *Straw Hat Revue*, I knew he was a showstopper. His odd behavior puzzled me. But everything came clear on opening night in Boston. Danny was onstage, playing the ringmaster in a circus scene. It was his responsibility to introduce Miss Lawrence after he completed his song. He astounded everyone, especially the critics, as he suddenly performed "Tchaikovsky" in a new and different way from the timid rendition he had rehearsed. This time, displaying his hypnotic sense of rhythm, he zestily belted out the lyrics, listing the names of countless Russian composers. His performance stopped the show! He repeatedly bowed, inviting the audience to applaud on and on.

Those of us who stood near him whispered at him, begging him to introduce Miss Lawrence's song, but he never did. When the applause finally died down completely, Miss Lawrence stalked forward like a lioness to sing her number, which began "Jennie made her mind up, when she was three." In rehearsal she had sung it in a refined and ladylike British style and accent. Suddenly she was transformed into a ball of fire. She began to sing with a cockney accent and laughingly borrowed every lowdown, earthy gesture ever used by any stripper, plus some new gestures of her own. She, too, stopped the show cold. The audience, as well as everyone onstage and in the wings, went mad with delight and gave her a massive ovation. Sensing the feeling of competition between the two stars was genuine, the audience screamed and stamped wildly as they applauded. Miss Lawrence bowed and bowed to the audience, then turned to Danny, putting her nose up in the air as if to say, "I can top you any time I choose! I am the star of this show."

Danny had understood from the first just how powerful Miss Lawrence was.

He also knew that once the critics had seen his performance and reviewed it as a high point in the show, she could not exert pressure to have his number cut. Danny's song most certainly would have been trimmed early on if he had not played his cards so cautiously and expertly. He had proven himself the one performer in the show almost as wily and self-protective as Gertrude Lawrence. Everyone benefited, however, in that the public came to see the fun as it developed into an ongoing feud between the two of them.

Before *Lady in the Dark* closed for the summer (supposedly to allow Gertrude Lawrence to rest and escape from the oppressive heat of New York City to her home on Cape Cod), Nelson was drafted into the army. When he left for basic training, I was devastated. Without him, I felt lost. The dancer who replaced Nelson was smaller and lighter in weight, and the lifts suddenly became agonizingly worrisome for me. Then one night, when Nelson was on leave, he secretly came into the theater, slipped on the costume for the circus scene, and unexpectedly came from behind to dance with me. It was heaven. How I had missed the spontaneous, shared fun and zest of dancing with him!

Lady in the Dark was a gorgeous show, and the management announced they were determined to keep it that way to the end. The cast was warned there were to be no closing-night high jinks.

"We intend to see that the last performance before summer break will be as perfect as the first," we were told. But if ever the dancers in any company felt the need to let off a little steam, we surely did. There had to be something we could do that anyone standing guard at the various exits could not see. And so—in the exquisite wedding scene, the dancers entered as always, like angels in yellow gowns, holding bouquets of white flowers. We stood throughout the scene, smiling gently and benignly. Then we exited single file, past the one blind spot where we could not be seen by management. We looked up at the singers, who were standing in back of us on a circular, raised platform, singing their hearts out for the last time, and one by one, we each smiled sweetly up at them, revealing blacked-out front teeth. As we left the stage, we glanced ever so modestly at the stage manager who had been posted there to catch us in any misbehavior. The startled singers on stage choked back their laughter and struggled to keep singing the beautiful Kurt Weill music.

When *Lady in the Dark* reopened in the fall, I was told my salary of forty-five dollars a week would be cut to the minimum of forty dollars. Miss Lawrence had requested what she called "a much deserved raise," and apparently we were all going to subsidize it. I refused to accept the offer, thus forgoing the pleasure of being in the biggest hit show on Broadway. But I have no regret.

At about this time, I came to know Gertrude Hoffman, an old-timer in show business who was still active on the fringes. Gertrude, who placed girls in night-club jobs, offered me work on the West Coast. Since I had not seen my family for so long, I accepted. At the last minute, Gertrude explained, "You know, you will be performing there bare-breasted."

Stunned, I responded, "I could never do that!"

She fought with me about it, reasoning "Why not? Are you ashamed? You have nothing to be ashamed about. You have beautiful breasts!" Modeling for a serious artist was one thing; dancing topless in a club was quite a different matter.

In response to a request by Agnes de Mille, I started teaching a Graham class in Gertrude Hoffman's studio. Everyone was curious about Martha's work, since she had never allowed outsiders into her studio. Agnes brought along her partner, the director Joseph Anthony. When I was insistent on trying to clarify the small details in the floor work that to me were crucially important, Agnes asked me to move on, suggesting that she would like to see the tilting falls, or the diagonal skip. Because I knew it was a lost cause to expect anyone to master the floor work when studying only once a week, and that it was much too late for Agnes or anyone else in the class to learn the really basic coordinations of Martha's work, I would reluctantly acquiesce. Meanwhile, Gertrude Hoffman was frantically signaling to me, "Don't let Agnes tell you what to do!" I found it very difficult to teach with Gertrude and Agnes pulling me first one way, then the other.

In September 1943, I auditioned for *One Touch of Venus*, to be directed by Elia Kazan. Agnes was to be the choreographer. Sono Osato had been engaged for the leading role, and a most exquisite dancer from the ballet world, Diana Adams, had already been selected by Agnes for an especially lovely part. When Agnes told me I would be Sono Osato's understudy, I was flattered, but apprehensive. To me, the exotic Oriental Russian ballerina was the epitome of femininity and sophistication. During rehearsal, Agnes asked me to show the dancers "the skip," and "the tilting fall" that I had tried to teach her in class. I reluctantly obliged, knowing Agnes would not use the movements as they had been intended but would change them. The thought of her altering these movements horrified me. Demonstrating them for her made me feel sick to my stomach. I hated myself for being such a pushover and decided I would have to quit.

Every time Agnes called a break in rehearsal, the dancers crowded around her, joking and telling stories. I felt very much left out of it. No opportunity presented itself for me to speak to Agnes privately. I waited miserably for a time when she would be alone. Finally, I followed Agnes to the bathroom and took the booth next to hers. I felt we had a kind of privacy there, and over the partition I abruptly said, "Agnes, I'm quitting."

As we parted, Agnes said, "You know, John Martin asked me to use you in the show. He will be very disappointed to hear you are leaving!" Over the years, Agnes asked me again and again, "Why did you quit *One Touch of Venus?*"

I finally bluntly explained. "Every time you asked me to show the Graham steps, you then proceeded to change them. I felt you ruined them. I was feeling nauseated all the time."

Agnes looked at me in amazement for a moment before stating, "I never knew you were such a purist!"

When word got out in December 1943 that Hollywood producer B. P. Schulberg was coming to New York City to realize his dream of putting on the show *Marianne*, we all understood why he had selected Helen Tamiris to be the choreographer. Helen was a bold, liberated young woman, who proudly announced her revolutionary political beliefs both onstage and off. When working as a choreographer in the WPA, she had lived up to her ideals and in the process astounded everyone by being one of the first choreographers to use themes of the black experience.

It was at the audition for *Marianne* that I got to know Helen personally. She greeted me enthusiastically, bubbling over with excitement about the work we were all going to be doing together. For *Marianne*, which dealt with a story set in France around the time of the French Revolution, Helen relished the idea of portraying scenes involving people gathering together to express rising feelings of dedication and hope. Her red curls bounced and rebounded all over the place as she spoke. Her sparkling eyes flashed with excitement, and when she fixed them on me, I was mesmerized. I felt like a captured butterfly, pinned to a wall.

Rehearsing in *Marianne* turned out to be a hopelessly depressing experience, however. Under B. P. Schulberg's direction, the cast was arranged in a series of tableaus. He placed us individually, composing groupings as if the camera would be doing all the moving. Apparently he could handle neither action nor transitions. We were frozen in positions. The mob scenes were static, without any energy. Company members became impatient. There was mumbling, followed by grumbling signs of frustration, culminating in chaos. Helen's dance interludes for the show were full of vigor and action, but it was all in vain. The show never made it to New York City.

I had seen Helen dance once in the 1930s on the stage of the old Mecca Temple, which later became the New York City Center. There were a number of different dancers on the program, but she was the one who stood out. It startled me to see a modern dancer jump so high, with such wonderfully taut, stretched knees and feet pointed so vigorously. Martha had always been disdainful about "dainty little pointed toes," but I liked the feeling of gusto and zest in Helen's performance. I was told afterward that Helen had been trained at the Metropolitan Opera Ballet School before going into modern dance.

I was definitely aware that Helen had never been, and never would be, accepted by the "Big Three" at Bennington—Doris Humphrey, Hanya Holm, and Martha Graham. I also knew that Helen had made an unsuccessful bid to join forces with them in 1930, and again in 1931. In those years she raised money to rent the Craig Theatre and invited a number of modern dancers, Martha and Doris among them, to participate in a group venture. With a touch of embarrassment, mixed with glee, Martha had described to me how Helen was outfoxed when it came to scheduling the order in which the dancers would appear on each of the various programs. Martha successfully managed to lay claim to some of the very best spots on the schedule.

Then I heard Helen's side of the story. She told me that she had found herself placed in the least desirable opening spot, the time when people were barely settling into their seats. I could not help but wonder how Helen ever thought she could in any way expect Martha Graham to behave in a generous, idealistic, unselfish manner. Helen was not *that* naive.

The first time I saw Jack Cole was on television, performing with the beautiful Kraft sisters as his partners. I knew he had been at Denishawn, and in

Charles Weidman's men's group, and that he had made a serious study of Hindu dance. The way he inventively set the oriental-flavored movement to jazz music was fascinating and utterly original. He possessed a fabulous sense of rhythm. Jack was the first choreographer to dance in sneakers to popular music. I had heard he demanded much of his dancers, and I wanted to be challenged. In late 1944, I learned that he had begun rehearsing *Allah Be Praised*. I told him I really wanted to work with him and pleaded to dance for him.

"The show has already been cast," he replied, "but if you want to dance in the chorus, you're welcome. It will be pretty innocuous, but that is all I can offer you." I gladly accepted.

Jack had a distinctly devilish look that was intriguing. He wore his hair combed forward and cut into a point on his forehead. When he choreographed, he demonstrated what he wanted. He leaned forward, with his haunches angled out sharply in back of him as if he were sitting in the air, like a satyr. He held his bent elbows close to his sides, shoulders forward and down. Strangest of all were his hands, which seemed completely relaxed, as they hung down limply from his wrists. The fireworks were in the speed with which he moved, accentuated by sudden stillnesses. With just his heels throbbing against the floor, he would slowly lower himself, torso slanting back, into an incomplete back fall, breathing out, out, out, as he went lower and lower.[5] Then suddenly he would take off at top speed, skidding about the stage. The movement patterns were exciting and very sensual. His feet moved or slid along the floor under him in a way that was always lateral. There was no elevation at all that I can remember.

Fiery Anita Alvarez was the lead dancer for *Allah Be Praised*. Only she, of all the dancers, could skid along the floor and rise up out of it while wearing her bowler hat tipped over her forehead, with the brim partially hiding her provocative little face.

Jack once said to me, "Anita is like salt and pepper. She adds flavor and taste to what I do. The rest of you are like sugar. Too sweet!"

In a satirical strip number, a takeoff on burlesque, Jack became frustrated because he couldn't get us to do the movement with the insinuating, snakelike bite he wanted. He had cast me in a top-hat tap-like dance, in which I was to be reckless and hoydenish, but he felt I was too delicate. One dance especially drove him almost mad. In it, we sat in imaginary saddles that swayed and rebounded as we went galloping around the stage constantly using small whips. As we rocked and readied ourselves for the gallop, Jack had us slap our thighs harder and harder (until they were badly bruised). He had us gallop faster, faster, and faster still. He was never satisfied. This dance reminded me of Martha's race-horse-theme dance, *Course*. Martha had believed "less is more," and we never actually slapped our thighs after the first rehearsal. Her gallop was a stylized triplet that skimmed the floor. Jack's gallop was a dupal rhythm that never got off the floor. If only Louis Horst had been there to teach Jack how to stylize and abstract movement patterns.

Jack became almost frenzied in his attempt to create a new American popular dance style; but he was not able to achieve the wild energy he sought. It was heartbreaking to watch his anguish mount as he worked. The dancers were filled with compassion for him. Most of us knew he had been taking "uppers" prescribed by a doctor. He had admitted to me privately that he was also using "downers" to try to get some rest at night. When the dancers heard that Jack had walked out the stage door and had gone directly to the railroad station to board a train for Hollywood, we were stunned, but in a way relieved. The dancers pulled all the loose ends together for him as best they could. *Allah Be Praised* opened in New York City at the Adelphi Theater to good reviews.

Seven

The
Limón
Trio,
1944–1946

IT WAS AN ANXIOUS time for everyone in the early 1940s, as young men all around us were called to serve in the army. One by one they disappeared, first to the training camps and then off to the European or the Pacific front. When word got out that José Limón had been inducted, there was much concern in the dance world. An important figure in the Humphrey-Weidman Company, José was acknowledged to be an outstanding American male dancer. The principal concern was that if José were sent overseas, it would be unlikely he could maintain the level of technical excellence he had worked so hard to achieve. This fear must surely have motivated both Doris Humphrey and José's wife, Pauline Lawrence Limón, to devise a way to create a pressing need for him to remain, at the very least, in the New York area. To firmly establish in the public eye a clear vision of both the performing and choreographic talents of José Limón, they immediately initiated plans to launch the Limón Trio as a showcase for José.

I had never actually spoken to Doris Humphrey, so I was taken completely by surprise when she appeared backstage in my dressing room, following a performance of *Allah Be Praised*.

"I have been following your career," she declared. Doris knew about all the shows I had been in, though I doubt she had seen any of them. It was common knowledge that she was no longer interested in show business.

"Haven't you had enough of the Broadway scene? Aren't you getting a little tired of what you see going on in show business?" she inquired, half-laughing and a bit sympathetic.

From the point of view of the choreographer, especially a serious artist such as Doris Humphrey, working in commercial theater could be a devastating experience. I was reminded how I had watched with horror as Agnes de Mille was verbally harassed by management, before finally being fired. In successive shows, it had always been painful for me to watch one choreographer after another being put through the wringer as they struggled with the many competing and conflicting interests of costumer, set designer, composer, arranger, stars, directors, and the producers who actually controlled space and time allotments.

Although I had felt sympathy for the choreographers, I could not quite bring myself to tell Doris I simply did not identify with their position. I was a dancer. Once a show opened, I put the stresses of the rehearsal period behind me and was blissfully happy onstage. When the music rose from the pit and the stage lit up, it became a magical world for me. Being in a Broadway show was like basking in sunshine. It meant dances that were often fun to do, at best in front of full houses. Onstage I could relax and feel free. Applause was a sure sign of approval. I had found a safe haven, protected by the proscenium. Me, tired of show business? Never!

"Don't you feel ready by now to come back to the world of concert dancing?" Doris pressed on. I had come to believe that modern dancers must not only dance but also be innovative, creative choreographers in tune with the times. Broadway was my refuge, far from the nightmarish challenges of the modern dance world. I turned my head ever so slightly from side to side, and Doris shook hers in mirrored response as if to say, "Unbelievable."

Then Doris smiled and her blue eyes widened as she said, "We were just wondering if you would like to dance with José."

"José?" I laughed in surprise. Who wouldn't want to dance with the handsome, noble-looking José Limón? Still, I wavered. It would be a big step for me to venture back to the concert field. I had not forgotten the agonizing, single Sunday concerts with Martha.

"We thought you might like to just try it," Doris continued. "Things would not be settled until you are really sure you want to do it, and we are sure it will work. Beatrice Seckler is already set to be the third member of a trio we are planning. Let's see if we all feel comfortable working together." I hesitantly agreed to give it a try, but I was still uncertain.

Doris turned to leave, and as an afterthought and perhaps a bit diffidently she said, "There is one other thing, by the way. You would be dancing with José, without Bea, in the army shows that he is obligated to do at various ports of embarkation in this area. I won't be having anything to do with these shows. The preparation will be completely up to you and José."

Doris looked openly relieved as I replied, "I am sure we can put something appropriate together. I have already performed in army shows with Gus Schirmer's troupe."

"Do you have an evening gown you could wear?"

"Yes," I nodded. "I have a beautiful, dark blue gown that was made for me by Irwin Corey's sister one summer at Tamiment. I wear it with long, red velvet gloves."

Doris seemed to be apologizing as she said, "You wouldn't mind doing these shows?" She could not possibly have guessed how much I welcomed the idea of entertaining the troops. Two of my brothers served in the armed forces. Jack was with the U.S. Air Force in the Pacific, and David had been a pilot in the RAF. David had been shot down over Germany in 1942, and we still were uncertain whether he was alive. The opportunity to dance for the soldiers sold me on the whole idea. David, my guiding light, would have been proud of me for making the time easier for the boys waiting to go overseas.

"One more thing," Doris said before leaving. "Although everyone who works with me takes classes at the Humphrey-Weidman Studio, it will not be necessary for you to do so. I know that you were very close to Martha. Perhaps you would feel uncomfortable studying Humphrey-Weidman technique." I was touched by Doris's sensitivity. I did go to the studio to watch a class, and though it looked as if it would be a lot of fun with its jazzy music, somehow I felt I couldn't do it. Class work was a serious matter to me. I continued taking ballet classes every day at the School of American Ballet. That did not seem disloyal to Martha.

Coming from a background with Martha Graham to dance for Doris Humphrey was like entering another world. I came to the first rehearsal feeling nervous. Beatrice and I waited around endlessly. I warmed up repeatedly. Beatrice was relaxed and at home with Doris's work patterns. I was feeling caged, wondering "What on earth am I doing in the Humphrey-Weidman studio?"

Then Doris asked me to come closer and explained slowly and deliberately, "The way I work is that I plan everything very carefully. I just cannot jump into things. Some people say that I am cold and analytical. Actually, I am desperately shy. I care very much about dance and dancers." At once the ice was broken. I, too, was painfully shy and cared deeply about dance. I felt a rapport with Doris, and relaxed completely.

We started working to a Vivaldi concerto. Doris and Pauline sat together by the piano. I could hear them quietly discussing the basic form of the dance. Beginning with the entrance, they planned out the development of each section of the work verbally. Sometimes José joined them, but mostly he was working on a theme for himself. Doris had the three of us get up and move quite freely in a circle, as Pauline played the opening theme on the piano. They decided that was not what they wanted, so we sat down. Doris tried and discarded a few other devices, such as having us come in side by side, or in a triangle with José leading, or in a line. Yes. They decided we should enter in a line, one behind the other. Then we each turned consecutively, making a sharp three-quarter turn left before sweeping diagonally downstage.

Doris looked at me and said, "That seems right to me. You know, the only thing more important than a good beginning is the ending. We must find just the right ending. I will have to think about that very carefully." Doris's approach, the idea of a dance being visualized and blocked out in advance, was something I had never before experienced.

Doris seemed to be mentally sketching out the entire dance on the floor—like an artist using charcoal to lightly block out shapes and proportions in a painting. With the skeleton of the dance in her mind, Doris proceeded to flesh it out with many tiny, tableau-like positions done at breakneck speed. Levels changed. Angles changed. Speed changed. Suspensions were added. The patterns were sharp and intricate. I felt jolted all about. She constantly tested and replaced the body designs, as if hunting for the right-shaped pieces to fit into a jigsaw puzzle. With a little verbal persuasion, Doris's designs gradually began to fit together beautifully to form a finished picture, framed seamlessly by the Vivaldi music.

Whereas Doris appeared to be most concerned with the structure of the music, Martha had almost always worked without music. Louis's influence had been strong that the music should evolve as accompaniment, accentuating, following, not initiating, the rhythmic patterns of the dance. Martha searched for actions that had a kind of passion, combined with a sense of inevitability about them. She was always looking for symbols of intense energy, and plumbing for deep, hidden levels of feeling. Martha extracted the content of human action and attempted to translate it into abstract form. There were no poses.

Doris's emphasis on clarity of position rather than on coordination and transition was startling to me. Martha had always planted a seed of each transitional movement pattern ahead of time, and the movement grew out of it organically. Doris left it for us to develop the transitions for ourselves, and I soon found I was adept at discovering ways to get from one position to another. One by one the strange shapes became more defined, and linked together like a series of action photographs, designed to be seen very clearly from the front. Doris's insistence that both the face and the design were to be directed to the front was astonishing to me. With Martha, we didn't face front much at all. Martha had been emphatic that the back or the side of the neck could be startlingly eloquent. When Martha choreographed, the thought that the audience was sitting in the fourth side of the square of the stage rarely entered my mind. I never had thought of her choreography as a design facing the front. To me, designs were still infinitesimal beads in a chain of movement, not moments of suspended motion. Martha had trained me to think of movement as something physical, connected with flow. She might segment a movement later and cut it off, but we always knew what flow of movement had been fragmented. Although people did not think of Martha's work as flowing, I certainly did. At first it was awfully hard for me to work as Doris did, but once I came to understand how Doris intended to marry the sounds and the designs, I found it exciting and tremendous fun.

One section of the Vivaldi was slow and sustained. Doris told me my special quality would be featured there. She had me perform very slow arched back bends, using the "ecstatic" body (as Martha termed it). José picked me up on one side of him, then lifted Beatrice on his other side, and turned us both around and around and up and down, like horses on a merry-go-round. José was certainly a strong partner. He always danced full-out. The dance culminated in a fast segment begun by Beatrice, who had extraordinary nervous energy, speed, and a sharp, angular way of moving. I thought of Beatrice as a Picasso-like figure, with alert eyes that looked all over the place at once. She would not do much in rehearsal, but Doris tolerated Beatrice's marking, knowing that in performance she would come alive.

This was in direct contrast to Martha, who had explained, "It is essential to establish the muscular memory that will stand you in good stead when the time of performance arrives. The mind sometimes goes blank under pressure."

One day when we were rehearsing the Vivaldi concerto Doris stopped everything and called me and José aside.

"I am afraid that we have a very serious problem," she said. "This trio is not going to work unless we can find a way to do something about the timing. José, you know the music. You can play it. You can hear it in your head, and feel it so deeply that you are inclined to anticipate it. You are coming down a little bit ahead of the music. Dorothy, you wait until you hear the music, and then you come down lovingly on it. That makes you a little late. Beatrice is always absolutely accurate. What we have now is a canon—first José, then Beatrice, followed by Dorothy. I find this absolutely intolerable. José, you will have to hold back, and Dorothy, you must anticipate! Unless you work in unison, we must give up."

From that day on I would look at José, and he would look at me. We did not smile or anything, but we did silently communicate. I was tremendously appreciative of Doris's tactful restraint in handling the situation. She had a clarity that enabled her to communicate a problem and point the way to solve it. There was no ego to block the way. Another choreographer probably would have done it differently, saying, "Dorothy, you are late again! José, you're anticipating!" And we all would have ended up hating one another. Doris had worked it out so that we danced as a unit. In performance, the audience would sense that we were not just rhythmically together, but truly together. I loved the Vivaldi concerto and was blissfully calm and secure dancing in it as the music swept us along. It was pure dance. So satisfying. I had never before had the experience of performing to classical music.

One evening as we waited for José to join us in the studio, Doris spoke about her favorite subject—the art of choreography. "Choreographing is a skill, not an accident. You have to learn to work according to a plan. The plan must be like a recipe that you, yourself, have honed and tested until you know precisely how it will come out. Creating a dance is similar to baking a cake, a perfect cake."

She said we must learn what ingredients would please and interest an audience for a "work." Martha's dances were not created as in a recipe or a formula. They grew in a silent, mysterious, sometimes agonized way—more like a birthing process. I never thought of Martha's dances as "works," although I often thought of them as works of art.

I wondered about the parallels between baking a cake and the creation of Doris's Vivaldi "work." I concluded that José provided the flour (the staff of life) as well as the egg yolk (the seed of life). There was no question that Beatrice was the baking powder that made the batter rise, bubble, and become as light as air. She also whipped the egg white into a froth of vivid energy. It is hard to be objective, but I would take a wild guess that I brought the sweetness—honey, brown sugar, or maybe maple syrup—along with a flavor, perhaps ginger. I loved ginger. I added a touch of softness, too, like partially melted butter. Doris was the master baker who blended and mixed our talents to create her distinguished "work." The icing for the cake was left to Pauline, who had a genius for costuming. The luxurious velvet costumes she designed for the Vivaldi added much to the courtly quality of the finished dance.

The second work was *Eden Tree*, loosely based on the characters of Adam, Eve, and Lilith. Doris began with what she called a "breakfast dance" where José and Beatrice played a nice married couple, called "the man" and "the wife." They performed a lyric, loving, comfortable duet together. I danced the part of Lilith.

I asked Doris "Who am I?"

"You can be a snake or the woman who persuaded the man to eat the apple. You have to decide for yourself," she said.

For my entrance, I was to come from behind a section of transparent green curtain that gave me the feeling of emerging either from deep in the forest or from underwater. I was to be seen, but not fully revealed. As I came forth from behind the curtain, I would be alone at center stage, then move straight forward toward the audience. I had decided that my Lilith would be a smoothly moving, but powerful, cobra.

Doris was extremely interested in stage designer Arch Lauterer's ideas on the impact of location on the stage. At Bennington, I had heard him present his theories, of which areas were the good places to be onstage, and which area was more or less powerful as far as the audience was concerned. He explained the meaning to the audience if one moved on a diagonal path, as against a path that went straight across the stage, or straight forward, or in a circle.

Doris said to me, "The best entrance anyone could ever have is straight forward from upstage center to the foot lights." As I saw that she was giving me the perfect entrance, I realized this was the same entrance Jerry Robbins had given me in "Hometown."

I was waiting to see what Doris would have me do for my entrance, when she asked, "What do you feel you should do here? What movements would you like to use as you come forward when you make this entrance?" No other choreographer had ever asked me what I wanted to do.

I replied rather shyly, "I feel I should walk slowly and smoothly."

"Yes," said Doris, "just come directly forward very slowly and move your arm some way to establish the character you are portraying." As I walked softly straight forward, I brought the back of my right hand up under my long hair, pushing it out and letting it fall slowly. I then carried my hand forward and out to the side in a sort of figure eight. With my forefinger, I drew a line up through the center of my body, pausing at and passing through each of the chakras described in Oriental religions, before extending the gesture to the audience, and finally down. I repeated this movement very deliberately twice more, as I pressed steadily forward. The curving pattern of my arm in the air had a weaving, hypnotic quality. This movement, combined with the direct gaze I had learned from Martha, made me feel as if the cobra in me was mesmerizing the audience.

"That's good!" said Doris, "Now, let's try it with the music." Pauline played the music for the entrance, and I attempted to adapt what I was doing to it.

"No! No! No!" Doris moaned, "You're not supposed to do that." I was startled. I did not understand why she was so upset.

"All the quality you had is gone," she explained. "You have lost the sensuous walk. Now it's like nothing at all. Just gesturing." Again I tried to do it, but I couldn't.

"Let's go back," said Doris, "and do it without the music. We must establish the rhythm of your walk and your gestures, and set on what count each step comes, and how the gestures fit in." Doris counted quietly for me as I moved.

She established for me where the accents in the arm patterns were, and how long each movement took.

"Now," she said. "Hang on to those counts and to the quality of what you are doing, and Pauline will play the music very quietly underneath it." Thus Doris set the movement *against* the music. It was a valuable lesson. She showed me that I did not have to fit into the musical pattern, as I had done with so many different choreographers on Broadway. For the first time I realized that I did not have to adapt myself, or be obedient, as if I were still a child. I felt powerful and in control, and I was profoundly grateful to her for valuing my innate talent. Doris gave me a sense of confidence and a feeling of stature I had never before experienced.

Once Doris was satisfied with the entrance of Lilith, we began to work on the snakelike seduction duet between Lilith and "the man." José was so solid, like a tremendous wooden fence that I could climb. I curled around his shoulders and slid this way and that down his torso. José could have been active, but he chose to be impassive, as he dutifully portrayed a dignified male figure. In the face of José's passivity, I felt strangely free. Unselfconsciously, I moved quite aggressively. I had the impression that he disliked his role and resented me. José never revealed his inner feelings in rehearsals with Doris, always remaining polite and professional; but I sensed he felt demeaned playing a less-than-heroic role and would certainly have preferred a more macho theme with Spanish qualities such as pride, or arrogance, or even cruelty.

For the third dance, Doris thought that an Americana finale might balance out the program. She suggested that José, Beatrice, and I each select a folk song we would like to dance to and bring it to the next rehearsal. Choosing a song was a problem for me. Luckily, I happened to be at a party where the guests included puppeteer Bil Baird and his wife, Cora. She and I had been students together at the Neighborhood Playhouse in 1930. Bil, an angel of a man, was informally singing and playing his guitar.

I plucked up my courage and asked him, "Do you know a folk song that might be appropriate for a dance for me?"

He thought about it and replied, "I know one that would be just right for you," and he played and sang "If I Had a Ribbon Bow."

I searched everywhere for the music and finally found it in a John Jacob Niles collection. It was spelled in the old English usage, "Ef I Had a Ribbon

Bow." The words and music were very appealing to me. Even though I was not from the rural hills of Kentucky, my background was such that I could very much identify with the unsophisticated country girl described in the lyrics.

This time at rehearsal when Doris asked me, "How would you like to start the dance?" I was ready for her.

"Perhaps I could begin sitting on a bench, dreaming about my true love," I suggested.

"What movements would you make," Doris asked.

"I could follow the lyrics of the song, and indicate a ribbon bow in my hair," I said, as I lifted both hands over my head and mimed tying a bow.

Doris shook her head, "What you are doing is out of the question. It is just too facile. You have to create the person in the song for the audience. This girl never even owned a ribbon. She would just put her hand up in a sort of crumpled-up fist, trying to imagine what it might be like to have a ribbon bow." Doris, who enjoyed experimenting with coordinating words, music, and movement, wanted each of us to speak the lyrics of our song as we moved. I started in a sort of singsong way, beginning the words with the music as the phrase began.

"No! No! It won't work like that," Doris insisted, "You must listen to the music, to the melody, to the way it soars, and time the words in a more natural way. Do not sustain the sounds or stretch out the words as a singer would." She made me understand that I had to let the melody go by, and then come rushing in with the words, almost at the end of the musical phrase.

As I spoke "*Ef* I had a ribbon bow to bind my hair," my upstretched arm came down, the hand not quite touching, but sort of feeling, toward the top of my head. Then when I brought my hand down and around my waist to make a sash, Doris pointed out that I was again doing too much. She edited out the excess. First there was the dream, then the realization that my hands were empty. I respected her judgment and took her suggestions without the slightest hesitation. For the repeat, Doris changed the tone completely simply by putting the emphasis not on "Ef" but on "I," and using the "Ef" as an upbeat. Thus it became "Ef *I* was like a city girl," and my voice and movements became stronger and more assertive, flirtatious and bold, brazenly rejecting a young man.

Then Doris had me come back to reality, and sink down onto the bench. The first melody was played very softly again. This time I did not say the words, but only let my hand almost do the ribbon and sash gestures. On "my own true love would think me fair," I crumpled over to the back to hide the fact that I was crying. The music was like a little echo. It must have been very poignant, because actually I was not pretending. Doris had helped me tap into the fact that I was still a simple country girl at heart, and I, too, had not had any pretty clothes when I was growing up.

"Ef I Had a Ribbon Bow" was only a small fragment of the finale in which each of us had a song. We had entered together, moving in a square-shaped formation. One after the other, we came forward to verbally introduce the character we would be portraying. I described how I came from the hills of Kentucky where the bluegrass grows. Beatrice told how cold it was where she lived, and José presented his character, Charlie Rutledge, a robust, happy-go-lucky cowboy. José did not enjoy speaking onstage.

After the introduction, I danced my song. José's section followed, and Beatrice's was last. José participated with Beatrice in the dialogue and asked her questions, such as "Where did you sleep last night, my own true love?" Beatrice's natural inclination for vibratory movement fitted in perfectly, with "I slept in the pines where the sun never shines, and I shivered in the cold, deadly cold." When she shivered, the whole audience would shiver with her and be swept up with laughter and compassion. After José and Beatrice were finished, I joined them onstage, wearing a long, wide, violet-colored grosgrain ribbon tied around the waist of my blue sailor dress. We did not anticipate how enthusiastic the audience would be to see that I had my fancy sash. It was a bright, cheerful climax for the program.

In the rush to accomplish her goal for José, Doris paid a great personal price. She was constantly being torn by the conflicting currents of trying to balance the urgent demands of José's career and the needs of her young son. Again and again, just as she was deeply involved in creating something, the phone would ring. Her son, at home alone, would be calling the studio and begging her to come home. Doris was also bearing the stress of knowing her husband was in danger from German submarines while serving as an officer on a transport in the Atlantic. She was also experiencing a great deal of physical pain because of severe arthritis. Doris worked under all these pressures without funding. One night she was near tears as she confided in me her desperate disappointment that she had been unable to arrange the kind of financial support being bestowed on Martha Graham.

With José's every available moment devoted to rehearsing with Doris for the Trio, it gradually became evident that there would be no time to work out the duet José and I were required to perform for the army shows. Whenever I asked José to schedule a rehearsal for the two of us, he would brush me aside saying, "Later. Later." He obviously found the whole idea of army shows an intolerable burden.

When we finally did get together at the last possible moment, he impatiently rejected every idea I offered for the dance. The beguine we hastily threw together turned out to be an embarrassing experience for me. Whenever I looked at the servicemen, I thought of David and Jack. I wanted to entertain the boys and hear them laugh and enjoy themselves. Instead, I felt ashamed of the meager, mechanical dancing José and I were doing. I began to dislike José for being so ungenerous and self-involved.

My relationship with José was always professional, but without any real rapport. With Doris, José had always been all attention. Her every word was treated with the utmost respect. He appeared to worship her. His behavior was courtly, brimming with Old World charm. When Doris was absent he was a different person, completely unreachable. He would go through the motions of seeming genuinely concerned about my well-being, often taking both of my hands in his and holding them tightly as he asked, "*How* are you?" Then again, "How *are* you? How are you *really*? Are you *well*?"

Each time I would reassure him, "I'm fine. Fine."

José's intensity was overwhelming, but I was never really sure if he honestly wanted to know how things were with me or not. We never had much conversation other than pleasantries about the weather and such. When we danced together in the Trio, it was different. We shared an intense love of movement, and this made it a pleasure to dance with him. Even though I felt that the beguine José and I were presenting was hopelessly dry and dull, I never challenged him. I was convinced nothing could be done, but I bitterly regretted the missed opportunity. I did not want to do anything to endanger my position in the Trio. Working with Doris was such a rewarding and extraordinary experience for me, I did my best to put the fiasco of the army shows out of my mind.

These army shows, which began in 1944, included a variety of comics and singers, plus José and me. The civilian performers traveled together in a special bus to the various installations, where José would meet me. There I changed into my blue sequined evening gown and long red gloves. It must have been hard for him to be paired with me dressed glamorously and colorfully, while he was required to perform in his drab army uniform. I always imagined that José saw himself as a danseur noble, or perhaps even Louis XIV of France costumed as the Sun God, lighting up the world with his golden rays. The stage was always set up with microphone wires lying all over the floor. When I asked José to have the wires removed for our duet, he shrugged, "It doesn't matter." But it mattered a great deal to me. How could I relax and dance well for the soldiers while I was watching out for the wires? José kept repeating, "It doesn't matter. They're all just waiting for Margie to come on."

The high point of the show was Margie Hart, a stripper who was not allowed to strip. She was gifted with the most extraordinarily large and beautifully shaped breasts. Margie was just naturally provocative and had us rocking with laughter as we watched her in action. Everyone knew that the rules forbade disrobing in the show; nevertheless, Margie wore her stripping costume. She came onstage and danced around a little, humming and laughing as the boys eagerly watched her closely. Soon her fingers would start to move a little over her costume, until they came in contact with one of the straight pins that held it all together. As she found the first pin, it just seemed to accidentally come undone. Her eyes would connect with one serviceman, then another.

She seemed to be innocently asking, "What should I do? Should I take a chance? Yes?" Then she would glance quickly into the wings to check, "Are *they* watching?" One pin and then another would just seem to slip out.

Then the fun would really begin as pins flew every which way, and strategically placed sections of her gown fell off. Margie's husband was the lieutenant in charge of the shows, and he was backstage yelling and laughing, "Don't do it, Margie! Don't do it!"

But his voice was soon completely drowned out by the cries from the boys out front. "Take it off! Take it off!"

Margie's husband would come rushing out just in the nick of time, to wrap her in the curtain, and sweep her offstage as she waved goodbye. Margie was just what the doctor ordered. The boys trooped out of the auditorium laughing happily.

One evening after a show, as we walked toward the bus waiting to take us back to the city, I could see a long line of servicemen loaded down with gear, marching silently in the darkness. Instantly I knew, this was the real thing. As I waved goodbye and blew kisses to the soldiers whose loved ones couldn't even know it was their time to go overseas, I felt like crying. Suddenly I heard a tremendous roar. I turned to see Margie standing behind me. Her feet were wide apart, and she was indicating in slow motion the most powerful, huge, crazy, lighthearted bumps that you could ever see. The sound of laughter and whistling spread from one end of the line to the other as the soldiers marched off into the night. They loved Margie, and she loved them. Margie, like me, was a country girl who had grown up on a farm; however, she was uninhibited, and I was not. Margie told me she would one day like to return to farm life and was sending all her money home to Papa to buy cattle for the family ranch.

Following one of the final army shows, I needed to check something out with José. I ran after him, calling, "José! José!" I could not catch up with him but thought I saw him enter a tent, and again I called his name. There was no response. I lifted the flap of the tent and peered inside. José was there with a young man. José turned on me in a towering rage, accusing me of spying on him and invading his privacy. I felt crushed that he thought I would intentionally intrude. Privacy was something I deeply respected. From that time on, José barely even glanced at me. Under his polite veneer of absolute courtesy, I sensed a burning hatred toward me, such as I had never before experienced.

The Trio performed in many areas of the United States, including Chicago and Eloch, Illinois, St. Louis, Missouri, Jacksonville, Florida, Trenton, New Jersey, Baltimore, Maryland, and New York City. Only when we performed in New York City did José, Bea, and I receive equal billing on the program. For the out-of-town engagements, we were the Limón Trio. José was credited as the choreographer. In his first, most favorable review in the *New York Times*, John Martin did not refer to us as the "Limón Trio," but rather as "a new trio." He listed our names equally and referred to us as "young artists of substance and vision." John also said, "Its [the new trio's] work was so impressive that it must be taken seriously into account in any estimate of the future of the dance hereabouts."

By January 1946, when we performed at the 92nd Street YM-YWHA in New York City, José had been mustered out of the army. It was a joyous time, with the world at peace. John Martin wrote superb, tremendously encouraging reviews of the Trio. He singled out for praise certain features of Bea's work and said "there should be more of Beatrice Seckler." Then, after referring to my "radiant performance" in "Ef I Had a Ribbon Bow," John suggested, "there should be more in this vein." Little was mentioned about José's dancing, but John did laud José's choreographic efforts, without realizing that the credit should rightly have gone to Doris. When I read the review, I knew it was not going to please José, and certainly not Pauline.

When I arrived at the next rehearsal, Doris barely greeted me. She appeared very upset. I had never seen her like this before. José and Pauline ignored me. Not a single word was spoken about John Martin's comments. I felt uneasy. Finally, Doris stopped working with José and took me aside. With great stress in her hushed voice, she stated that "someone" had criticized my duet with José in *Eden Tree* as being unforgivably cliché. In fact, John Martin had stated in his review that the duet was surprisingly *not* cliché. Doris then said that she would not be available to rework this duet. It would be up to José and me to change it so there would be no physical contact whatsoever between the man and Lilith. This meant it would be a completely different dance! José was nearby, listening. He reacted by hissing out his breath. I saw at once that the hostility I had felt for quite some time from José in regard to the army shows was now fully extended to me in the Trio. There was no question in my mind that we would never be able to re-choreograph this duet without Doris's presence and help.

The air was thick with feelings of animosity at the next rehearsal. Only Bea greeted me. Doris had already started on a new work, with José as the centerpiece. She was creating a dance certain to be the perfect vehicle for him, a major work to make him happy once again and give him an opportunity to show off his performing skills. Doris paused briefly from her work and silently handed typewritten copies of the poem "Lament for Ignácio Sanchez Mejias" by Federico García Lorca to Bea and to me.

"Just look it over," Doris said to us both.

The words "at five o'clock in the afternoon" were underlined each time they appeared on the copy that Bea was holding. On mine, there was a long, complex description of how death came to a bullfighter in the ring. I was not familiar with the poem, and I dreaded the thought that I would have to speak these words to an audience. Doris and José were struggling to discover a basic theme for him that would capture the feeling of the bullfighter described in the Lorca poem.

As I watched, I saw a side of José that I had not seen before. Hidden fury, anger, and resentment filled the stamping footwork patterns that established his character. This role would be perfect for him.

After a long time, Doris turned to Bea and said, "You will read the one line 'At five o'clock in the afternoon' every so often. Drone it out in an impersonal, flat, monotonous voice, like a church bell tolling at a funeral. Yours is the voice of fate."

Doris then turned to me, saying, "Your voice must project a building sense of drama, of tragedy. I want you to read your lines in a highly passionate and emotional manner."

I was already feeling so emotional I was clenching my teeth, trying desperately to maintain control of myself. With a mounting sense of horror, I read how the bullfighter was gored, and the way he died in the ring. When I came to the part about "gangrene coursing through his veins like a green trumpet," I struggled with a rising feeling of queasiness.

Doris kept calling out to me, almost hysterically, "Do it again! Louder! Louder! Stronger! More intensity! More feeling!" I was repulsed, but at Doris's command I shrieked, almost out of control, "GANGRENE COURSING THROUGH HIS VEINS LIKE A GREEN TRUMPET." I began to feel severely nauseous. Bea repeatedly recited her one line, punctuating my discourse on the death of the bullfighter.

At the close of rehearsal, all that Doris said to me was, "Your reading was not nearly powerful enough! You will have to work on getting much more emotion into your voice!"

I could see the handwriting on the wall. This was going to be a solo work for José. Bea and I would not be dancing. I suddenly realized that without the requirement of doing the army shows, José's need for me had ceased.

From the time of the formation of the trio, I had been aware that the always practical Pauline was a tiger where José was concerned. At times I felt Pauline was distinctly hostile toward me in a veiled, but malicious, sort of way. Because of the sudden change in Doris's attitude, I suspected that Pauline had won Doris over to her way of thinking. I was devastated. Working with Doris had been a revelation. She was the supreme coach, devoted to dance. She worked unstintingly. I had trusted her absolutely. Under her skillful guidance I had gained confidence and stature, both as a performer and as a person.

I had been so happy in the Limón Trio, that I was blind to the fact that, in their haste to create an entertaining and successful program to showcase José, the result was not appropriate for him. The only exception was the Vivaldi, which had been built around him, and in which he felt comfortable. Ironically, the three roles Doris had created for me all suited and pleased me immensely. After all the trivial, lighthearted dancing of show business, I found the powerful dancing in the Vivaldi totally rewarding. Doris recognized both my strengths and my weaknesses, and she dealt objectively and constructively with them. She had done everything in her power to help me in a truly professional manner. Working for her had been a joy, and I had bloomed under her care. I had rarely felt as secure or as satisfied with the way I was performing as I did when I was in the Limón Trio. Doris may have been a little too successful with me.

At the next rehearsal I told Doris quite simply that I was leaving the Trio to go back into show business. I had the perfect excuse. Jerry Robbins had come backstage after a performance of the Trio in the Humphrey-Weidman studio theater. He could not have been warmer as he complimented me on my work and asked if I would like to take over Sono Osato's role in *On the Town*, since she was considering leaving the show. Even though Jerry had assured me he would change the choreography to suit me, I hesitated to accept. I still could not forget the satire he had done of me at Tamiment that had shattered my self-image. Nevertheless, I used Jerry's invitation as my reason for resigning and babbled on a bit to Doris about furthering "my career."

In truth, I never had a shred of ambition and actually had no intention of accepting Jerry's offer. Doris did not protest. She did not so much as say "give us time to make adjustments." I suspect she was relieved. If it had been presented to me that José needed material that suited him, I would have spoken the Lorca poem, because I did love to speak on stage. As Doris and I talked, José and Pauline were standing together at the far end of the studio. Pauline was facing me, glaring at me with cold, dark eyes. I shuddered. I was reminded of the time at Martha's summer home in Silvermine, Connecticut, where the two huge black snakes were curled around each other at the well, heads raised threateningly, eyes glistening. I felt I was being shut out with no word of explanation. Their hostility was the reason I resigned.

The Limón Trio had toured for a period of two years, whenever José had a furlough. The fact that the Trio came off so successfully, with such a high level of professionalism, was no accident. It was a kind of miracle. The planning and all-consuming passion on the part of Doris and Pauline was supported by determination and almost superhuman drive on the part of José. Everything had depended on his being able to get off the army post and come into the city for rehearsal. He came whenever he could in the evening, and we worked far into the night. It was a grueling schedule for him. He must have been made of iron to do it.

José brought in the themes for his solos, and Doris worked with him very sternly. He was deeply musical, as was Doris. She was the perfect coach for him. In training José to be a choreographer, Doris molded, shaped, and developed the phrases and patterns, while pulling the dances out of him. Doris was a giving person, who willingly and unselfishly subordinated herself to enhance his reputation and to elevate him to the more important positions of choreographer and company director. In actuality, it was Doris who filled both roles. She unequivocally was the root of the experience.

In speculating on who may have suggested me as a possible third member of the Limón Trio, something tells me that it most likely was John Martin. Only he would propose the idea that a dyed-in-the-wool Graham dancer like me be taken into the Humphrey-Weidman fold. As the first dance critic on the *New York Times*, John had created a niche for himself, encouraging, helping, guiding many of the modern dancers—even scolding them at times. He had told me he was devoted to Doris Humphrey. He also stated that the modern dance world needed a strong male dancer. John Martin had an overview that no one else had at that time, and it would have been like him to envision that I might be just what the Limón Trio needed. I was well known to the public, having already appeared in six Broadway shows. I was considered a glamour girl and had been covered in *Pic* magazine with an article devoted to my feet, of all things. "The most beautiful feet in New York," they claimed. An alluring four-page spread in *Look* magazine also had added to my status, especially when John Martin was quoted as saying I was "the most naturally beautiful dancer in New York City." If indeed John did suggest me, how ironic it would be that his glowing reviews may have contributed to the circumstances that led to my leaving the Limón Trio.[1]

Eight

The School of
American Ballet
and the
Broadway Scene,
1945–1948

BEGINNING IN THE mid-1940s, quite a number of Martha Graham dancers could be found in ballet classes at the School of American Ballet on Madison Avenue. We felt very comfortable studying with our friend, Muriel Stuart; however, the teacher I most adored was Anatole Oboukoff. He gave us unusually beautiful adagios, many from the classical repertory in which he had performed. I especially loved the way he covered space when he demonstrated pas de basque. Like many others, I developed a deep affection for him in spite of his rather sour manner. If anyone said to him, "Good Morning. How are you feeling today?" he would mutter in guttural tones, as if clearing his throat, "Awful. Awful."

But I could sometimes detect a slight twinkle in his eyes. At the start of class, he would usually walk past the long line of dancers at the barre, correcting hand positions, wrists, elbows, heads, and necks, all the time murmuring to himself,

"Awful. Awful." One day he stopped next to Anna Sokolow. His hands went up, and his voice rose higher and higher until it echoed through the school as he shouted "Awful! Awful!" He stormed out of the studio. When he returned to class with the school administrator, Miss Ouroussow, in tow, he pointed to Anna's feet. They were bare. Anna's feet were rather large in relation to her tiny frame, and they were not pretty. Anna was asked to put on her ballet shoes or leave the classroom. Mr. Oboukoff recovered his sense of equilibrium and continued to teach the class. From then on, the modern dancers in his class always made certain to wear ballet shoes.

It might have been Muriel Stuart who recommended that I teach the weekly Plastique classes, which were intended to prepare the students to work with modern choreographers. I did not wear the traditional ballet attire when teaching, but instead wore the stunning white turtleneck leotard and wraparound skirt that Pauline Limón had made for me when I was with the Limón Trio. I think it was Pauline's costume design that sparked a trend in dance wear.

In the Plastique class, I tried to energize the lovely, rather delicate little creatures and to introduce the concepts involved in contraction and release. It was immediately clear that what I was doing was not merely foreign, but indeed abhorrent to them. I decided to try an experiment that Martha had once used so successfully in Seattle. I asked the students to sit on the floor, legs to one side, take in a huge breath, and then shout out the word "No!" loudly, clearly, percussively. They certainly were not shouters. I was so intent on explaining the importance of the shouting as a litmus test to check themselves in moving on a breath, that I had not seen Mr. Balanchine enter the studio. As I demonstrated once again how they were to expel the breath while shouting "No!" the students were staring, but not at me. They were looking wide-eyed at Mr. Balanchine, silently beseeching him to rescue them from this dreadful situation.

He made his presence known, sniffed a couple of times, then leaned down and whispered in my ear, "Couldn't you teach them to say 'yes'?"

I replied instantly, without thinking, "I teach them to say 'no,' Mr. Balanchine. *You* teach them to say 'yes'." He laughed, and I laughed, and he smiled at the class as he exited. For a moment I entertained the thought of explaining to him how with Martha we had explored the rhythms in sobbing and laughing, but then I remembered him saying once, "It is really quite the same in dance if you are sad whether the cow kicked over the milk bucket or if your grandmother just died. It's only a matter of degree. The appropriate response for both would be to cover your face with your hands."

Mr. Balanchine came into the studio again when I was teaching a one-sided skip that flew diagonally across the studio. I was trying to get the students to dig down into the floor and thrust themselves pell-mell forward, covering a lot of ground on each step. I urged them to skid along the floor with arms beating down, then flying out.

Afterward Mr. Balanchine asked, "Why don't you vary the skip once you have taught it to them?"

I looked at him in astonishment. I would never think of changing it! "How do you mean—vary it?" I questioned.

"You could bend the arm that swings forward, or you could turn the head the other way," he suggested.

I flinched. How could I turn my head the other way when the whole focus was to press out over the audience with the chin and forehead looking directly at them over the shoulder? A straight arm, flung out in front marked the line of the momentum forward. How could I change that?

Mr. Balanchine persisted, "Think in terms of a glass of iced coffee, rich and dark. Pour cream into it, and you will see it becoming all creamy and soft. If you take the cream out, it will become dark and rich once again. You can vary the skip, and then put it back again the way it was."

I was overwhelmed by his readiness to share the enormous creativity that sprang out of him. Although I could see he was right, I felt that the skip belonged exclusively to Martha, and only she could change it. Nevertheless, I appreciated his attempt to help me unlock the obedient attitude toward Martha that I still clung to.

At Mr. Balanchine's request, Miss Ouroussow extended an invitation to me to feel free to attend as many classes as I could at no charge. I gratefully and ecstatically accepted this generous offer. From then on, I attended two or three classes a day and also observed classes for the advanced students and distinguished guests. It was quite a sight seeing the beautiful Tamara Toumonova in class. Her mother was there watching, boldly complimenting and applauding her daughter as if she were the only one dancing.

Sometimes we would be in the classroom at the barre when Mr. Balanchine would quietly enter and proceed to teach the class himself. This did not happen often, but each time was a memorable experience in that he clarified basic concepts in the most illuminating way. One day he walked down the barre, making small corrections as we did tendu battement.

He shook his head when he reached me and murmured, "Turnout." Then he said, "Elastic," and made a stretching motion with his hands, "about four inches long." He dropped down toward the floor and touched the inside of the heel of my working foot and said again, "Elastic." He gently pulled the imaginary elastic on my heel to bring the leg forward until only the tip of the toe remained on the floor for a perfectly turned-out position. Then he deftly moved the imaginary elastic to the little toe of the same foot and pulled it through first position to point in back, holding the turnout from the hipline to the tip of the toe. He repeated the process to be sure I understood, saying, "Always the elastic pulls." Not only did this image create turnout, it also gave me a pleasurable sense of perfect alignment that I would never lose.

Another day Mr. Balanchine said to me, "Port de bras," as he took my hand lightly and shook it, to loosen the hand and separate each finger. He repeatedly tapped the tip of my thumb and middle finger together to demonstrate correct alignment of the hand and fingers, then he guided my hand through a figure-eight motion several times and said, "Seagull."

Using his two hands, he suggested the head of a seagull by locking his thumbs together, and closing the other fingers to create the feeling of feathered wings. He spread the feathers wide and demonstrated how seagulls glide on air currents. He separated his hands, and with fingers closed and thumb in line with the middle finger his hands floated like birds as his arms moved forward, opened to the side, and came down, until middle fingertips touched in low fifth position. His fingers opened slightly, thumb again aligned with middle finger, to create the desired perfect curve extending through the arm, wrist, and delicately narrow hand.

It was such an honor when Miss Ouroussow informed me, "Mr. Balanchine feels you are a born teacher. He wants you to teach a beginners' ballet class for children."

Miss Ouroussow commented dryly that some of the students were already quite adept at technique. "They will get bored," she said. "It's the fragile, little, plain Janes who develop slowly, that we watch." I was surprised by this, but in time I saw that it was true. Students that Mr. Balanchine watched over were nourished secretly, and they developed in the most extraordinary way, like orchids or other rare and exquisite plants.

Although I had performed extensively, I had not had a career in the ballet world. It did not take long for me to recognize that I would never be really accepted by the teaching staff. Each instructor at the school had their own individual way of teaching. For example, the great *ballerina assoluta* from Russia, Alexandra Danilova, taught pas de basque in a rebounding, aerial way, with arms opening high above her head. Pierre Vladimiroff, who had partnered Anna Pavlova, taught it emphasizing ronde de jambe on the floor with a rather elaborate port de bras. I was greatly in awe of them both. When they opened the door to the studio where I was instructing beginners and stood there audibly criticizing my having chosen to teach pas de basque with a deep forward surge in the manner of Mr. Oboukoff, I felt painfully inhibited about my own teaching.

Lincoln Kirstein requested that I arrange a simple dance sequence using the young students for a semiprofessional production of a historic pageant to be presented in New Jersey. He also assigned me to select and rent the needed costumes from Brooks Brothers. For the run-through, we traveled to New Jersey. There we were dismayed to find that the costumes I had rented did not fit. Tanaquil LeClerq, who was very young at the time, was upset that I had not ordered tights and toe shoes for her. The director kept brushing aside my polite requests for stage time. I was utterly unable to assert myself and insist on breaking into the rehearsal so that the students could leave. We waited endlessly. The director never got around to us. Parents and students were angry. Coping with the unstructured situation, and being responsible for caring for the children on the train and in the theater, was just too much for me. The whole episode turned out to be an embarrassing fiasco. I knew I had let everyone down, especially Lincoln Kirstein.

The ultimate pleasure for me at the School of American Ballet lay in being granted permission to watch Mr. Balanchine choreograph. He used images the way Martha had used them in Seattle, to color and transform movements into new and original patterns, and to communicate action. When Tanaquil LeClerq was rehearsing a leaping combination in a circle, he suggested she think of a baseball diamond rather than a circle, and slide each time into bases. There was no static landing, just gliding through the air, skidding into and out of each base. With this image in mind, she skimmed along the floor. Three girls were standing in back and to one side of Tanaquil, mechanically going from pose to pose in a simple port de bras.

Mr. Balanchine gently explained to them, "Weeping willow branch, a breath of air will lift it gently. Breeze subsides, branch sinks softly to the other side. Breeze comes again, lifting gently up, then passes." The images he gave were fragile, like Haiku poems. Only the truly talented dancers retained the exquisite delicacy and clarity of the image. He was like Martha in that they both thought and talked imaginatively in unpressured, hushed tones. There was no sense of haste with him. He laid the groundwork for what he envisioned, and then it would evolve over time, seeming to grow by itself.

Ruthanna Boris, dancing in *Concerto barocco*, first opened my eyes to Mr. Balanchine's exquisite sensitivity to music. As a visual person, I saw the movement patterns first, then heard the music. With Ruthanna, it was as if the sound of music were made visible. Ruthanna's artistic interpretation of the choreography was a heavenly introduction to the idea of shapes and sounds moving in space together. Mr. Balanchine came to my rescue musically when I was preparing a solo to *Bachianas brasileiras no. 5* by Heitor Villa-Lobos, sung by Bidu Sayo.

Anna Sokolow had suggested that the theme for my dance be a legend she had heard while traveling in Mexico. Anna had seen a huge rock with a carved hollow in it and was told the story: that in ancient times a young girl was chosen to participate in a worship ceremony. At the end of the ritual, she would cut out her own heart and pour her blood into the hollow in the stone. Anna blocked out the floor plan for me, beginning with an entrance through the forest. I was to say farewell to every bird, flower, and small creature. I constantly stopped, changed focus, and incorporated everything I could remember ever having seen in the forest as a child. I easily filled the form of the music, made it come alive, and found myself endlessly inventing in response to the heartfelt vocalization supported by eight throbbing cellos; but I was distressed that, without a score, I was unable to count or analyze the music.

I asked Mr. Balanchine what I should do. He watched me perform, then he encouraged me to move instinctively in response to the music. "Don't worry. Just count to yourself 'one, one, one, one, and so on.' Follow the melody, and go with it. It will become clear to you."

As I danced, I associated the movements with changes in the beautiful sound of Bidu Sayo's voice as it poured out of her. I flowed with the sounds, suspended and hung onto the sounds, then rushed by them to stop suddenly. Although I knew that Louis would not have approved, I was happy with this solution. It worked. At Mr. Balanchine's suggestion, I attended a Dalcroze class for ballet dancers from the school taught by John Coleman.

Late in the summer of 1945, my former partner Nelson Barclift called to announce, happily, "I am back from the Pacific, and I have been mustered out of the army. To top it all, I have been engaged to do the choreography for a big Broadway show."

I was stunned. Nelson, who had always been so happy-go-lucky, was taking on a huge responsibility. I listened in disbelief as he continued, "This is going to be a very important show. Orson Welles is the director, and Cole Porter is doing the music. The name of the show will be *Around the World in 80 Days*. Will you help me?"

I was tremendously impressed, but distinctly frightened for him. How could Nelson undertake this huge task so lightheartedly? "Of course," I replied, "I'll help you if I can."

I went with Nelson to watch an audition. Orson Welles was there, wearing a cape and high-button boots, and carrying a cane. He was a powerhouse in the way he operated. I was fascinated, but at the same time horrified, to hear him making disparaging remarks to the people auditioning. He was utterly lacking in courtesy as he high-handedly rejected aspirants. In fact, he was downright heartless.

At the first rehearsal, Orson entered the hall and called out in that powerful, magnificent voice, "Rise and shine." Everyone shivered with excitement. Orson was not just intensely purposeful, as Martha had been. He was a tornado. Early on, Orson set out to create the atmosphere of Egypt by suggesting a sense of climate with sounds and smells. He gave everyone stage business to do: to enter laughing, quarreling, chasing each other, fighting, begging, crying, stealing. He gave them sounds to make and pointedly told performers, "*You* are thieves. *You* are beggars." He enumerated endless cues, for example, "As this occurs, you do that. After. . . . When. . . . In between. . . . While so-and-so does this, you move there."

The stage throbbed with life, heat, color, action, and many evocative sounds he made himself. Everyone went through the action, related to one another, followed the floor patterns, changed levels of sound, said their lines as if they had been mesmerized.

"*Cut!*" Orson then commanded. "Now repeat the scene from the very beginning!"

No one could remember anything of what it was they were supposed to do, not even when or where to enter. With everyone depending on cues that would never come, they could not re-create what had been done before. The cast had been spellbound! Everything that Orson had set was gone—evaporated into thin air. All that remained was an agonizing sense of anxiety and indecision.

Orson proceeded to verbally demolish the cast. Like a monstrously peevish little boy who liked to do terrible things, he took lines of dialogue and action away from some performers and gave them to others. He took the role of Meerahlah away from a young dancer and announced that he wanted me to dance it. She was distraught.

I felt painfully embarrassed and protested to Orson, "I am not right for the part. Why don't you hire a professional belly dancer to do the role?"

"No! No!" he bellowed. "That would be boring and much too obvious. I want you to do it. That is what we call counter-casting."

I simply could not bring myself to refuse Orson. I took on the part of Meerahlah, feeling secure that Nelson would not ask me to do anything inappropriate.

Before the opening in Boston, Orson worked alone with the stagehands in the huge opera house. He had just finished making the movie *The Third Man*, and now he wanted to realize his dream of incorporating radio and movie techniques into a stage show. There would be no slow curtains or lighting changes for him. He had five stage areas with curtains that fell precipitously. He was working feverishly with props and lightning-fast scene changes to create the impression of traveling around the world. Cities moved across the stage on a treadmill, at breakneck speed. To simulate the passage of a train over the mountains, Orson had scenic film projected on the backdrop. He employed a toy model train to appear to cross a suspension bridge, which then collapsed, causing a mock train wreck. Orson loved such startling theatrical effects and had countless surprises planned for the show. Eventually Orson had to use his own money to pay for additional time to coordinate all this. We heard there were six freight-car loads of special effects in Boston that were never even unloaded, apparently because there was no room for them backstage in the Boston Opera House.

While Orson worked in the theater, we all remained at the hotel, waiting impatiently to be called. It was days before we were finally permitted to enter the theater. At that point, there was nothing Nelson could do about adjusting spacing on that vast stage. Orson was insolent, inconsiderate, and gave him no time on stage. Nelson finally gave up and left, leaving me in charge.

The main character, Phileas Fogg, was played by Arthur Margetson. The character I played was to cause Phileas Fogg to lose a wager by detaining him in his race to encircle the globe in eighty days. Orson stopped rehearsal to show me himself exactly what delaying tactic he wanted from me.

"None of that abstract Martha Graham stuff!" he warned.

Then he demonstrated the demonically suggestive hip-swinging movements he had in mind for me, accompanying himself with, "Oom-tiddy, oom-tiddy, oom-tiddy, CRASH!" I nodded coolly and marked it carefully—left, right, left, pull to the right, and crash to the left. In performance I looked straight out at the audience with a fixed level gaze as I meticulously swung my hips in the required "S" curve. On the pull to the right, I aimed with the bow and arrow precision we had worked on in Martha's class. My gaze shifted to Phileas Fogg for the crash, and as our eyes met, I let go. My aim was perfect. Right on the mark.

His monocle fell, then very politely he would say, "No, thank you!" We got a huge laugh. But Orson wasn't pleased. He handed me a small prop chair made of plywood and commanded me to hold it in my mouth by one leg, and balance it straight up in the air. I experimented with it, once, and got a mouthful of splinters. As I spat them out, I handed the chair back to him, saying coldly "I can't do it, and I won't!" Orson bowed in defeat, but that would not be the end of it.

The feverish pace of staging had been anticipated, but because the costumes had arrived too late for dress rehearsal, the dancers were completely unprepared for the hectic costume changes. The first scene took place in London, where the dancing girls wore corsets, bustles, bonnets, and high laced-up boots. There was simply no time to remove this elaborate attire and dress for the desert scene. I alone was ready, waiting in the wings on opening night, when the cue came for the desert scene to commence.

"Where are the other dancers?" Orson demanded. Then he promptly shoved me onto the immense stage and hissed, "Get out there and improvise!"

With great presence, the orchestra leader had someone quietly extemporize on the drums. I moved back and forth across the stage, making figure eights with my arms and wrists, with memories of Ruth St. Denis vaguely in my mind. All the while, my eyes were glued to the exit. I silently begged to be allowed to get offstage. Orson was glaring at me from the wings. I moved rather timidly toward the exit.

"Get back out there and *do* something," Orson commanded. "*Anything!*" (I did not rise to the occasion and grasp this golden opportunity as I could have.)

Orson never missed out on an opportunity to be in the spotlight. He incorporated his own magic act into the show, appearing on stage in a cape and turban. There were many props, including boxes containing rabbits and doves. He began to show his bag of tricks on opening night in Boston, but each time he opened one of the boxes, they were empty. Nothing worked. If the necessary prop was not incorporated into Orson's cape, it wasn't there. Enraged, he stormed offstage, shouting at the stagehands and the person in charge of props.

The reply was, "Oh, we thought you'd already done that scene and we put everything away." The stagehands had been so abused by him, they sabotaged his act.

On opening night, stagehands were frequently caught placing props or removing them when the lights came on. They were invariably embarrassed and would exit the stage awkwardly. As the curtain came down abruptly, it hit one of the stagehands on the head. One critic wrote that the stagehands had made more appearances than anyone in the cast, and had gotten more laughs.

Immediately before the next matinee, Orson told me to call the dancers onstage. In a martyred tone of voice he announced, "The show is *dying* while I am offstage, especially during the dance in Egypt." Hadn't he noticed that we had been getting a very good hand at the end of that dance?

"*You*," and he pointed to me, "are going to have to cut forty-five seconds from the dance." With that, he produced a stopwatch and made us run through the dance.

Then he stopped us abruptly. "I have already arranged with the orchestra leader to cut the next forty-five seconds from the music commencing at this point." We ran through the movements for the forty-five seconds in question, and he stopped us again.

"At precisely this point you will pick up the dance and continue to the end. This change is effective immediately! The matinee is about to begin."

"But Orson," I protested, "we must at least have time to figure out how to get to the places where we will have to be when the music picks up."

All the dancers rallied around me in support, but Orson categorically refused. He called out "Curtain!" and the performance began. When the cut came, the dancers were dashing madly to where they had to be, some even crashing into one another. It was insane.

Afterward, I begged Orson for a rehearsal, but he flatly refused and stalked off into the audience in his costume in the midst of the performance. I followed him in my costume, reasoning to myself, "If he can do it, I can do it too!" Again I begged for a rehearsal. He roughly and adamantly refused. I gave up.

Working with Orson was like being in a battle zone. Constant crises occurred in the show. The girl who was to be cut in half in the magic act was paralyzed with fear. The musicians in the pit cringed as Orson performed his sword-throwing stunt, hurling swords in all directions. One night out of town, Arthur Margetson was lifted off the top of the elephant in the hunting scene, and he was left hanging, forgotten, up in the wings. He had to be rescued and taken to the hospital in an ambulance. We thought he had had a heart attack.

In Arthur's absence, Orson happily took the opportunity to step into his role. First he made a little speech to the audience explaining who *he* was, and who it was that he was replacing. He stated that he did not know the lines, or the entrances or exits. The audience was enchanted with him and his majestic voice. We in the cast were captivated too. A few days later, Arthur Margetson returned to the show, just at the time a young male singer had to drop out because he had the flu. Orson cheerfully stepped into the newly vacant role and explained to the audience that, since he could not sing, he would call upon the nearest chorus boy to sing for him. The audience was charmed, as if hypnotized by him.

Mary McDonald, a marvelously rhythmic dancer with whom I had worked in *Allah Be Praised*, came backstage to visit me. She was then appearing in *Charlie's Aunt*, starring Ray Bolger. I was impressed with her description of how Ray Bolger often remained in the theater after the show to work on ways to capture any slight serendipitous accident that had occurred in performance and incorporate it into the action. She told me how his performance was full of tiny jewels that grew ever more polished all the time, to the delight of the audience. I wished that Orson could have been like that. If only he could have valued his tremendous gifts and not squandered them as he did.

When Orson suddenly and unexpectedly closed the show, we all stood in line with him onstage as he made a final speech, in which he said, "Actors die a little every time the asbestos curtain comes down at the closing of a show."

We all knew this was true, as we stood there with tears streaming down our cheeks. But were the tears in recognition of the tragic, hideous waste of all that talent? or was it just such a relief that the nightmarish ordeal was finally over?

In the winter of 1946, shortly after the end of *Around the World in 80 Days*, I was offered a small part as the wife of one of the main characters in the musical *Park Avenue*. Our choreographer was Eugene Loring, who had worked previously in Ballet Caravan for Mr. Balanchine and had created a number of original ballets, including *Billy the Kid*. He came to rehearsal totally prepared, even having floor plans marked on the floor. Whereas other choreographers used dancers like puppets to work out the dances, he had the movements thought out in advance. I liked and respected his quiet, deliberate way of working. For this play, he told us, we were to behave always in an elegant manner, because much of the action took place on Park Avenue or in the drawing room of an estate in Southampton, Long Island. Specifically, we were not to touch the furniture.

Eugene hired the accomplished Matt Mattox, who was very strong in jazz as well as in ballet, and crafted a beautiful duet for the two of us. It was not at all a dance of seduction, like the duet I had done with José in *Eden Tree*, but rather we were equal partners. Set to blues, it was very elastic; we pulled apart and flew back together. Eugene choreographed an exciting rhumba for another couple, but as far as the rest of the show was concerned, he was at a loss. He said he felt uncomfortable and hated "happy dancing."

In total frustration, Eugene confided in me. "They won't let me move any of that elegant furniture," he said, "and there is no room on the stage for the dancers."

When we were out of town, Eugene gave his notice. I was terribly disappointed; I hated to see him go. Arthur Schwartz, the show's composer, invited me to lunch and asked if I would take over as choreographer. "Oh, no!" I replied, "If Eugene can't handle it, I certainly can't."

Arthur prodded me, "Don't you know anybody else? Haven't you worked for anyone who is bright, positive and sophisticated?"

I thought to myself, "Jerry Robbins has already turned the job down. Who else could possibly do it?" I hesitantly suggested, "Helen Tamiris is bright and positive, but she's not exactly sophisticated."

Helen was summoned immediately, and I was delegated to assist her. Whereas Eugene had waved his hands vaguely in the air saying, "I hate happy dancing," Helen announced that she hated "*sad* dancing" as she waved *her* hands vaguely in the air.

"I like vigorous, happy dancing," Helen announced. "I want you all to stand with your feet wide apart, and wave and shimmer your hand vigorously."

Actually, Helen seemed desperately lost without Daniel Nagrin to assist her. I tried to help, whispering suggestions just to get the dancers moving: chassé, run high, run low, spin, perform simple steps from square dancing, and devices from Balanchine like winding in and out under the arms. Before long, Helen had the dancers jumping all over the furniture and falling on the floor. No one attempted to stop her. No one could stop her.

"This is bright, vigorous dancing!" she exclaimed, as she sat close to George Kaufman, trying to dazzle him with her bright blue eyes. "See that! See how she comes through under his arm? Isn't that marvelous? See how they gallop around in a circle? Isn't that great?" She went on and on, trying to sell it all to George Kaufman as "wonderful," and he seemed to be buying it. It drove me wild to see her showing off these elementary devices, which I had half-laughingly thrown out to her. I felt embarrassed I had recommended her.

Helen had taken a sudden, violent dislike to one of the female vocalists and was ruthlessly critical and sarcastic in her comments, to the point of being brutal. The poor girl left the stage sobbing and begging for someone to call her boyfriend, a well-known comic, to come and take her back to New York City. She was hysterical and even went so far as to try to roll herself up in an old rug on the floor in the wings. I was standing behind Helen watching this pathetic scene, and my heart went out to that rather inexperienced young singer.

When Helen turned and saw me with a couple of sympathetic tears running down my cheeks, she was livid. The next day, Helen staged a new scene in which I was to direct a wedding rehearsal, showing everyone where they would stand. Throughout the scene, I would never turn to face the audience. Then she took away my lovely costume in muted shades of brown, orange, and copper, which had been designed specifically for me, and replaced it with a bright red dress with a cutout midriff, which had been made for someone with a gorgeous, slim figure. I felt uncomfortable in that dress.

Only one dance choreographed by Eugene remained in the show. It consisted of graceful, gliding, leaping, figure eights in the half-light around the girl and boy singers, as they sang to each other. Betty Lowe and I danced it, costumed in white shirts embellished with a hint of silver, paired with grey skirts. I felt we created a feeling of shimmering moonlight surrounding the lovers. When Helen decided Betty and I should wear oxblood-colored shirts for the dance, it ruined the mood. That was the last straw. I protested.

Helen shot back that I had a star complex and screamed, "Dorothy just wants to stand in the middle of the stage in a white fur coat like a Hollywood celebrity."

It so happened that I did own a white fur coat, which Mother had bought for me at a thrift shop in Victoria. I had kept it in a box because it was out of fashion and shedding terribly. The coat was long, flared at the bottom, and so large it wrapped all around me. At a run-through in New York City the next day, I donned that coat for the bridesmaid scene in which I would never turn to face front. I performed the scene perfectly. George Kaufman and all the others who had heard Helen blasting me the day before were sitting out front. They laughed so hard, tears streamed down their faces.

Once the show opened in New York City, we all settled down to enjoy the run. The star, English actress Leonara Corbett, was generous and likable. She set the tone for the show and everything ran smoothly. It was like a show should be, a sunshine place. One evening, someone told me Bobby Alton was out front.

He had come to visit the girl with the stunning figure, whose red dress had been given to me. The next day, that girl told me Bobby had commented that I had become a very good performer. I was thrilled and remembered what fun it had been working with him. He was the only dance director I had known who had a real sense of humor about what he was doing. How I wished that I had thought of him to replace Eugene as choreographer.

The short run of *Park Avenue* on Broadway was not nearly long enough to make me forget the nightmarish rehearsal period. This, combined with the unpleasant experience of *Around the World in 80 Days*, led me to question if I would ever again want to submit to the indignities of another Broadway show.

An opportunity to leave New York City for a time presented itself when Ernie Glucksman came backstage to see me following a revival of *Picket Line Priscilla* in 1947. I had never forgotten how kind he had been to me at the Berkshire Country Club nearly ten years earlier. Now Ernie was the social director at Green Mansions, a summer resort in the Adirondack Mountains of New York. I knew one of the owners of Green Mansions, Lena Garlen, whom I had first met in 1939. At that time Lena had invited me to perform there. I had already been offered a job for the summer at Tamiment, however, and she withdrew her invitation.

"It would be unethical for me to take someone away from Max Liebman," she had said. I never forgot that incident, and I held Lena in high esteem because of it.

Ernie explained to me that he was working to implement a festival of the arts at Green Mansions for the summer season. It would include singers from the New York City Opera, and concert dancers under the direction of Doris Humphrey. He invited me to participate as both a dancer and a choreographer. I was interested in his offer, but, although I implicitly respected and trusted Doris, I was still shaken by what I perceived as having been exploited by José when I was in the Limón Trio. I asked Ernie to check with Doris, how she would feel about working with me again. It wasn't long before Doris informed Ernie it would be fine with her, and I eagerly signed a contract for $500 for the ten-week summer period.

This was an especially timely opportunity for me, because my marriage to

Jeremy had reached a crisis. He had recently said to me, "We have to talk." Whereupon he sat me down and patiently explained, "Dorothy, you are a schizophrenic."

Then he handed me a slip of paper with the definition of schizophrenia written on it, just as he had copied it from a dictionary. I read the words, and I knew that term was not true of me. I listened in disbelief as he pledged to care for me and support me for the rest of my life. I was stunned. Dismayed. Frightened. In response, I told him that I had just been offered a job for the summer at Green Mansions and felt I should accept it and take that time to think things through.

Rehearsals with Doris began in New York City. When I saw how difficult it had become for her to get around because of the pain of her arthritis, my heart went out to her, but regretfully I was unable to get beyond the professional relationship and express my feelings. Doris prepared *Shakers*, her beautifully crafted dramatic masterpiece of choreography, for presentation on the Thursday night concert program at Green Mansions. The basic theme of *Shakers* was "shaking out the sin" and required constant, vigorous shaking of the hands, combined with a bouncing and rebounding walk. Mark Ryder, from Martha Graham's company, played the role of the minister exhorting us to rid ourselves of sin by shaking it out ever more forcefully. To move in this way constantly jarred my breasts. Whenever Doris focused her attention elsewhere in the studio, I clutched my breasts with my hands to support them; otherwise, I stoically bore the discomfort as best I could. Martha had once attempted to create a special brassiere for me, but she had not been successful.

Just before Decoration Day, we all traveled by train to Green Mansions to prepare for the big holiday weekend. Ernie Glucksman surprised us by announcing at least one of us was expected to perform the following night in the variety show. No one was prepared. I hastily put together a solo I called *Mirage*, set to a recording of harmonica music. In the dance I lay flat on my stomach, facing the audience, arms wide on the floor of the stage. I flung my legs this way and that as if waves were washing me to and fro. I rose and rode the waves, then sank down and melted into the surface of the ocean. That night at dinner, I was served a slice of cake with "Beautiful Mirage" written in icing. At least the baker had liked it.

I had hoped that Doris would pair me with Mark Ryder, but she didn't. She assigned as my partner Herbert Ross, a tall dancer who had been in Broadway shows.¹ I thought he was rather elegant. He reminded me of the character Anna Sokolow called "the Renoir man" in the French movie *Grande Illusion*. Happily, he turned out to be a joy as a partner. Herbie and I discovered we had a lot in common. We both had been in many shows and had danced for Agnes de Mille. Throughout the summer Herbie took over some of the choreographic tasks I had been hired to do. He contributed many openings and closings for the Saturday night revues, as well as complete dances (including a hornpipe). Herbie, though he was young, had the taste and poise required to do the job. In the competitive atmosphere of Green Mansions, I found him unthreatening and welcomed his efforts.

For the Thursday night dance concert, Doris again rehearsed us in *Shakers*. Then she worked on a square dance theme, but she was not satisfied and gave up on it. Doris directed a satiric Charleston, in which Bea Seckler exhibited her very real talent for comedy.

Deep in the Forest—my version of the Mexican legend set to music by Heitor Villa-Lobos, *Bachianas brasileiras no. 5*—was presented as part of the first concert. The stage was dark, lit only by pools of light, similar to the designs Jean Rosenthal had used for Martha. I costumed myself in a long, tobacco-colored jersey dress, decorated with a huge vine that I had picked from Lena Garlen's porch. The vine was entwined around one shoulder, across my torso, and cascaded diagonally down the skirt. In performance, after bidding goodbye to one imaginary forest creature after another, there was a silence during which I rose from the ground, sank and rose again, trembling, my hands tracing out the form of antlers in the air. As the music became fiercely compelling, I felt driven to the final deadly act. I drew back. I was unready, yet I found myself dragged forward. I ran away but was obliged to begin again. When the music became ecstatic, I arched up into a circular back fall, spinning on the floor, rising and falling again and again. Finally I gathered myself together and walked forward quietly toward the audience. With the tips of my fingers tracing the area of my heart I cut upward, through my center, took out my heart, and offered it in sacrifice to the audience. My head went up and my leg raised in a high side extension as the curtain fell. There was an absolute blast of applause. At that moment I felt as if the audience encompassed me, and we were one. I just wished Anna Sokolow could have been there to see how wonderfully the basic structure she had mapped out for me had come together.

In addition to performing in the Thursday night concerts, the dancers were expected to do a staggering amount of work for the Saturday night revues and the Monday night variety shows. We choreographed opening numbers, finales, and dances for songs. Rehearsals ran from 9:00 A.M. until lunch and resumed again from 1:00 until 6:00 P.M. On nights when we did not perform at Green Mansions, some of us would be asked to entertain at neighboring resorts. Although I worked long hours, I never tired. I felt endlessly fulfilled. I loved it.

Very late at night when the stage was clear, I worked alone on a new solo for the concert program. It was inspired by the movie *Man of Aran*, which had moved me deeply. Again I chose music by Villa-Lobos. I had in mind to dance the feelings of a woman, who, while walking quietly on a beach, comes upon the wreck of a storm-torn fishing vessel. It was well after working hours when I explained to Jerry Henchke, the man in charge of sets, that I needed the suggestion of a wrecked sailboat.

"It has to be a wreck?" he asked.

"Yes," I replied.

Jerry, who was always kind and helpful to me, pulled out a high platform that someone might have used for making speeches. Then he pushed a narrow ramp up against the platform, so that it slanted steeply down to the floor like a runway. The element I was most concerned about was the rigging. Jerry found a thick rope like the ones used to tie up ferries, and hung it high in the wings above the platform. The rope hung in a long curve, neither loose, nor taut, and he fastened the end firmly to the floor not far from the base of the ramp. When he brought out a tall, narrow flight of steps that led up to the high platform, I saw that my set was complete. He adjusted the rope to allow me to swing far out, yet keep my feet locked on the ramp. In this magical world I spun down that rope a million times—turning, twisting, falling out into space—then somehow wrenching myself back to recover center, before falling out into another direction, as if swept overboard. This reckless battle with waves and wind was movement I had never before explored. I frequently lost all sense of time, and missed the last jitney back to the quarters where the social staff lived. I slept in the costume room, under the area where the guests danced far into the night. The pounding over my head would have kept the average person awake, but not me.

Each evening before he left work, Jerry set up the stage for me. One night Doris came to see what I was doing. She sat at the rear of the dark theater for a while, then came down front and asked, "What are you going to call your dance?"

"The Rope Dance," I said simply.

"I think you should call it 'Woman by the Sea,'" she stated, "and you'll do it in the Thursday night concert."

Doris was walking out of the theater slowly, painfully, when she paused and struck me speechless. She said, "Do you know, Dorothy, I think you work harder than any other dancer I have ever known."

Woman by the Sea was beautifully lit at the concert, and it came off powerfully. It was a proud moment for me, a personal triumph that could only have been accomplished in the protective environment of Green Mansions, for an audience that I felt cared about me. I did not expect to dance it elsewhere.

One day, Ernie announced that a special guest was on his way from Hollywood to perform at Green Mansions. "His name is Paul Villard, and he is taking a six-week leave of absence from MGM, where he is being groomed for stardom."

Then Ernie looked at me and stated, "Dorothy, you will surely recognize him."

We were rehearsing in the theater when Paul Villard walked in. Ernie was right. I did not remember his name, but I had never forgotten that strikingly handsome young man who had sung and played the accordion for the guests rocking on the porch after dinner at the Berkshire Country Club way back in the summer of 1938. I recalled that I had refused to date him then. In the intervening years, he had become a big success. As I stared at him, I noticed that the dark curls on top of his head were gone, and his scalp was sunburned and peeling. He no longer seemed quite so alarmingly self-confident. In fact, he appeared a little sad. I don't know just why, but I went up to him and gave him a hug as I said hello. I surprised myself. It was unusual for me to be so demonstrative.

After I had finished dancing at that night's performance, I dressed and went out front, curious to see Paul Villard's act. Ernie was treating Paul like a star, providing him with a powerful microphone, and a pin spot that picked up Paul's white merchant seaman's cap and the jewels on his accordion. Cream-color curtains were arranged to create an intimate frame, a cameo, in front of a backdrop of black velvet. Paul took all the time in the world before beginning, first pushing his cap back, then tipping it down over his eyes. He opened and closed his accordion, played a few notes, then adjusted the straps as he looked the audience over, checking to see if they were all paying attention. One more adjustment of the cap, and finally he began with an original song. He sang songs and recited poems about life on the sea. He had an ear for melody, effectively lingering before ending very softly and precisely. After his closing song, "So Long, It's Been Good to Know You," he went offstage to huge applause and calls of "More! More!" When he reappeared without his accordion, the audience accepted that he was finished. The staff singers were bewildered, saying they could not understand how he so charmed the audience. I understood. Paul was a natural; he was not just a singer, he was a born entertainer.

I went backstage to compliment him, and he laughed at me. Then he asked, "Would you like to go for a soda?"

I nodded. When he said, "Right! Let's go," I thought he meant just the two of us. But he didn't.

I found myself squeezed in next to him in the front seat of his red convertible, along with half the staff performers, all sitting on top of one other. It reminded me of the joy rides with my brothers, Mums, and The Skipper. I impulsively slipped my hand around Paul's wrist as he drove, just as The Skipper had linked my small hand around his wrist so long ago.

After performances, members of the social staff would go to the canteen and sit at one of the long tables. Lena Garlen was often there, and whereas I was very much aware that she was an owner of the resort, to Paul she was like family. She warmly agreed to Paul's request that I eat with him in the main dining room with the guests. I looked forward eagerly to the delicious meals with endless choices, wonderful fresh fruits, salads, and unbelievable desserts that had not been available in the staff dining room.

Green Mansions had provided an exquisite haven for me, but all too soon the summer ended. I had gone there thinking of it as a trial separation from my husband. Spending the summer with people from show business, and being out-of-doors, had allowed me to regain some of my self-esteem and spontaneity. Now I was sure I could not go back to playing the stifling role of the chic—but silent—wife of a successful advertising man. As the time approached to face the real world in the city, I dreaded the inevitable confrontation with Jeremy.

Ruthanna Boris came to my rescue, referring me to her lawyer. It meant a great deal to me when my brother Windham came to New York at this time when I really needed him. Together we had lunch with Jeremy, who promised me seventy-five dollars a week and volunteered to stage the necessary "scene" to enable me to get the divorce. Jeremy found an apartment for me at Madison Avenue and Fifty-fourth Street, conveniently within walking distance of the theater district, Pilates Gym, and the School of American Ballet, where I continued to study and to teach children.[2]

Anna Sokolow called me one morning to say that she had been chosen to teach a class in Movement for the Theatre for Elia Kazan at the Actors Studio. Mr. Kazan had asked Anna to invite me to join his class. I knew the Actors Studio was going to be very special. It was a privilege to be invited to participate in this first session, and I gratefully accepted. There were actually two classes. Bobbie Lewis was teaching a group in which Marlon Brando was a student. The work in Mr. Kazan's group was riveting. Outside the studio, it was different. After hearing Mr. Kazan boldly claim, "There is no woman I cannot have," I felt his maleness was akin to that of a satyr or a minotaur. I had never before known a man in whom I sensed such undisguised, raw sexuality, with no hint of sensitivity, tenderness, or gentleness. He presented himself as cold as ice—all ambition and ruthlessness.

During the spring semester, Elia Kazan had to leave temporarily to accept an Oscar in California. He arranged for Hollywood director Martin Ritt to come east to teach the class. Mr. Ritt was a large, enthusiastic man, who presented the work very differently. In a scene from *Golden Boy*, which involved a young fighter who had studied the violin as a boy, Kazan had dismissed a particular student's interpretation of the role, saying "It was his mother who had hoped and dreamed her son would play the violin. His one obsession is to have both the money and the power to buy what he wants—women, luxuries."

Mr. Ritt saw the same scene acted by the same young actor, and he observed that the violin may have been his mother's dream for him, but then again, perhaps he really loved music and still harbored a secret longing to become a concert violinist. In that case, the fighter would have had a conflict about using his hands as a weapon. Mr. Ritt insisted, "*You* have to decide how you are going to play the scene. It is crucially important that *you* decide this for yourself."

When Mr. Ritt called upon the students to perform an "action," the words were not important. We could recite a nursery rhyme or even gibberish while doing it. "Mary Had a Little Lamb" had been used over and over by the time Mr. Ritt called on me. I took a chance and used the words from "Ribbon Bow." He let me get as far as "Ef I had a ribbon bow to bind my hair; ef I had a fancy sash, my own true love would think me fair."

Then he stopped me cold. "What you are showing us is your *reaction*, not an *action!*" He explained, "You have to have a plan of action in your mind. What are you going to do? Tease? Attack? Flirt? Flaunt yourself? What floor pattern would you use for your plan of action? At what speed? What could you do with the ribbon?"

He suggested possible floor patterns: S-curves, zigzags, rushes. The possibility for action was there in the song, but I had seen it as dreaming. Now I saw that this was what Martha had meant when she spoke of using action words—verbs and adverbs—and altogether eliminating nouns and adjectives. A few days later I performed at a folk song festival at the Brooklyn Academy of Music, and the insight Mr. Ritt had given me worked. My voice was clearly heard by people sitting in the last balcony. I was no longer dreaming. I felt indebted to Martin Ritt for having given me the key to unlock my strong projection.

When MGM did not renew Paul's contract, he returned to New York City to perform at Le Ruben Bleu. He invited me to meet him at the Wellington Hotel where he was staying and then go out for dinner. I soon discovered that, just as at Green Mansions, dinner invitations included not only me, but many others.

Conversation at the restaurant usually continued until closing time, after which we often went to Pearlie Adler's apartment. Pearlie and her sister Lulla, granddaughters of the great Jewish actor Jacob P. Adler, were known as "the turtle doves." Pearlie called me "angel eyes." Paul had been bewitched by their aunt, Stella Adler, when he was a teenager and she was a guest at the Blue Bird Inn in Lakewood, New Jersey, at a time when Paul's mother ran the inn. Paul recalled sitting on the stairs of the porch, watching in awe as Stella talked, laughed, and shared confidences with his mother. Stella had grown up as the "golden girl" in her father Jacob P. Adler's Yiddish theater company.

Stella and her husband, Harold Clurman (director, writer, critic, and leading initiator of the Group Theatre), were each in their own way dazzling conversationalists. Harold's rapier wit was delivered with the utmost grace, punctuated by a slight stutter. Stella was very daring and would not be outdone. Her brother, Luther Adler, held us spellbound as he described the desperate times of the pogroms in St. Petersburg. Jacob Adler had fled Russia in 1883, when he was twenty-six, and miraculously had made his way across Europe through the fires of persecution. This feat had required bold, resourceful, and sometimes unbelievably reckless, creative measures, which Luther narrated in vivid terms. Stella, Harold, Luther, Pearlie, and Lulla were all consummate storytellers. They told tales of their beloved Odessa, which Lulla claimed was a magical city from which had sprung the source of all their color, warmth, and grace. They all loved to hear these familiar stories repeated.

The stage, it seemed to me, was not the center of the Adlers' lives. The stories were the core. These stories had been told over and over in this close-knit, courageous family whose emotions were wide open. Nothing was hidden. To be with them was a warm, wonderful experience, like sitting near a bonfire on the beach. As gusts of laughter crackled like flames, my frozen heart showed signs of melting. The Adlers were filled with love for one another, with an overflow for others as well. Pearlie and other well-meaning friends privately cautioned me that, like the Adlers, Paul too had fallen in and out of love many times. This demonstration of open caring was new to me.

A new door opened for me at the School of American Ballet when Mr. Balanchine invited me to teach a very special class of young boys, some of whom were children of dancers. I felt honored, and I welcomed this opportunity, but I did express anxiety at the prospect. Mr. Balanchine told me not to worry, explaining that he wanted me to teach only the most basic elements. My specific task was to teach these potential danseurs how to stand with dignity, walk with presence, run freely, and make simple gestures with energy and a sense of authority. Of course, I could do all those things well, because that was exactly what Martha had taught me to do. Mr. Balanchine proceeded to show me very specifically how I was to present the barre work. Pliés and tendus were to be done facing the barre always. That was how he had been trained for the first year, and he said it would "set them straight." He wanted me to repeat each step only four times and showed me how fast (actually, how slowly) and how carefully each move should be executed. I was also permitted to teach glissade and pas de chat. Mr. Balanchine was adamant about what I was not to teach. There were to be no complex steps, no turns, no beats, and absolutely no tricks!

In class, there was no question about it. The boys did not want to face the barre. Perhaps they felt as I had when I was small and had been forced to stand in the corner and face the wall as punishment. They did not like to move slowly. They wanted desperately to gallop about the room, compete, and learn tricks to show off to their friends. It was not an easy class for me to teach, but I tried my best to follow Mr. Balanchine's directives. I kept the boys on a tight leash, but there was no joy in it for any of us under the restrictions imposed upon me. Mr. Balanchine had always been gentle, sensitive, and helpful toward me, but I was much too shy to approach him and tell him how hard I was struggling with the class, and that I felt the boys needed a male teacher.

Elise Reiman and I often talked together in the waiting area outside the office at the School of American Ballet. Elise had studied with Adolph Bolm and had performed extensively. She jokingly told me her one big claim to fame was that her exquisitely slim legs and beautiful pointe work had resulted in her doubling for Loretta Young's legs and feet in a movie. Elise and I laughed a lot, mostly at ourselves. Mr. Balanchine was clearly fond of her, and when he would catch sight of us, he would join us. On one occasion I was wearing a stylish suit from Bergdorf Goodman. It was made of a soft black wool, and the jacket had an attached shoulder-length cape. Mr. Balanchine turned me around to see how it was designed.

"Hmmm," he smiled. "I see we have a black angel with us here today." He told me he was preparing a small group piece for a benefit at the Waldorf Astoria, and he asked if I would like to play the "white angel." He said he was going to be the "black angel." The movements Mr. Balanchine had me do for this event were quite simple, but I found the music terribly complex. I was amazed and impressed by the young dancers who were so at home with the music, readily picking up their cues. How different this was from training with Martha Graham where we had learned to move to counts.

Si-Lan Chen was also attending class at the School of American Ballet, and she talked me into sharing a concert again with her. This time it would be at the 92nd Street YM-YWHA. I had dances ready. There was *Sicilienne et Rigaudon*, which I had first presented at Tamiment and later in the Limón Trio, as well as *Deep in the Forest*, and *Woman by the Sea*, both of which had gone so well at Green Mansions. I would complete my section of the program with a suite of three folk songs, "Whistle, Daughter, Whistle," "Horses Ain't Hungry," and "Ef I Had a Ribbon Bow." I had written to Doris requesting permission to use "Ribbon Bow," but by performance time I had not yet heard from her.

Just before I was to go onstage to perform, I was told I had an urgent telephone call from Doris Humphrey. It rattled me terribly to be hearing from her at the very last minute. Was she going to say no? As I anxiously ran to answer the phone in the foyer, I was shocked to see Anatole Oboukoff sleeping on a couch. Someone said he had been there for an hour.

I picked up the telephone and with great relief heard Doris say, "Yes, of course you can use 'Ribbon Bow.' It's yours."

I ran backstage in time to hear someone excitedly call out, "Mr. Balanchine is here!" The cool, assertive Si-Lan Chen had given tickets to Mr. Oboukoff and Mr. Balanchine. Embarrassed, I tightened up. As if all this were not nerve-racking enough, the Victrola backstage overheated and buzzed loudly, ruining the Villa-Lobos music for *Woman by the Sea*.

Afterward, I was told that Mr. Balanchine left during the first intermission, following my *Sicilienne and Rigaudon* and the disastrous *Woman by the Sea*. The second half of my program went adequately, but I was devastated. Without purpose, I had gone through the motions of one dance after the other. All rapport with the audience was gone. Instead of concentrating on the dances, I was consumed with, "What are the people in the audience thinking of me?"

Paul was there with his friends. Looking at what I was doing through their eyes, I could see only the minuses, none of the pluses. My skills as a performer, my sense of security, my focus out across the footlights, evaporated. For the first time, I became painfully self-conscious on the stage.

The next day, feeling heartsick, I went to class at the School of American Ballet prepared to face that word "awful." Mr. Oboukoff never even mentioned to me that he had been at the concert. Mr. Balanchine, however, was warm and said he liked the "Rigaudon." He generously offered constructive suggestions on how to make the footwork more complex and faster. He did not mention *Woman by the Sea*, and I was too ashamed to say anything. I knew I had been gifted with talent and abundant stamina, but I lacked the necessary fiercely indomitable spirit of Martha or Agnes or Anna. The demoralizing outcome of the concert, combined with my recent disheartening experiences in show business, convinced me that neither the concert dance world nor Broadway was for me. Then came Anna Sokolow's phone call.

"I will be choreographing a show based on *The Legend of Sleepy Hollow*, and I am counting on you to be in it. You're the perfect country girl. You'll fit right into the setting of *Sleepy Hollow* just as you did in *Everywhere I Roam*." With Anna at the helm, I felt sure that things would be different this time. I trusted Anna. I had absolute confidence in her. She had never let me down. I said "Yes."

Then I approached Miss Ouroussow about being out of town with the show.

"You do know," she said, "that you will have to decide which you would rather do. Perform or teach. You cannot be on the staff here unless you are present consistently. This is essential with the children's classes."

I liked and respected Miss Ouroussow so much, and of course I understood her position. Feeling morbidly depressed and desperately embarrassed about the outcome of the concert, I foolishly gave up a treasured opportunity at the School of American Ballet. I fled toward the sunshine of the footlights and the world of make-believe, without even a word of explanation or appreciation to Mr. Balanchine. I just could not face him.

Anna selected Edward Starbuck, a dancer from the Ballet Russe, as my partner. His appearance was startling. He resembled a Greek god, with hair that looked sculpted, arranged in small, tight curls all over his head. His blue-gray eyes were exceptionally large. He stared wide-eyed like a blind man, revealing not a flicker of pleasure or rapport. At first I was extremely shy with him, because I realized it was not easy for him to be dancing for a modern choreographer like Anna, and working with a modern dancer as a partner. He was professional, but impersonal. I saw this lack of interest as a challenge and was almost obsessed with the need to make contact with my new partner.

Anna had called a Sunday rehearsal. I rather think that dancers of my era rarely knew what day it was. But since this was Sunday, I questioned my partner just as we danced apart, "What did you have for breakfast this morning?" As we came back together again, I inquired, "Lox and bagels?" At the next opportunity, I asked, "Bialy and cream cheese?" Then, "Kippered herring?" Lo and behold, the next time we came together, he smiled!

From then on, I racked my brain to come up with delicacies I had heard of, but never even tasted—frog's legs, squid, pigs' knuckles. Even a hint of a smile was enough for me. Ultimately, he accepted me, and I think he even enjoyed dancing with me. Being partnered by a soloist from the world of ballet was a big challenge, and I was grateful to Anna for having made this experience possible.

Anna choreographed a dream sequence around Gil Lamb, the tall thin leading man who played the role of Ichabod Crane. As the curtain opened, Ichabod was asleep in a huge old-fashioned bed. He was wearing a long nightshirt and a nightcap. I was hiding under his bed. I wore a white starched camisole, and a starched and ruffled white petticoat with lace trimming. I rolled out from under the bed, and I reached up one bare leg insistently wiggling first my toes, and then my whole foot airily in a figure-eight pattern. Ichabod's head came up, and his knees too. He seemed wide awake. I quickly found my way up onto the bed and sat up on his knees. It was my role to introduce him to the characters in his dream—Indians, Quakers, and the stern minister Cotton Mather. I danced with them, and Ichabod joined us, cutting a very humorous figure. The reviews of the show in Boston were mixed, but they singled out this lively scene as a high point.

Rumors began to circulate that a distinguished director was being brought in to sharpen things up. The stage manager, Ben Kranz, and I had worked together in *Everywhere I Roam*. We were both onstage when who should come strolling in, carrying a long cigarette in a slender cigarette holder, but Marc Connelly, our new director. Ben and I looked at each other with alarm. We put our arms around each other's shoulders as we moaned, "No! Oh, no! It can't be true! This is the end, the absolute end of this show."

Anna must have gotten the message earlier and had disappeared. (Directors and choreographers always seemed to feel perfectly free to leave a show whenever it suited them.) This time I, too, desperately wanted to leave. The dancers in the company warned me not to resign before the opening. Chorus Equity rules required giving two weeks' notice. Failure to do so would mean expulsion from the union. I still wish I had followed my instincts and walked right out the door when Marc Connelly came in.

Everything about Marc Connelly was offensive to me. His lordly manner and patronizing attitude toward the cast implied we were all his inferiors. He had already seen the show and had obviously laid his plans. He greeted me with, "You know, *dear*, that 'goody, goody' dance you do on the big bed?" I had figured it would be one of the first things to go. But no, not exactly.

He stated, "We are going to make it into a *real* showstopper!" With my teeth resolutely clenched together, I waited quietly to see what he had up his sleeve.

"I have ordered a new costume for you." I groaned inwardly. I loved my costume.

"It's going to be a knockout," he said, "a sophisticated, beautifully fitted, black lace corset with long garters to hold up the black lace stockings; high-heeled, black, laced-up boots; and long gloves. Instead of romping around with those stupid Indians and Quakers and old Cotton Mather, you will lead Ichabod Crane around the stage, teasing him as you strip off one glove, then the other, dropping *everything* as you go, until at the very end of the music. . . ." He paused. Why was he hesitating? What on earth did he have in mind for me? "You both climb onto the bed, and *you will give him your flesh!*"

He quickly added, "But the audience won't actually *see it*, because the curtain will close just at the last possible moment."

I asked him coldly, "And what about the stagehands? Will *they* get to *see it*? And what about Anna's choreography? Will Anna be here to change it?"

Marc replied, "You will choreograph it yourself."

I thought wistfully of Imogene Coca's marvelously comic strip, with the camel's hair coat within another camel's hair coat, and I wished I was back at Tamiment.

Before I knew it, my new costume was ready. The black lace corset did not fit, but it did remind me of Martha Graham's mother and the wet paint on the toilet seat. With the corset came a capelet that tied in front, a parasol, and a sort of a bonnet. Everything was black. I hate black. I associate it with funerals. When I put it all on, I felt I resembled the portrait of Whistler's mother.

Feeling an absolute idiot, loaded down with all this paraphernalia, I obediently crawled under the bed in readiness for the onstage run-through. On cue, I climbed up on the bed, and halfheartedly struggled to open the parasol. I removed one long, black glove and tossed it away, then the other glove, then the parasol. All the while I thought of how Margie Hart had done her strip so easily and lightheartedly. There were no straight pins in my corset to slip out easily. I was trapped and miserably embarrassed. I gave up in disgust. I walked offstage as the music continued to play. When rehearsal was over, everyone else was hurrying out to eat before the opening, but I was too upset to think of eating. I shrieked hysterically, "*I cannot and will not submit to that man's outlandish command that I strip!*"

Suddenly, I noticed my white petticoat and camisole hanging forgotten on a hook on the wall. I knew then exactly what I was going to do. I calmed myself and carefully applied my makeup. I put on the white costume while the girls with whom I shared the dressing room were onstage. When the stage was dark, I hid under the big bed to wait for my entrance. As the scene began, I came out from under the bed, right on cue, but wearing my white costume. I danced my heart out with Ichabod Crane, the Indians, the Quakers, and old Cotton Mather. We gave it all we had, and we got a really big hand at the end.

I was told later that Marc Connelly had been in the audience, shouting and screaming, and had to be carried out. The notice went up, and the show closed immediately. I fully expected that I would be put out of the union for insubordination. What I had done, I did in full knowledge that it was unthinkable. As it happened, Equity was totally disinterested.

For me, defying Marc Connelly was like jumping off a high cliff, and landing on a ledge three feet down. But the outcome did not change my decision that I never, never, never wanted to be in another Broadway show. I had been burned enough. There were offers, but each time I said, "Thank you, but no thank you." The Broadway stage was no longer the safe, sunshine place it once had seemed. I finally understood that Doris Humphrey had been right about the commercial theater when she first spoke to me backstage at *Allah Be Praised*.

Hooray for What! 1937. Dorothy *(left of center)* leading the hitchhikers.

"In the Shade of the New Apple Tree," *Hooray for What!* Dorothy is seated on the stage, second dancer from right.

Hooray for What! Ed Wynn with the "Apple Tree" girls. Dorothy is third from right.

Straw Hat Review. 1939. *Left to right:* William Bales, Dorothy Bird, Jerome Robbins.

Straw Hat Review. Left to right: Alfred Drake, Dorothy Bird, Jerome Andrews, Albia Kavan.

The Limón Trio. *Left to right:* Dorothy Bird, José Limón, Beatrice Seckler in "the Vivaldi," *Concerto grosso,* choreographed by Doris Humphrey. *Photo by Gerde Peterich, courtesy of the Dance Collection, New York Public Library for the Performing Arts, Astor, Lenox, and Tilden Foundations.*

Dorothy as Lilith in *Eden Tree*, choreographed by Doris Humphrey for the Limón Trio.

Dorothy Bird in "Ef I Had a Ribbon Bow," *Three Ballads*, choreographed by Doris Humphrey for the Limón Trio.

Around the World in 80 Days. Dorothy as Meerahlah. *Performance photo by Richard Tucker, courtesy Julia Tucker.*

Principals from *Park Avenue.*
Dorothy Bird on left, Joan Mann
on right. *Left to right*: Robert
Chisholm, Raymond Walburn,
Arthur Margetson, Charles
Purcell. *Photo, courtesy Museum
of the City of New York.*

Closing night at *Around the World in 80 Days*. *Left to right:* Arthur Margetson, Orson Welles, Dorothy Bird, unidentified, Victoria d'Cordova, Mary Healy, remainder unidentified. *Performance photo by Richard Tucker, courtesy Julia Tucker.*

Paul Villard. He was known as "the Bogart of song."

Nine

Marriage, Motherhood, and Teaching, 1947–1988

HAVING WORKED so easily and comfortably together at Green Mansions during the summer of 1947, Herbert Ross and I decided to team up for a night-club act. Herbie suggested that our theme could be a spoof of society ballroom dance exhibitions of an earlier time. To prepare, we went to the Museum of Modern Art and studied silent films of Vernon and Irene Castle, and Rudolph Valentino. Herbie and I rehearsed at the Hotel des Artistes in the studio of Anita Peters Wright. We tried to capture the distinctive mannerisms we had seen and make them light and amusing. In the tango Valentino had been tigerish, lowering himself as he lunged, with thigh muscles bulging satyr fashion. But Herbie was tall and straight, like a delicate praying mantis. When Herbie crouched, which was not easy for him, he allowed each leg to shoot out in back of him before swinging the leg around to the side. His steps were maddeningly long, causing me to stagger backward almost into a back-fall position near the floor, as if in submission to his masterfulness. Trying to appear deeply emotional, I was actually choking back my laughter. Not Herbie. He was all intensity and temperament.

We auditioned for an agent for an engagement at the Rainbow Room. I had always found it an ordeal to audition for agents. This one looked at me coldly without enthusiasm or interest. As I opened the act with a brief introduction welcoming everyone to our *Tea Dansant*, the agent puffed steadily at his cigar. I was reminded of Louis Horst and his scathing remark, "Are yuh pregnant yet?" Suddenly nothing seemed amusing. In rehearsals, I had been so happy just dancing with Herbie and laughing at what he was doing, it never occurred to me that what I was doing was not the least bit funny. I instantly regretted that in the tango I had not focused on my English heritage and followed Beatrice Lillie's example in *Carmen*. Her sort-of-Spanish costume with the ruffles in all the wrong places, the shoes tied childishly with big bows on her insteps, and her spirited claps, but petulant stamps, always brought down the house. Even with a red rose clenched between bared teeth, I could not have been more un-Spanish. Perhaps we would have been slightly more hilarious if I had eaten the rose.

After the audition, Paul, who had accompanied me, said, "You weren't funny at all when you had the rose between your teeth, and you were puffing. I hate to see dancers puff! In a nightclub, patrons can hear you puff. Maybe the time has come for you to retire?"

I died a thousand deaths. Paul was totally at home in nightclubs, having had repeated lengthy engagements at the Vanguard Downtown, and Le Ruban Bleu. I, too, had performed in nightclubs—the Samovar in Montreal, and the Village Barn and the Glass Hat in New York City.[1] But I had not felt at home. Men in the audience sometimes reached out to touch me, and I would shrink back. I must have been mad to think I could work in a nightclub again, even partnered by the skillful and sophisticated Herbert Ross. I needed the protection of the proscenium. I panicked. I left Herbie a brief note saying, "I know you will go very far. I am terribly sorry, but I just can't go through with it. I am quitting."

Soon after this, Paul and I returned to Green Mansions. Ernie Glucksman welcomed us. Paul and I could always be counted on to stop the show with "Susie Brown" and "Venezuela." Mata and Hari were already under contract there for the summer, but it was quite different from the time at Tamiment years before when they had been forced to rehearse at the first tee. At Green Mansions they were assured of star treatment.

When Paul and I returned to New York City, I needed to find work. Teaching at the School of American Ballet had added immensely to my prestige and confidence, but I knew I could not return there. Instead, I again approached Dr. Kolodney, who welcomed me back to teach children's classes at the 92nd Street YM-YWHA. He assigned me many groups, packed with children, and I poured all my love of dance into these classes. I also taught for Anna Sokolow in Great Neck, Long Island.

Paul had many singing engagements, and once when he came home from working in Montreal, he told me he had read in the *New York Times* that Martha Graham would be giving a lecture at Town Hall. He insisted that we go together to hear her speak, and that I must introduce him to Martha. Although I had participated in many lecture demonstrations with Martha, this would be the first time I had ever sat out front. It would also be the first time I had seen her in years. In her lecture, Martha described the wrist as a thermometer of feeling that an audience reads quite unconsciously, and how changing the placement of the bones of the hand and the angle of the wrist could send many different messages. She was always sensitive to body language, having been taught to observe it by her psychiatrist father, and had often mentioned this to us.

She portrayed abstraction as a process we could liken to enjoying an orange. We could hold the orange in our hands and feel the roundness, the texture of the skin, the weight of it. We might smell it and enjoy the fragrance. We could peel the orange, throw away the rind, separate the segments, and eat them one by one, spitting out the seeds. The combined taste, smell, color, and nourishment constitute the abstraction of an orange. If the orange had been squeezed, the juice would be the essence of the orange. Martha said that the audience does not need to know the details of how you arrived at your goal. She cautioned us to not spell it out for them. What is to be communicated must be absolutely pristine and uncluttered.

Martha had spoken so vividly that a large part of the audience went backstage afterward to visit with her. There were a number of celebrities, including

Katherine Cornell. Paul and I stood a little to one side, awaiting our turn. I was quite sure that Martha had seen me, but I detected no sign of recognition, and I thought, "Maybe she doesn't want to speak to me."

I felt like an outsider and drew Paul away. We were halfway down the passageway leading from the stage to the street, when I heard running steps, and then Martha's voice calling, "Wait, Dorothy. Come back! I want to talk to you. Don't leave. I'll only be a little longer."

I felt suddenly as if the sun had come out. We went back and waited for her. Martha was very warm when I introduced her to Paul. The whole time we talked, she held on to Paul's hand. I still found myself overwhelmed by her magnetism. Finally, I could not help but pull Paul away from her.

In the summer of 1949, Paul and I returned to Green Mansions to entertain. It had become a home away from home for us, with Lena and Sam Garlen our extended family. Lena stood in for my mother to give me away when Paul and I were married on August 19, in the garden of the Justice of the Peace in Warrensburg. Ernie Glucksman was Paul's best man. I wore a white shirt, blue dirndl skirt, and white sandals. My small bouquet was from Lena's garden. Before the ceremony, we picked corn from the farm, the baker made us rolls, and someone gave us a steak. The bartender provided a bottle of Scotch for a wedding toast. Following the ceremony we boarded a speedboat, along with Paul's sister Jean and several close friends and found the most perfect beach on beautiful Paradise Bay on Lake George for a cookout. It was the best wedding ever. On Monday we returned to work at Green Mansions.

The following summer, 1950, after we once again entertained at Green Mansions, Paul and I traveled west to visit my brothers and their families—Mike in Oregon, and Jack in Seattle, Washington. Finally we traveled to Vancouver Island to introduce Paul to Mother and Windham. Mother and Paul liked each other instantly. Together they sang Irish songs, and Paul was very good to her. On the return trip to New York, Paul kept insisting that "a woman is just not a complete woman unless she has a child of her own."

I laughed at first but was beginning to believe he might be right. Although I was eating only tea and toast and hard boiled eggs, somehow I had not recognized the fact that I was pregnant. It wasn't until I was in our New York City apartment house, flying down the stairs two at a time, and tripped, but did not actually fall, that I felt something was different.

I thought, "Could I be pregnant?"

My doctor confirmed it, but then he warned me, "You are bleeding. You could have a miscarriage. It is imperative that you discontinue teaching immediately." Sadly, I offered my resignation to Dr. Kolodney.

Paul was off to Montreal once again for a club date, and I had time to fill. An artist friend of the Adlers, Norman Raeben (the son of Sholem Aleichem), had arrived in New York City from Paris. The Adlers arranged for him to teach a sketching class at a studio in the Carnegie Hall building, so we all enrolled and brought friends. A marvelous teacher with a sardonic wit, he was fanatically against the slick and facile in the arts. Norman liked us to find shapes—not the shapes of the body, but the shapes of spaces around the body. Sometimes they were enclosed by parts of the body, as when legs are wide apart.

As he taught, he interspersed stories about his personal contacts with many of the greats in the early years of modern art. I saw many parallels between modern art and modern dance in the concepts he was offering. Norman rekindled my enthusiasm for many of the ideas Louis had presented, and now, they finally became understandable and acceptable to me.

After class, Norman and the students went around the corner to his favorite restaurant, the Russian Tea Room, and we sat together at a long table in the rear section. We consumed bowls of borscht with sour cream and drank tea from a glass, as the old-timers had done, holding a lump of sugar between our teeth. The conversation flowed as we questioned our master teacher far into the night. Norman insisted that all the jokes that were constantly being shared in Yiddish be translated into English for me, the only non-Jew in the group. As everyone attempted to please him by including me in everything, they would often say, "You know, Norman, it is totally impossible to translate *this!*"

But he would insist again that they must dig deeper and give the carefully hidden, obscure, true flavor of the humor. What an extraordinary experience it was for me to be included in all this intimate warmth, love, and laughter. I came to see that such camaraderie was strongly binding and more comforting by far than anything I had ever experienced onstage.

The child I was about to bear grew strong within me and kicked strenuously. I drank two quarts of milk a day, ate fruits and vegetables, and gained forty-five pounds. I was so big, the neighbors expressed concern that I might burst. The baby was a boy, so sturdy that when the nurse asked the doctor if she should take him to the nursery, the doctor replied, "Oh, let him walk. He's big enough."

Paul, our new son David, and I were living in Forest Hills when two men in black suits barged unannounced through the door of our garden apartment and identified themselves as being from the FBI. They questioned Paul about his background relating to progressive causes, citing his entertaining at fund-raising events for Loyalist Spain many years previously. Paul quite innocently replied, "I was never very active in political affairs."

Paul was shown a list of names and told, "You need not corroborate that any of these people had been involved with you at the fund-raisers." But Paul was asked to say if any of the people on the list were *not* to his knowledge ever active in the left-wing movement. He was pressed to name friends or associates who might have been connected with progressive causes. The intruders explained that if Paul would add two new names to their list, he would not be questioned further. Paul adamantly refused, and the men left.

David was not quite three, when he and I were home alone one evening, and he suffered a severe attack of croup. I called the doctor and waited for her to arrive. It was bitterly cold outside with deep snow on the ground, and still falling. I had no way of knowing that the doctor's car had broken down. When she finally came, we wrapped David in blankets and made our way to the hospital in a borrowed car. David died in my arms.

At first I didn't understand. I was screaming at the doctor, beating on her chest, repeating "Do something! Do something!" Then I became numb with grief. They wouldn't let me take David home. When Paul arrived at our apartment, I told him what had happened. He was dazed. Our dog, Jimmy, ran outside, howling. Barefoot, I ran after him in the snow and brought him inside. Jimmy rubbed himself along the floor on his stomach, keening, crying for David. I felt it was my fault. I was shattered, but I could not cry.

Martha came to the funeral services. She wore a big black hat and black cape. She entered dramatically, with hands clasped, and paced as if she were choreographing. Martha stood next to Paul and me beside David's casket. As I looked down at the small figure in the little white box, Martha put one arm around me and her other arm around Paul. She whispered to us something about "the miracle of the seed," then said, "You must have another child at once." Feeling that this was not an appropriate time to talk of such things, I pulled away from her and refused to sit with her. Martha sat down next to my friend Milly Johnstone. Later, Milly told me that Martha had confessed to her, "I feel very guilty because I knowingly kept Dorothy a child."

When they put my sunshine child into his grave, I felt my life was finished. I did not want to be comforted. I could not be comforted. Paul's sister Jean took us to her apartment in New York City. She gave us her bedroom, and she slept on the floor. We never again returned to our Forest Hills apartment. Friends packed everything for us and put it in storage. Floods of flowers came. People brought food and made endless pots of coffee. Martha sent money. Doris wrote a note of condolence and suggested I return to the concert stage. I tried to write notes to thank everyone for their kindness, but my tears kept dripping all over the pages. I gave up. It was impossible for me to write or speak about it. I was an empty shell.

One of our friends, Freyda Adler, was married to an analyst, Kurt Adler, the son of the great psychoanalyst Alfred Adler.

Kurt asked me, "Do you feel it was your fault that David died?" I nodded. He told me that many women felt as I did, and he suggested I talk to him about it.

I responded, "No. It's too late. It would not help now to talk about it. But thank you."

Kurt countered with, "Paul told me he feels as if he died with David."

I was so caught up in my own grief, I had not even asked Paul how he felt. I had barely noticed that Paul could no longer sing.

I questioned Paul, "Would you like to see if we could have another child?"

"Yes," was his direct reply. In a flash of certainty I knew soon after this that I was pregnant again. That day I substituted for Anna Sokolow at the Actors Studio. I taught the class, focusing throughout on putting energy into the open, vulnerable areas of the throat. I was showing the students, just as Martha had shown me, how to communicate grief as well as ecstasy with an open throat. Only now it was genuinely real to me. The students were spellbound as I demonstrated the rhapsodic quality of the open throat, evincing abandoning oneself to life. I knew I had opened myself up to all possible pain, yet I was not afraid. I was not even concerned that I was forty-three years old.

The day that a pregnancy test confirmed that Paul and I were to be blessed with a second child, we attended a party at Pearlie's place. There was whispering all around the room, and everyone was smiling as they looked at us. Showing great sensitivity, no one said anything. But eyes were shining. When Paul officially told everyone our good news, they took turns hugging us, embracing us with love. I had not realized until then what a big load was being lifted from everybody else's shoulders. Now we could all look forward, not back.

Suddenly, there was a knock on Pearlie's door, and when it opened everyone burst out laughing in amazement. Marlon Brando entered. He was looking for his beloved teacher and coach, Stella Adler. I had seen his name plastered all over the front pages of that evening's newspapers, "Marlon Brando Missing," "Marlon Brando Disappears." Here he was, so slim and handsome in his beautifully tailored grey flannel suit, standing in Pearlie's living room, smiling at Stella.

"What happened, Marlon?" asked Stella. Marlon was openly angry as he described how he had been on the set for *Spartacus* while they were shooting background scenes. He pictured for us a scene in which powerful black men with oiled skin wielded long thick whips that they lashed and cracked through the air. Marlon had gotten into a big ruckus with the producer, stating in no uncertain terms that the scene was tasteless. He said he did not intend to star in a racist movie. Then Marlon walked off the set. He told us he had come home to New York from Hollywood to be with people whom he respected and who understood him and valued his talent.

In the course of the evening, I went into Pearlie's bedroom to rest. Paul lay on the bed next to me, and Marlon came in and laid down on the other side of me. Marlon had heard about our losing David, and that I was pregnant. His sensitivity to our situation, even though we had only just met, was very kind and comforting. In that strangely hushed voice, Marlon talked on and on about Hollywood, and again poured out his feelings of frustration and revulsion about the appeal to crudity and violence being so carefully established on the set of *Spartacus*. Marlon told us that he enjoyed playing drums. He said he especially admired Alvin Ailey and his work and had often played the drums for the dancers. I felt bonded with Marlon, having myself protested against tasteless or unseemly things in the theater.

When Sam Garlen heard the news that Paul and I were expecting a child, he invited us to Seven Keys at Loon Lake in the Adirondack Mountains for the summer. This was a new place he had bought and developed when he and Lena had agreed to separate. Sam provided Paul and me with a room in a boathouse on the lake. The clientele at Seven Keys included many sophisticated, intellectual, artistic people. Movie director Sidney Buckman—whose distinguished career had been cut short in Hollywood by his being blacklisted as a result of the McCarthy hearings—was there for the summer. Somehow Sidney was able to persuade Paul to sing again, for the first time since David's death.

Our second son slipped gently into our midst at Doctors' Hospital in New York City.

Pearlie whispered to me quietly, "He's like a little Buddha, so serene and full of wisdom."

I turned to Paul, saying "He is my gift to you. You must choose his name." Paul chose the name Casey, after the many down-to-earth people who bore that name—Casey Jones, the railroad man; Casey at the bat; and Casey the captain of the tugboat. The day we were to bring Casey home, Paul stopped at the cemetery to place flowers on David's grave. Ironically, it was January 15, the first anniversary of the day that David had died. Casey brought us both very gently but firmly back into the world. He filled our lives with love and laughter and slowly healed our broken hearts.

In 1955 Mrs. Morgenthau, director of the Neighborhood Playhouse, telephoned and asked if I would come to her office. When I shyly went in to see her, I was jolted to hear her say, "Oh, dear! Dorothy! I must have gotten you and Bonnie mixed up AGAIN! It was Bonnie I had meant to call, to discuss an opening on our faculty. I hear she has been doing very interesting things with children. Well dear, since you are here, why don't you tell me what YOU have been up to lately. Have you been doing any teaching?"

I told Mrs. Morgenthau about the children's classes at the School of American Ballet and the 92nd Street YM-YWHA. She then offered me what I considered an ideal job, teaching in the Junior School on Saturday mornings. That meant Paul could look after Casey, freeing me to work. And, very important, I would have an opportunity to repay the generosity of Mrs. Morgenthau and the Lewisohn sisters by passing on to others much of what had been so freely taught to me at the Playhouse.

But disaster was about to strike.

The House Un-American Activities Committee (HUAC) came to New York City to stage their hearings. A young actress, a friend of ours we thought, had been interrogated by the committee. She was terrorized into naming Paul, and even incriminating her own brother! Her reward was to go free. Shortly after this, Paul was subpoenaed to appear at the HUAC hearings. I was desperately, deeply distressed, constantly trembling for fear that our troubles somehow would rub off on my friends. Paul's friends had already been implicated. When anyone called me on the phone, I would refuse to talk for fear the wire was being tapped and they would be questioned and drawn into this nightmare.

I went with Paul to the courthouse on Foley Square, where he was required to testify. The authorities admitted me with great reluctance, warning Paul, "No friends! No relatives. Only your wife."

Seating was reserved for a noisy crowd of rabble-rousing hecklers, who behaved almost as if they were attending an execution at the time of the French Revolution. I was stunned to see the senators casually strolling about, reading and chatting throughout the entire proceedings. In a bored, mechanical way, they questioned the witnesses, "Are you now, or have you ever been a member of the Communist Party?"

Joseph Papp, along with others from the world of the arts and entertainment, successively took the stand. Badgering these well-known people guaranteed coverage in the media. Newspapers reported that Paul was being questioned. Publicity—as well as an ever-expanding list of names to be investigated for disloyalty—was essential, to ensure that abundant funds would be appropriated for the inquisitors' witch-hunt.

Paul was sworn in. His hearing had been failing, and he could barely understand the questions. The interrogators had no patience with him at all. A lawyer from the Emergency Civil Liberties Union sat near Paul, who had been instructed to refuse to answer under the Fifth Amendment. I had wanted Paul to claim the right to refuse to answer on the basis of the First Amendment. But this would have cost a lot of money, which we did not have. Instead, Paul had to respond to the very first question, and every subsequent question in exactly the same way. That was the law. With the opening question, "Are you employed, and who is your employer?" Paul "took the Fifth." He was not about to tell them he had a job with Lena Garlen at Green Mansions.

The proceedings of the House Un-American Activities Committee were designed to alarm the public. It wasn't that most of the people testifying had done anything of importance politically. It was just a part of a process of intimidation. Those people questioned who "took the Fifth" were treated as if they were criminals and declared "Reds." In Senator McCarthy's climate of fear, innocent people were threatened, and many careers were instantly destroyed. Shortly before the hearings, Paul had made several very successful appearances on the Arthur Godfrey Show, and as a result was asked by Gary Moore to join the cast of his daily television program. Following Paul's testimony at the hearings, Gary Moore contacted him to say, "I'm sorry, Paul, but there is nothing I can do." Paul had been blacklisted.

We packed Casey, Jimmy, and whatever we could of our belongings into a car given to us by a relative, put the rest in storage, and set out for California hoping to create a new life. We didn't make out much better than the Joads. After a cross-country journey in which everything that could go wrong did go wrong, we returned to New York City. Faithful friends created a job for Paul, but the whole experience had been too stressful for him. He suffered a massive heart attack.

As Paul lay in the hospital in an oxygen tent, one doctor told me, "We do not expect him to live."

Another one said, "At best, he will most probably spend the rest of his life in a wheelchair."

I was frantic with worry. Again good friends stepped in to help. They cared for Casey while I was at the hospital, and as Paul remarkably began to recover they helped me contact the Jewish Family Service, which arranged for Paul to go to the Cardiac Home in Yonkers for six weeks of rest. Casey and I moved to Long Beach, Long Island, aided by Paul's sister Frances and her husband, Jack. All of our worldly goods were stored in a garage, except for the upright piano. We squeezed it into our tiny apartment so that Paul could play while he recuperated at home.

When summer came, we had to move out of our cozy winter rental in that beach community. Paul found a small house for us in nearby Merrick. The house had been hopelessly neglected. Wallpaper was torn and peeling, and in the bathroom the plastic tiles were hanging here and there like loose baby's teeth ready to fall out. The floor had heaved up in many places, but I did not care. There was a garden full of flowers and trees, and Casey would be attending a wonderful school. When Paul offered a ten-dollar deposit, the real estate agent laughed, but he accepted it. With the help and support of Paul's family—Jean supplied the down payment, and Jack and Frances offered a new refrigerator, a washer, and a dryer—we moved ahead with the purchase.

The secretary at the real estate office sat me down and said, "To obtain a mortgage, we will need information about your source of income."

Paul was still unable to work. I told her about my teaching on Saturdays at the Playhouse, the job at the South Shore Arts Center that Bonnie had steered my way, and my work at the Five Towns Music and Art Foundation. The salaries were all minimal, and I quietly murmured something about being paid every ten weeks for two semesters. She frowned. I swallowed hard.

"What else?" she asked. "Did you forget anything? This is not quite enough income."

I said half-laughingly that I had applied to teach in adult education, and I came up with two jobs that I had heard about, one in the Bronx and another in downtown New York City. Apparently no one ever checked, and we got our mortgage. But then we had to meet the monthly payments.

Paul's former employer had been more than generous, but finally the medical insurance ran out. My teaching and Paul's occasional club dates were not providing enough earnings. Paul tried to operate a mail order business from home, but it fizzled out. Ernie Glucksman sent us a gift of money that put food on the table. Having money to buy milk for Casey was a constant worry. Bearing on my shoulders the weight of responsibility for supporting the family was a new and frightening experience for me.

At this point, just when I was so distressed, Mrs. Morgenthau offered me a job teaching the summer course in Movement for the Theatre at the Neighborhood Playhouse. It would be every day, five days a week, for an enrollment of young adult hopefuls from all across the United States and Canada. This course would certainly have to be very different from the successful Saturday children's classes

I had been teaching. I felt distinctly apprehensive at the prospect as I gratefully accepted the offer.

I was in a muddle of indecision as I had to develop an appropriate curriculum, but I confided my fears to no one, not even Paul. I tried desperately to make up lesson plans, but I could not settle on what I should teach. As I was anxiously pondering what to do, the telephone rang. I picked it up and heard, "Hello . . . Dorothy?"

I immediately recognized that husky voice. There was no other voice like it. "Hello, Martha," I said.

It was the first time Martha had ever called me on the telephone. My head was spinning. Why was she calling me now? It was more than twenty years since I had left her, and in the interim we had rarely spoken.[2] Yet it was once more just as it had been when I first came to New York City to work with her, and she had been so very good to me. I felt close to her, as if no time had passed at all.

Martha first asked, "How is Paul?" Somehow she knew all about his heart attack.

I told her, "He is doing well."

"And Casey? Is he all right?" she asked.

"He is fine. The joy of our lives," I replied.

Then she got to what was obviously the main reason for her call. "Is everything all right with you? Are you teaching a lot?"

I knew then that someone must have told her we were struggling financially. I told her of my various teaching positions.

She asked me curiously, "Do you wear ballet shoes when you teach?"

"No," I laughed. "I am still a dyed-in-the-wool Martha Graham dancer. I wore shoes only when I was teaching ballet at the School of American Ballet."

She asked about my modern classes, and I told her that I usually start with simple exercises like the ones Joseph Pilates had given me to do at home on a mat. I mentioned that I had studied sensitivity training with Charlotte Selver and was trying to incorporate some of her work into the classes.[3]

"Charlotte reawakened me to the worth and tremendous importance of what you taught us," I said.

Martha brushed that off, along with my work at the Actors Studio. She was not interested.

"I teach contractions and releases just the way we did them in Seattle, and I use some of those marvelous animal images you used. I remember everything you did in Seattle," I said proudly.

"I have forgotten it *all*," Martha retorted. I knew how much Martha hated to look back, yet I dearly loved to look back.

I confessed, "Because I am unable to inspire my students to do the work with sufficiently high energy and clarity, I sometimes find myself falling into the trap of showing off and entertaining them, rather than really teaching. I'm ashamed of that, but when I try to be stern, I feel it comes across as petulance. I can't seem to motivate them to discipline themselves the way you do. With all the studying and performing I have done, I know I have so much to offer, but no sense of selectivity. Right now I am preparing to teach a summer course at the Playhouse, and I cannot decide what and how to teach acting students." I asked her if she could help me sort it out, guide me. I totally trusted her judgment and waited quietly until she spoke.

"I know exactly what you must do," Martha said. "You must not teach the way I do. You must learn to teach the way Louis teaches. He gets students to do everything themselves. He gives them a problem and challenges them to work it out. Then they show him what they have done."

She suggested that I first give the students a warm-up on the floor, followed by basic ballet exercises in case they need that style for the lords' and ladies' roles, then simple exercises in the center and moving in space—nothing more elaborate than walking, running, and skipping. After that, I should ask them to take partners or form groups and have them work out their own brief patterns of movement.

"Give them a theme, and have them color it with an emotion, possibly anger, fear, or curiosity," she said. "Tell them they must decide among themselves which way to face and how to move. Use words like *identical, consecutive, mirror image, rounding, straightening, rising* and *lowering*. Teach them to see movement by asking questions and let them discover it all for themselves. Help only the ones who really need it. Have the students take turns showing what they have done, while others watch. You could then show them how to vary the theme by changing one element—turn the head, or raise one arm. Simple things. Keep it very simple! They will love it! And it will take up a lot of time. I could never do this myself, because I would charge in and take over right away! I couldn't stand waiting for them to do it. I have no patience. But you are patient. You can do it. You are generous and won't frighten them out of their wits as I would. You will be very successful." Martha's phone call had come at a most critical time. I went right to work, preparing class plans for each day of each week of the course.

At an orientation meeting before the summer course began, Mrs. Morgenthau explained that the faculty was not to make judgments of any kind about the students. We were to ignore physical attributes, since the pretty blonde who appeared as if she would make it on Broadway was just as likely as any other to leave show business, have babies, and move to the suburbs. The most awkward and ungainly student might one day become a playwright, director, lighting expert, stage designer, costumer, manager. The primary duty of the faculty was to throw out ideas and information, as if casting grain on the ground. Some students, she said, would be ready to accept these ideas and use them immediately. With others it might take years before the ideas would germinate in them. She was emphatic that the administration would handle all disciplinary matters, and she insisted that any complaints be referred to that office. What a relief! I was free to concentrate on teaching.

Initially I did develop a teaching style based more on what Louis had taught than on Martha's work, but gradually I branched out as I grew to value my own varied experiences. With the support of the most perfect accompanist, Ted Dalbotten, who had also studied with Martha and Louis, I was able to inspire students to do some very creative work, not by asking them to copy me, but rather by encouraging them to discover for themselves how to solve problems, to experiment. I strove to empower the students, and to develop in them body eloquence, as Martha had done for me. I used Louis's pre-classic dance forms, not to teach theme and variations as Louis had done, but rather to introduce the changing style, manners, and social behavior in different periods of history. A person could not suddenly become gallant or formal. It was necessary to experience a sense of the period.

We examined how costumes accentuated and transformed the body, as well as affected behavior. The men learned to bow with dignity and style, using hats, elaborately, with great flourishes. Women bowed modestly, barely dropping their eyes, or bowed low to make the other person feel taller. The women practiced handling fans, wigs, jewelry, and imaginary trains. I taught both men and women, as couples, the intricate moves needed to handle long gowns. They played at maneuvering in reverse directions without stumbling, learned how to back up and criss-cross, and rehearsed how the man walked around the woman and assisted in manipulating her skirt so that nobody tripped. We danced the galliard brazenly or modestly or flirtingly. Many of the classroom examples were supported with marvelous illustrations from rare books provided by the Playhouse's devoted librarian, Alice Owens.

We used many props: capes, hats, scarves, skirts, canes, and so on. When costumed, students moved into material that sometimes extended the body line or wrapped the body, thereby discovering how to respond in entirely different ways. At times, we threw very lightweight chiffon scarves up into the air, and the students would spin to the floor to get under the scarf as it landed. They allowed the body to slip under the material and respond to the lightness of it.

The key word is *allow*. An exercise originated by Anna Sokolow is the perfect example of this *allowing* the body to respond naturally. In it, one person runs to the center of the room and takes a very strong stance. The next person runs around and around, then shuts their eyes and turns into the original figure, before stopping to rest lightly, keeping eyes closed. A third person runs out and around and rolls into the sculpture, resting lightly against the others. This is repeated until about seven people form the sculpture. The remaining students in the class walk around the human sculpture and observe the extraordinary grace that people have when they are not posing—when they *allow* themselves to fit in instinctively. At this point, the participants in the sculpture, still with eyes shut, lower their bodies while supporting one another slightly, perhaps lowering to the floor. Then they draw themselves up as a unit. This adjusting to one another as a group allows their own individuality to melt into the whole design and become as one.

We explored Arch Lauterer's ideas of space onstage, by making entrances and exits from each aperture in the wings, from the footlights and back. Discussion ensued about how different it feels to the audience if a path is diagonal or circular. A diagonal across the stage is good for relating something from the past, such as sentimental memories, because it never really contacts the audience. A path across the footlights is good, being nearest to the audience. Every spot on the stage has a value. Some are unimportant; others are more noticeable to the audience. We practiced using the stage space boldly, forthrightly, wistfully, or in cruel, cunning ways.

Experience has taught me that self-discipline serves as the container, while freedom and spontaneity form the content that flourishes within the container. Because the safety net of self-discipline had permitted a sense of spontaneity to bubble up out of me in the theater (where, to me, work and play were one), I set out to fulfill the meaning of the term *playhouse*. The ability to play is a gift some performers have in abundance and is an essential element in the theater. My goal, in endeavoring to complement the necessary discipline with playful times within a specific framework, was to set the students free to be themselves, each different from the others. As an example, I had students go to the barre to "shake the ladder." Martha had once described to us how in the days of melodrama actors would use this device in preparation for an entrance. I had often used this technique to energize myself before making an entrance, and I knew that it works wonderfully. The students laughed at first, but some did begin to boom out their voices vigorously in a vibratory manner as I urged them on.

These same students were privileged to be in Sandy Meisner's class. A drama teacher of great stature, Sandy demanded absolute discipline and complete dedication to the work. I understood and respected his position. Some of Sandy's students, girls especially, were in total terror of his tongue. By introducing the element of play, I hoped to armor the more fragile or inexperienced students, who might otherwise be open to intimidation and be inclined to freeze up.

I explained how performers need to spark the imagination of the audience and light up the stage by singling out elements and making them visible. It is not sufficient to just go through the motions. Great performers are never mechanical; they always fill the movement. I asked Ted Dalbotten to gather the men together around the piano and discuss music, while I took the women to the far end of the studio.

I began by showing the women a print of Picasso's *Les Demoiselles d'Avignon* and asked, "Why do you think he chose to shape the breasts the way he did? Was it to make you see them?" They shrugged.

As an experiment combining play with singling out an element, I suggested, "Let's see if you can erase the image you have in your mind of your own breasts, and replace it with a new and different shape. Could you possibly think of your breasts as peaches, all velvety? Or perhaps large, round, slippery grapefruits? Maybe they could be two lemons, small and sour. Purse your lips, shape your mouth for lemon juice. Can you feel the shivers coming from the sour taste? Press out your lips like nipples. Try oranges. Rounder? Sweeter? Fragrant?"

Keeping an eye on the men gathered around the piano to see that they would not come over and inhibit us, I asked the women to perform a modern port de bras, such as the one I had used when dancing the role of Lilith in *Eden Tree*.

I challenged them, "As you perform the arm movements, think of your breasts as oranges. Change to grapefruits. Do you see that you need more room for grapefruits?" By now they were all laughing.

"See how the arm patterns change subtly with each different shape. Think pears. Juicy, fragrant ones, with the stems pointing out." It was a raunchy Orson Welles who had described one of the dancing girls in *Around the World* this way. I showed them kiwis, a fruit that was new on the market, and suggested that every time they opened an arm, this prickly little devil would be revealed. From that day on, I only had to look at the girls and raise my eyebrows slightly, and they would come alive.

To further encourage the students to look at shapes—not geometric shapes, but rather the strangely individual and human ones—I used reproductions of the work of Picasso and Braques and introduced Norman Raeben's ideas about shapes. I tried to explain the term *haptic*, which Picasso had used when referring to communicating vigorous, violent actions and feelings.[4] For a painting to create a haptic response required suggested motion, intense energy, and distortion. Emil Nolde was the artist I chose as an example of the use of colors. I prodded the students to see through the eye of the artist by asking questions: Can you see movement in the design? do you sense Picasso having conversations with his model? can you see the contrast between Picasso and Braque? what do you feel intuitively about the colors in Nolde's paintings? are they warm or cold? ominous?

I showed the students the strikingly original painting by Marcel Duchamps that Martha had told us about long ago in Seattle. It was called *A Nude Descending Stairs* and had been in the Armory Show in 1913. The students tried to capture in movement what the artist had wanted the viewer to see in the segmented designs of the body. I explained, as Martha had, that this was probably the result of the earliest motion picture images, which did not flow smoothly but seemed to jump from frame to frame in a somewhat jagged manner. Duchamps appeared to have discovered the way-stations through which the movement of walking downstairs actually flowed. I asked my students first to move down imaginary stairs and to notice what was happening in their joints. Then they were to exaggerate the actions and changes of positions in a stilted, grotesque way (which they accomplished with obvious delight). Through observing the irregular patterns of movement occurring in each other's body, they soon realized that they, too, could use the idea of segmenting movement to capture the eye of the audience.

A sequence of three paintings by Piet Mondrian provided the most perfect illustration of the evolution of abstraction. The first was *Landscape with Farmhouse*. It showed a summer's day with tall, graceful trees reflected in water as if a breeze had fluttered over the surface. In the background stood a solid square house and adjoining building, all with peaked roofs. The students worked in groups. Some stood on ladders and benches to represent the swaying, curving tree trunks. Others lay on the floor on their backs, feet reaching up toward the feet of those standing on ladders and benches. They were trying to reproduce the reflected patterns in the water as they copied the movements of the people above. Still other students made themselves square and blocklike, forming the shapes of buildings. It was a madhouse of complexity and did not have the least hint of the serenity of the painting. The students gained a deep respect and appreciation of Mondrian's achievement, bringing all the elements together with a sense of harmony, unity, and simplicity.

The second painting, *Horizontal Tree*, pictured a gnarled and leafless tree, anchored deeply into the ground, its overlapping branches extending to each side of the canvas and beyond. Two students undertook the task of feeling secure and rooted, reaching out their arms as if they were being swept high and low by rushing rain and wind. Others joined in to extend the branches. Still others traced out small squares of sky, side by side in rows, like unframed windowpanes that seemed to flatten out the background and add to the side-to-side pull of the branches. Being rooted, it was hard to reach out endlessly while at the mercy of the elements. By observing all this in the mirrors, the students grasped the concept of suspended movement.

The painting called *Rhythm of Straight Lines* was the epitome of abstraction. Here trees became upright parallel black lines on a white page. Horizontal lines stretched from side to side, with a blue square toward the top, suggesting sky, or a yellow square for sunlight. Mondrian had achieved absolute simplicity and total discipline. It was challenging for the students to move in this way—nothing but straight up, down, and across. Through this exploration the students were able to grasp the idea of the simple basics of growth up or sideways. The concept of abstraction became abundantly clear.

In 1974, my longtime friend from the Berkshire Country Club, Lillian Solomon Diamond, gave me a copy of *The Thinking Body*, by Mabel Elsworth Todd. I found this book fascinating, containing a wealth of valuable concepts and inspiration for teaching. I immediately incorporated a myriad of her ideas about sensitivity, body alignment, breathing, and weight into my classes.

The very first pages of the book showed an illustration of evolution called *Fish to Man* by Dr. William K. Gregory. This triggered in me a long-forgotten memory: when Martha had presented us with the idea of walking like a crocodile with a long, heavy tail. She had explained that before man was upright he was long, walked on all fours, and could not lean back. In relating this exercise to man's rising upright, Martha had us support ourselves on two feet, not four. We inclined the body forward slightly from the hip hinge, focusing on the spine, to balance the tail off the ground. The hip hinge did not come forward, nor the knees lock. Instead, the abdomen contracted to permit the hip hinge to remain slightly back. This allowed all other hinges to be free. Martha cautioned us to not lean too far back in order to protect the vital internal organs from possible slashing. We conjectured that when humans finally did stand up, they balanced too far back.

It was extraordinary how many concepts in *The Thinking Body* had parallels with the work Martha Graham had done in the very early years. The explanations in the text detailing the use of each body part corresponded with Martha's progression of exploring the use and alignment of all parts of the body. Martha focused first on the feet—toes, ball of the foot, arch, heel—before moving upward to the ankle, knee, thigh, and muscles on the sides of the legs. Special attention was given to the hip hinge and its response to rebound and breath, and how it created an impulse. Martha addressed the carriage of the rib cage, shoulders, and balancing of the head on the top vertebra of the spine.

Much time had been spent on the breathing rhythms. We allowed air to come in passively, then forced it out. The in-breath was not the energizing force; the out-breath, which Martha related to a bellows, was the source of energy. The explanations in *The Thinking Body* regarding the balancing of the body, the creation of momentum, the response of the body to breathing, elements of sustained movement, and moving on the breath, I had experienced them all in Martha's classes in Seattle in 1930.

There was a great deal on walking in *The Thinking Body*. The text included a detailed analysis of walking, and how to propel the body's weight forward. There is an illustration of the image Martha had presented in class in Seattle that we picture legs—many legs—as spokes of a large wheel moving forward, turning, progressing.[5] I found much that was in common with the walking we had done in 1930 in preparation for the premiere of *Primitive Mysteries*. As we rehearsed, Martha had cautioned us to neither tense the shoulders nor lift them. She suggested we picture a milkmaid bearing a piece of wood carried across her shoulders to support the weight of two buckets.[6] She had us first stand, then walk, as if we bore two heavy buckets filled with milk balanced on a yoke. I felt my chest lifted, and my shoulders and hands pulled down with the weight of the buckets. Martha had used a number of the animal and mechanical images that I discovered in *The Thinking Body*. But Martha did not employ the technical language—the names of muscles and bones—even though, as the daughter of a doctor, she probably knew more about anatomy than the average person.

At the performance of the Graham Company sponsored by the Asia Society on May 19, 1988, I asked Martha Hill if she thought Martha Graham had been in contact with Mabel Elsworth Todd or her ideas.

Martha Hill vehemently responded "NO!" and stated it was "an outrageous idea."

I could not understand her impatient reaction, but I did not press her. I was personally convinced it was true. Only recently I learned that Mabel Elsworth Todd was researching the material for her book in the 1920s (possibly with a mentor whose name I do not know) and published a portion of the text in

1929 under the title *The Balancing of Forces in the Human Being*, as a syllabus for her students at the Teachers' College, Columbia University. I sincerely believe Martha Graham had been exposed to some of this material early on. It is said that ideas hit different people at the same time. Maybe that is what happened, but I wonder.

Teaching in the studio that had originally been designed and built for Martha at the Neighborhood Playhouse was a privilege and a great joy that lasted for a quarter of a century. There, as well as in colleges, universities, and my own community, my role as an artist teacher was not only to impart a skill and instill habits of self-discipline, but also to give as a gift to the next generation all that I could of the marvelous warmth and excitement of a life in the theater.

Throughout the 1960s and 1970s, I taught modern dance in the Adult Education Program of the Merrick Public Schools on Long Island. Many of the students became lifelong friends. Several went on to careers in theater, physical fitness, and dance teaching, and most of them still exercise.

My friends rallied around me in the late 1960s when Renny Sternberg, administrator of the Nassau County Office of Performing and Fine Arts, latched on to me to serve as chairperson for a proposed Nassau County Dance Committee. These women, along with key volunteers Doris Peck and Pepe Semler, worked with me to initiate a fantastic community effort to promote dance in our own hometowns. Bertha Weinstein, with her talent for organization, provided leadership for enormously successful Festival Days for Young Dancers. These events drew hundreds of dance students, who participated in workshops featuring top-level guest teachers. Over a period of years, performances by local dancers as well as nationally known professionals such as the American Ballet Theater, Norman Walker, Cora Cahan, Matteo, and many other notables were presented by the committee.

With funding from Nassau County, Long Island Lighting Company, and the New York State Council on the Arts, the dance committee created a performing company of between eight and ten young dancers. Our program was called "What Is Dance?" and was presented in more than 350 in-school demonstrations. I directed the modern dance portion and wrote the script, which likened dance to sports. Usually I spoke the narration. At times, opera star Mimi Benzel was our guest narrator. As slides of athletes were shown, the dancers illustrated relationships between their movements and those of the athletes. A favorite slide was of Edward Villella leaping over a proscenium. The modern dancers performed on many levels (floor, tables, chairs, stepladders) and in different kinds of environments, and were costumed in a variety of styles.

The modern dance was in contrast to a classical ballet segment directed by Christine Tietjen. Lighting effects were by Naomi Kaapcke, costumes by Bernice Gillenson, and sound by Muriel Sullivan. Joyce Greenberg arranged the bookings, and Patricia Gutmann was our business manager. Everyone pitched in to provide transportation for the dancers and to drive them to the performance site. The performances came off with flying colors, and we were swamped with drawings and letters from children and faculty. It was rewarding to hear that the New York State Council on the Arts considered ours to be the best in-school program of its kind they had ever funded. In 1972 Maestro Lazlo Halasz invited me to choreograph his production of *Amahl and the Night Visitors* using dancers from our in-school company. Frank Rizzo, Gian Carlo Menotti's director, termed it "the best in all *Amahl* productions."

In the 1960s I was also a founding member of Wantagh Community Arts Program. Our director, Anne Forman, requested that I serve as an artist-in-residence to introduce dance into the classrooms of the Wantagh elementary schools. In cooperation with teachers, I keyed movement experiences into the subject under study at the time. When the topic was weather, the children became trees tossed by a storm; or they rose from the floor, arms spreading wide like a sunrise; or they created the crackling of lightning along with rain and wind. Practical lessons about traffic and following rules became choreographic games: No Left Turn, Quiet Hospital, Slow School. Whether the subject was new math, science, or history, dance became a way of dealing with reality and instilling pride, while learning to work cooperatively with one another. It was a great joy to pioneer in this area and to see children using their whole bodies as a means of self-expression. I was especially rewarded that this work inspired several of my adult students to pursue careers in dance education.

Over the years I have been told that I had influenced people, with positive feelings carried over from their experience in my class. It was unintentional, perhaps intuitive, but it seems I could help people uncover and overcome inhibitions, thus allowing them to gain the confidence that freed them to succeed in many areas. I enjoyed it as much as they did.

In April 1981, I participated as a panelist at a major dance conference entitled

"The Early Years," held at the State University of New York at Purchase. It was there I proclaimed publicly for the first time, *"I don't know about anybody else, but I know that I love Martha Graham. I always have loved her, and I always will because she gave me a skill that carried me through my life, and she introduced me to the world of the arts."* The words came tumbling out of my mouth at breakneck speed. I had waited fifty years to say it, but I so desperately wanted the people in the audience—students, teachers, and friends of dance—to understand and to know.

People who had seen me onstage, dancing so blissfully, serenely, and radiantly happy, were often bewildered when they met me offstage and found me to be painfully shy, tongue-tied, and retiring. I froze, becoming both verbally and emotionally paralyzed. I have heard this condition described as being "encapsulated in a shell of self-consciousness." At the conference at Purchase, I believe I was able to speak as I did because I was again onstage, protected by the proscenium, basking in the sunshine of the spotlight, and facing a large, responsive audience.

For a long time, I had harbored ambivalent feelings about Martha Graham, ranging from pure gratitude to fear, terror, nearly hatred, but finally to love. I eventually came to realize that, without Martha's guidance and patience, I never would have had the fantastic life I have experienced. Martha's advice and encouragement during that extraordinary telephone conversation was her ultimate gift to me. She gave me the power to fully share with others my deep love of theater, dance, and the arts. When I needed help the most desperately, Martha again reached out to me with exceptional sensitivity, just as she had, once before in Seattle, reached out to loan me the magical exotic object that I thought was a necklace.

Notes

The direct quotations in this book are recorded to the best of my recollection, aided by entries I made at the time in my diary and on file cards. Although the exact words may have differed slightly, in all cases the content expressed is accurate.

Foreword

1. Arnold Genthe, *The Book of the Dance* (Boston: International Publishers, 1920; copyright 1916 by Arnold Genthe).

2. Ann Daly, *Done into Dance: Isadora Duncan in America* (Bloomington and Indianapolis: Indiana University Press, 1995), 128.

3. Genevieve Stebbins, *Delsarte System of Expression* (1902; New York: Dance Horizons, 1977), 113.

4. Franklin Rosemont, ed., *Isadora Speaks* (San Francisco: City Lights Books, 1981), 33.

5. Robert Henri, "My People" (1915) in *The Art Spirit* (1923; New York: Harper and Row, 1984), 144.

6. Emile Jaques-Dalcroze, preface to *"Exercices de Plastique Animée": Méthode Jaques-Dalcroze* (Lausanne: Jobin and Cie, 1917), 5–6 (my translation).

7. Irma Duncan, *The Technique of Isadora Duncan* (1937; New York: Dance Horizons, 1970), x.

8. See Nancy Lee Ruyter, "Dance in Education," in *Reformers and Visionaries* (New York: Dance Horizons, 1979).

9. Elizabeth Selden, *Elements of the Free Dance* (New York: A. S. Barnes and Company, 1930), vii.

10. Barbara Morgan, *Martha Graham: Sixteen Dances in Photographs* (1941; Dobbs Ferry, N.Y.: Morgan and Morgan, 1980).

11. Mabel Elsworth Todd, Foreword to "The Balancing of Forces in the Human Being: Its Application to Postural Patterns," in *Early Writings, 1920–1934* (New York: Dance Horizons, 1977).

12. Elizabeth Selden, *The Dancer's Quest* (Berkeley and Los Angeles: University of California Press, 1935).

13. Ellen Van Volkenburg Browne and Edward Nordhoff Beck, eds., *Miss Aunt Nellie: The Autobiography of Nellie C. Cornish* (Seattle: University of Washington Press, 1964), 206.

14. "A Tribute from Martha Graham," in ibid., 269.

Preface

1. Curt Sachs, *World History of the Dance* (New York: W. W. Norton Co., Inc., 1937), 447.

2. At the age of fifteen, Gertrude Hoffman ran away from the convent where she was a student, to perform in the operetta chorus of the Castle Square Theater. From the corps de ballet she went into vaudeville and became one of the first generation of American solo dancers of the late 1890s. Gertrude Hoffman was the first "art" dancer in vaudeville. She became a headliner in show business and performed in the *Ziegfeld Follies*.

1. Background, Family, and a Pioneering Lifestyle

1. The Bird Waterworks is mentioned in Adelaide Ellis, *Along Mill Bay Road* (Cobble Hill, B.C.: Firgrove Publishing, 1990), 29.

2. François Delsarte (1811–1871). Although Martha Graham had severed her connection with Denishawn School in 1924, she was definitely familiar with the Delsarte system that Ted Shawn was researching and teaching with such devotion.

2. Martha Graham at the Cornish School, Seattle, 1930

1. See "A Tribute from Martha Graham," in *Miss Aunt Nellie: The Autobiography of Nellie C. Cornish,* ed. Ellen Van Volkenburg Browne and Edward Nordhoff Beck (Seattle: University of Washington Press, 1964), in which Martha Graham described Miss Cornish as "a small, round, plump little lady with the dynamism of a rocket, and we were all terrified of her, of her tongue and in a way, terrified of her dream."

2. Ronny Johansson joined Denishawn in 1925 as assistant teacher.

3. The term *marking* refers to the common practice of dancers to indicate movements with hand motions, without actually executing them.

3. *Martha Graham's* Seven Against Thebes, *1930*

1. Mark Tobey was born in 1890 in Centerville, Wisconsin. He was a self-taught artist and first exhibited in Knoedler Gallery in 1917.

4. *The Neighborhood Playhouse, New York City, 1931*

1. The tentlike shape of the hands in *Primitive Mysteries* is shown very clearly in Barbara Morgan's photographs. While today this arm (with elbow slightly rotated and lifted) and hand configuration might be thought of as merely a decorative detail, we performed it with a sense of potential power and vigor. Martha incorporated an emphasis on the open armpit, which contributed to an airy feeling of flight and courage. We associated tightly closed armpits with timidity.

2. There would be neither time nor money nowadays to rehearse the walk for *Primitive Mysteries* for so many months, as we had done in 1930. The experimentation that Martha did at that time could never be accomplished today. In one of our last conversations in 1990, when Martha Graham was working on the Scott Joplin piece *Maple Leaf Rag*, she was near tears as she told me she was desperately distressed by the limitations placed on the dancers' schedules by the union. "My hands are tied," she said. Union rules dictated how many hours a day the dancers were permitted to work with her. Costume fittings and photography appointments were considered part of the working day. Lamenting that the dancers were becoming more balletically oriented, she said she could not require them to come to her studio for the daily morning classes, and many dancers went to ballet class before coming to the studio for rehearsal. It frustrated her that few of the dancers could communicate a sense of weight and how to propel it through space.

3. When Agnes de Mille read this manuscript shortly before her death, she told me she recalled that Martha Graham went so far as to order Michel Fokine to leave the auditorium.

5. *Performing with the Graham Group, 1931–1937*

1. I had always thought of *Celebration* as an experience of shared energy. In its reconstruction for performance at Brooklyn Academy of Music in 1994, the dancers appeared to be at a party. They evidently had been instructed to smile. The smiling, combined with the white taffeta-like costumes they wore, totally changed the impact. It became superficial and feminine, despite the inclusion of male dancers. Instead of

the original rebounding explosions of energy, what we had now was charming and lightweight. The elastic quality was less, and the propelled weight was less flung. There was more wrist motion. The audience seemed to love *Celebration* in its new incarnation, but old-timers including myself who had performed in the original did not.

2. The discipline and emotion in the reconstruction of *Chronicles* presented at the New York City Center in 1995 was astounding. Terese Capucilli evinced a strength impelled by fierce and violent feelings. The Martha Graham Company appeared more theatrical and at times more passionate than when I was a member. I had danced in the group in the original production of *Chronicles,* and I felt the group dancing in this 1995 revival appeared to have been fleshed out to advantage.

3. When the company was in San Francisco, Martha and Louis went to Alcatraz to visit Henry Cowell, who was incarcerated there, in order to discuss the music she wanted for *Immediate Tragedy*. In the Barabara Morgan book there are many photographs of the dance *Deep Song*, which was presented in New York City shortly after that summer at Bennington. I have always felt that this was another version of *Immediate Tragedy*.

6. *Dancing on Broadway,* 1937–1945

1. When Agnes de Mille read a working manuscript for *Bird's Eye View*, she informed me that I had misunderstood certain circumstances surrounding the gas mask incident in *Hooray for What!* Apparently Agnes, too, thought the gas masks in "Under the New Apple Tree" were repugnant, and they were frustrating to her as a choreographer. Agnes told me that using the gas masks to make a statement was the "great idea" of Vincent Minnelli. It was also his idea to have the dancers dressed in gray sacks to represent posts for the movable barbed wire fences on the battlefield. These posts conveniently raced on cue to new positions so that Paul Haakon could leap over them. Vincent Minnelli was enchanted with these concepts, and he was adamant. Agnes said that Vincent Minnelli had hired her, therefore, he was her boss, and she loyally stuck by him. When the going really got rough he checked into the hospital, leaving Agnes to carry the ball alone.

2. What people could not understand was that I was hopelessly obedient, and the rules against copying stopped me cold. It was as if movements were like letters in the alphabet. I could have used the letters, but the use of words or sentences (phrases of movement) would be copying or stealing. Copying, like indicating, was for me a cardinal sin. Over and over again I have heard that choreographers, Martha Graham and George Balanchine included, do indeed steal from every source—talented students, animals in a zoo, raindrops running down a windowpane, and so on. Martha claimed she found and combined movements that already existed and that might have been lost

or undiscovered. It was recognizable combinations or sequences of movements that were banned. I am quite sure that George Balanchine had seen Martha Graham's *Celebration* in 1933. I have always felt that he appropriated from *Celebration* the opening position of *Serenade* (1934), in which the dancers stand with feet close together in parallel position, one arm extended diagonally forward high, then abruptly turn their feet out into ballet first position.

3. I did not for one moment want to venture back to Martha's studio, until the time I was invited to help with the first reconstruction of *Primitive Mysteries*. At that time I was filled with trepidation as I entered the studio. Dancers in the company were not at all like the dancers in the early Graham Group. The girls now were so slim, delicate, and exquisite. And it was no longer androgenous. There were young, vigorous men. I knew I would not fit into this new world, but I wanted to be there because I had loved *Primitive Mysteries* so much. The apprentice dancers gathered around as I sat on the floor and described what it had been like in 1930 and 1931 when we were working on the dance. Soon other old-timers assembled. It was astounding to see how each of the former dancers remembered *Primitive Mysteries* differently. Everyone's memory was colored by their own special idiosyncracies that had become exaggerated over the years. Antagonisms sprang up. There was arguing about the counts. Each dancer did battle for her own style. Nina Fonaroff, dressed in pink tights and pink ballet shoes, pressed for delicacy. Ethel Butler was as passionate as ever as she remembered high abandoned arches. Gertrude Shurr was terribly intense, stressing high elbows, clenched fists, and raised tense shoulders in "Crucifixus." Sophie Maslow, meanwhile, was remembering with the music in a quiet way, and I felt she was on the right track, even though she had not been in the company the year we first worked on the dance. There was one apprentice dancer, Elizabeth Halpern, who was nearest to the way it had originally been—unforced and very clear. Without Mary Rivoire, on whom much of it had been modeled, I felt that the core of the dance was lost. Martha herself did not attend the rehearsals; she so hated the idea of reconstructions.

4. When Erick Hawkins joined Martha's company, everything changed. He introduced ballet classes for the dancers. With the addition of male dancers, the strength and vitality of the dance went into the men's roles. They were the strong, stable ones. The men, especially Erick Hawkins, did a lot of stamping, jumping, and slapping of the thigh. Instead of sturdy pioneers, the women now became slim, fragile, delicate, and feminine. The women's movements were less powerful, more reactive, and they performed air work with feet pointed. The technique became more decorative and elaborately choreographed. Dresses were still long and unrevealing, but more feminine. The men were revealed. Partnering became a new and important element. Sexual themes frequently predominated. Seduction became an element with commercial value.

5. Jack's was not a Graham back fall, but more like a Weidman one, except he never hit the floor.

7. The Limón Trio, 1944–1946

1. In the summer of 1995 I saw the José Limón Company perform at Art Awareness in Lexington, New York. I felt the company successfully retains much of the Humphrey-Weidman-Limón sense of power, momentum, and simplicity. I was impressed and pleased that young dancers of today are seeing in this company, under the able direction of Carla Maxwell and Nina Watt, an excellent representation of early modern dance.

8. The School of American Ballet and the Broadway Scene, 1945–1948

1. Herbert Ross achieved success as a Broadway and Hollywood director. Among his many movies are *Goodbye Mr. Chips, Funny Lady, The Secret of My Success, Steel Magnolias, My Blue Heaven, Nijinsky,* and *The Sunshine Boys.* He and his late wife, ballerina Nora Kaye, collaborated to create the smash hit film *The Turning Point.*

2. Joseph Pilates (1880–1967) was born in Germany. A frail child, he worked hard at body-building and as a teenager became a diver, a skier, and a gymnast. He developed an exercise system that merged mental and physical processes, as well as original equipment for stretching and building muscles. His ideas influenced all the major innovators in dance, including Ruth St. Denis, Martha Graham, José Limón, and George Balanchine. I never felt in better condition than when I worked out at Pilates Gym.

9. Marriage, Motherhood, and Teaching, 1947–1988

1. Paul's friend, agent Al Herman, had gone out of his way to secure an engagement for me at the Glass Hat in 1944. I felt deeply obligated to Al, so when Agnes de Mille asked me if I would like to dance in the show she had been hired to choreograph— *Oklahoma!*—I foolishly turned her down.

2. At times I had gone backstage with friends and introduced them to Martha following performances, and Martha always greeted me warmly. I never spoke to her alone, but I did write her long letters, in which I poured out my heart about the dances. Sometimes I even mailed the letters, and Martha sometimes replied. I heard that Martha once quoted from my letters and remarked, "It must be true, because Dorothy does not tell lies."

3. Charlotte Selver graduated from Bode School for Expressive Movement. She worked with Mary Wigman and studied extensively with Elsa Gindler. On the basis of

Gindler's work, she developed her own ideas, which she later named "Sensory Awareness," and introduced this through Esalen Institute to the Human Potential Movement. She has taught in many universities and has given graduate courses for teachers and special courses for handicapped students.

4. My scholarly friend Humphrey Fry, headmaster of St. Bernard's School and husband of Dini de Remer, researched the term *haptic* for me.

5. See Mabel Elsworth Todd, *The Thinking Body* (Dance Horizons, 1972), illustration p. 195.

6. See ibid., illustration p. 157.

of, 90–91; dramatic vs. rhapsodic qualities of, 51–53, 81, 233; "early work" of, 19–37, 42–54, 71–72, 88; and "ecstatic body," 71, 175; energy, explorations of, 33–37, 42–44; finances of, 77, 81–82, 90; Humphrey, Doris, compared with, 174–77; images, use of, 20–35, 50, 53, 190, 193–95, 244, 246–48; lecture/demonstrations by, 82–85, 98, 99, 229; as mentor, 37–41, 57–58, 61–64, 85, 99, 136, 239–41, 250; as mother figure, 59, 63–64, 78, 86, 89–90, 100–01; performances, preparation for, 54–56, 78; personality of, 71, 86, 92, 94, 101, 103, 105–07, 110, 116–18, 195, 250; rehearsals of, 53–54, 73–75, 78, 97; smiling, expulsion of, 23, 96; storytelling by, 26, 45, 51–52, 100, 243

Gray, Diane, 1
Green, Mary, 138, 144
Green Mansions, 203–08, 227–30, 237
Greenwich Village Follies, 100, 141

Haakon, Paul, 139
Harburg, Yip, 139
Hart, Margie, 183–84, 217
Hart, Moss, 162
Hawkins, Erick, 160–61
Henry, Hank 148
Heretic, 42, 72, 75, 78, 83–84
Hill, Martha, 58, 99–100, 107, 111–12, 147, 247
Hoffman, Gertrude, 166
Holm, Hanya, 89, 104, 168
Holmes, Peggy Anne, 150–51
Hooray For What!, 136, 139, 145–46
Horizons, 109
Horst, Louis, 71, 109, 115, 231: appearance of, 3; as composer, 75, 79, 91, 175, 195; and Graham, 38, 77, 78, 82, 83, 86, 89–91, 93, 97, 100, 101, 104; as mentor, 61–64, 88, 98, 135–37, 140, 145, 170; personality of, 65, 155; as teacher, 65, 67–69, 74, 93, 148, 240–41; as tormentor, 68, 87, 101, 144, 228
HUAC (House Un-American Activities Committee), 236–37
Humphrey, Doris, 99, 110, 168, 171–73, 188, 213: at Bennington, 105–05; choreographic methods of, 174, 176–81; compared with Graham, 174–76; at Green Mansions, 203–05, 207; musicality of, 178–80; personal difficulties of, 181–82, 185, 207; rehearsing with,

174–77, 185–87; sensitivity of, 173, 176, 217, 233

Immediate Tragedy, 116
Integrales, 97
Isaacs, Edith, 100, 104

Jacobson, George, 150–51
Johansson, Ronny, 16, 17, 34, 37

Kaufman, George, 201–02
Kaufman, Harry, 142, 144, 159
Kavan, Albia, 155
Kaye, Beatrice, 151
Kaye, Danny, 156, 164–65
Kazan, Elia, 166, 209
Kirstein, Lincoln, 193
Kollwitz, Käthe, 111
Kolodney, Dr. Nathan, 117–18, 229, 231
Kranz, Ben, 149, 215

Lady in the Dark, 161–62, 165
Lamb, Gil, 215
Lamentation, 98, 116
Lauterer, Arch, 105, 115, 177–78, 242
Lawrence, Gertrude, 161–66
LeClerq, Tanaquil, 193–94
Legend of Sleepy Hollow, 214
Lewisohn, Alice, 67, 236
Lewisohn, Irene, 67, 69, 72, 236
Liandre, Lil, 97
Liebman, Max, 154–55, 157, 159, 203
Limón, José, 171–77, 179, 181–88, 200, 203
Limón, Pauline Lawrence, 171, 174, 177–79, 185–88, 190
Lindeman, Edouard, 105, 108
Lloyd, Norman, 149
Loring, Eugene, 200–03
Lowe, Betty, 161, 202
Lyons, Annabelle, 146

Margetson, Arthur, 197, 199
Marianne, 167–68
Martin, John, 37, 74, 82–85, 104, 145, 167, 184–85, 188
Maslow, Sophie, 58, 81, 96, 98, 103, 107, 111, 113–14
Massine, Leonide, 93
Mata & Hari, 156, 228
Mattox, Matt, 200
Mature, Victor, 163
Mazia, Marjorie, 95
McCarthy, Senator Joseph, 237